Lecture Notes in Computer Science 9154

Commenced Publication in 1973
Founding and Former Series Editors:
Gerhard Goos, Juris Hartmanis, and Jan van Leeuwen

More information about this series at http://www.springer.com/series/7408

Jasmin Christian Blanchette
Nikolai Kosmatov (Eds.)

Tests and Proofs

9th International Conference, TAP 2015
Held as Part of STAF 2015
L'Aquila, Italy, July 22–24, 2015
Proceedings

 Springer

Editors
Jasmin Christian Blanchette
Inria Nancy & LORIA
Villers-lès-Nancy
France

Nikolai Kosmatov
CEA LIST Nano-Innov
Saclay
France

ISSN 0302-9743   ISSN 1611-3349   (electronic)
Lecture Notes in Computer Science
ISBN 978-3-319-21214-2   ISBN 978-3-319-21215-9   (eBook)
DOI 10.1007/978-3-319-21215-9

Library of Congress Control Number: 2015942786

LNCS Sublibrary: SL2 – Programming and Software Engineering

Printed on acid-free paper

Springer International Publishing AG Switzerland is part of Springer Science+Business Media
(www.springer.com)

Foreword

Software Technologies: Applications and Foundations (STAF) is a federation of a number of leading conferences on software technologies. It provides a loose umbrella organization for practical software technologies conferences, supported by a Steering Committee that provides continuity. The STAF federated event runs annually; the conferences that participate can vary from year to year, but all focus on practical and foundational advances in software technology. The conferences address all aspects of software technology, from object-oriented design, testing, mathematical approaches to modeling and verification, model transformation, graph transformation, model-driven engineering, aspect-oriented development, and tools.

STAF 2015 was held at the University of L'Aquila, Italy, during July 20–24, 2015, and hosted four conferences (ICMT 2015, ECMFA 2015, ICGT 2015, and TAP 2015), a long-running transformation tools contest (TTC 2015), seven workshops affiliated with the conferences, a doctoral symposium, and a project showcase (for the first time). The event featured six internationally renowned keynote speakers, a tutorial, and welcomed participants from around the globe.

This has been the first scientific event in computer science after the earthquake that occurred in 2009 and affected L'Aquila. It is a small, and yet big step toward the grand achievement of restoring some form of normality in this place and its people.

The STAF Organizing Committee thanks all participants for submitting and attending, the program chairs and Steering Committee members for the individual conferences, the keynote speakers for their thoughtful, insightful, and engaging talks, the University of L'Aquila, Comune dell'Aquila, the local Department of Human Science, and CEA LIST for their support: *Grazie a tutti!*

July 2015   Alfonso Pierantonio

Preface

This volume contains the papers presented at the 9th International Conference on Tests and Proofs (TAP 2015), held during July 22–24, 2015, in L'Aquila, Italy, as part of the Software Technologies: Applications and Foundations (STAF) federated event.

TAP 2015 was the ninth event in a series of conferences devoted to the synergy of proofs and tests. Abandoning the traditional separation of formal verification and testing as orthogonal research fields, TAP aims at the identification of common ground across the different research communities. In particular, both testing and proving follow the goal of improving the quality of software and hardware, but with different means. Therefore, TAP provides a forum for the cross-fertilization of ideas and approaches from the formal verification community and the testing community, abandoning earlier dogmatic views on the incompatibility of proving and testing. TAP offers a meeting place for researchers who combine proofs and tests in an interdisciplinary manner by taking the best from both worlds.

Since its first edition at the ETH Zürich in 2007, TAP has been organized annually with great success. TAP was hosted by the Monash University Prato Centre near Florence in 2008, the ETH Zürich in 2009, the University of Malaga in 2010, the ETH Zürich in 2011, the Czech Technical University in Prague in 2012, the Budapest University of Technology and Economics in 2013, and the University of York in 2014. From 2010 to 2012, TAP was co-located with the TOOLS conference series on advanced software technologies. In 2013, TAP became part of STAF, which was formed after the end of TOOLS.

For the ninth edition of TAP, held at Università degli Studi dell'Aquila, we initially received 28 abstracts, leading to 21 submissions that were considered for reviewing. After a rigorous reviewing process and a discussion phase, we finally accepted 11 long papers and one short paper. For each paper, we required at least three reviews from the Program Committee or from external reviewers assigned by Program Committee members. The accepted papers contribute to various testing techniques (model-based, property-based, grammar-based, bounded-exhaustive), fault localization, model-driven engineering, as well as model coverage, consistency, and validation, among others. Many papers rely on interactive and automatic theorem provers, including SMT solvers and model checkers.

We wish to sincerely thank all authors who submitted their work for consideration. Further, we would like to thank the Program Committee members as well as the additional reviewers for their enthusiasm and their professional work in the review and selection process. Their names are listed on the following pages.

TAP 2015 featured two keynotes: "Mind the Gap: At the Crossroads of Design, Implementation, and Foundations" by Einar Broch Johnsen and "Reasoning about C Concurrency and Compilers" by Francesco Zappa Nardelli. Furthermore, Carlo A. Furia gave an invited tutorial on "Testing, Fixing, and Proving with Contracts." Many thanks to the three invited presenters for accepting our invitations.

Finally, we would also like to thank the organizers of the STAF event, in particular the general chair Alfonso Pierantonio and the publication chairs Louis Rose and Javier Troya, for their hard work and their support in making the conference a success. We thank the Università degli Studi dell'Aquila for providing the facilities. We thank the EasyChair developers for allowing us to use their conference management system and Springer for publishing these proceedings. We thank CEA LIST and the Chair of Software Engineering of ETH Zürich for financial support.

July 2015

Jasmin Christian Blanchette
Nikolai Kosmatov

Organization

Program Committee

Bernhard K. Aichernig	TU Graz, Austria
Dirk Beyer	University of Passau, Germany
Nikolaj Bjørner	Microsoft Research, Redmond, Washington, USA
Jasmin Christian Blanchette	Inria Nancy – Grand-Est, France
Achim D. Brucker	SAP AG, Karlsruhe, Germany
Koen Claessen	Chalmers University of Technology, Gothenburg, Sweden
Robert Clarisó	Universitat Oberta de Catalunya, Spain
Marco Comini	University of Udine, Italy
Catherine Dubois	ENSIIE-CEDRIC, Evry, France
Juhan Ernits	Tallinn University of Technology, Estonia
Gordon Fraser	University of Sheffield, UK
Angelo Gargantini	University of Bergamo, Italy
Christoph Gladisch	Karlsruhe Institute of Technology, Germany
Martin Gogolla	University of Bremen, Germany
Arnaud Gotlieb	SIMULA Research Laboratory, Oslo, Norway
Reiner Hähnle	Technical University of Darmstadt, Germany
Bart Jacobs	Katholieke Universiteit Leuven, Belgium
Jacques Julliard	University of Franche-Comté, France
Thierry Jéron	Inria Rennes – Bretagne Atlantique, France
Gregory Kapfhammer	Allegheny College, Pennsylvania, USA
Nikolai Kosmatov	CEA LIST, Saclay, France
Victor Kuliamin	Russian Academy of Sciences, Moscow, Russia
Panagiotis Manolios	Northeastern University, Boston, Massachusetts, USA
Karl Meinke	KTH, Stockholm, Sweden
Alexandre Petrenko	CRIM, Montreal, Canada
Andrew Reynolds	École Polytechnique Fédérale de Lausanne, Switzerland
Martina Seidl	Johannes Kepler University Linz, Austria
Nikolai Tillmann	Microsoft Research, Redmond, Washington, USA
T.H. Tse	The University of Hong Kong, SAR China
Margus Veanes	Microsoft Research, Redmond, Washington, USA
Luca Viganò	King's College London, UK
Burkhart Wolff	University of Paris-Sud, France
Fatiha Zaïdi	University of Paris-Sud, France

Additional Reviewers

Dury, Arnaud
Hentschel, Martin
Lorber, Florian
Majdoub, Lotfi

Omer Landry, Nguena Timo
Pradhan, Dipesh
Soeken, Mathias

Abstracts of Invited Talks

Testing, Fixing, and Proving with Contracts

Carlo A. Furia

Chair of Software Engineering, Department of Computer Science,
ETH Zurich, Zürich, Switzerland
caf@inf.ethz.ch
bugcounting.net

In the mind of the practitioner, the term "formal specification" often conjures up ghastly images of impenetrable logic formulas that only highly-trained experts can digest. Our experience with using contracts indicates, however, that developing simple elements of formal specification embedded in the program text as assertions requires an effort that is generally compatible with standard development practices [2]. In exchange for it, even the very simple contracts that programmers write can improve the effectiveness of a variety of analysis and verification techniques.

In this tutorial, I presented a number of tools we developed for the Eiffel programming language that take advantage of contracts in various guises. AutoTest generates random unit tests and uses contracts as oracles to automatically detect bugs; it has been used to find hundreds of errors in standard libraries. AutoFix builds source-code patches that turn failing tests into passing tests, thus automatically providing program repair for real software faults. AutoProof supports the static full-fledged verification of functional properties in object-oriented software; it has been used to verify the complete functionality of a realistic general-purpose container library. The various tools demonstrate a variety of techniques both dynamic (tests and runtime checking) and static (correctness proofs), which all leverage contracts to improve their effectiveness.

Bibliographic notes. *AutoTest* [4] combines techniques to improve the effectiveness of random testing: adaptive generation strategies [1], test-case minimization [3], and guided object selection for precondition satisfaction [18]. In the latest years, AutoTest has been mainly used as a supplier of test cases to support dynamic analysis of contract-equipped software [9,17,20].

AutoFix [19] takes advantage of flexible fault-localization and fix generation techniques [8], and has been evaluated on over 200 faults from different code bases [7]. SpeciFix [5] is an AutoFix component that can fix contracts instead of implementations.

AutoProof [16] supports incremental static verification by including heuristics to debug failed verification attempts [15], extensive source language support [14], and a methodology to reason about complex object dependencies [11]. It has been used to verify, among other challenges, algorithmic benchmarks [12] and the full functional correctness of a realistic, general-purpose library of data structures [10].

AutoTest, AutoFix (with SpeciFix), and AutoProof are all integrated in *EVE*, the Eiffel Verification Environment, which provides a uniform interface that integrates the results of the various analysis tools [6,13].

References

1. Ciupa, I., Leitner, A., Oriol, M., Meyer, B.: ARTOO: adaptive random testing for object-oriented software. In: 30th International Conference on Software Engineering (ICSE 2008), pp. 71–80. ACM (2008)
2. Estler, H.-C., Furia, C.A., Nordio, M., Piccioni, M., Meyer, B.: Contracts in practice. In: Jones, C., Pihlajasaari, P., Sun, J. (eds.) FM 2014. LNCS, vol. 8442, pp. 230–246. Springer, Heidelberg (2014)
3. Leitner, A., Oriol, M., Zeller, A., Ciupa, I., Meyer, B.: Efficient unit test case minimization. In: 22nd IEEE/ACM International Conference on Automated Software Engineering (ASE 2007), pp. 417–420. ACM (2007)
4. Meyer, B., Fiva, A., Ciupa, I., Leitner, A., Wei, Y., Stapf, E.: Programs that test themselves. IEEE Computer **42**(9), 46–55 (2009)
5. Pei, Y., Furia, C.A., Nordio, M., Meyer, B.: Automatic program repair by fixing contracts. In: Gnesi, S., Rensink, A. (eds.) FASE 2014 (ETAPS). LNCS, vol. 8411, pp. 246–260. Springer, Heidelberg (2014)
6. Pei, Y., Furia, C.A., Nordio, M., Meyer, B.: Automated program repair in an integrated development environment. In: Companion Proceedings of the 37th International Conference on Software Engineering (ICSE). ACM (May 2015) (Demonstrations Track)
7. Pei, Y., Furia, C.A., Nordio, M., Wei, Y., Meyer, B., Zeller, A.: Automated fixing of programs with contracts. IEEE Transactions on Software Engineering **40**(5), 427–449 (2014)
8. Pei, Y., Wei, Y., Furia, C.A., Nordio, M., Meyer, B.: Code-based automated program fixing. In: Proceedings of the 26th IEEE/ACM International Conference on Automated Software Engineering (ASE 2011), pp. 392–395. ACM (November 2011)
9. Polikarpova, N., Furia, C.A., Pei, Y., Wei, Y., Meyer, B.: What good are strong specifications? In: Proceedings of the 35th International Conference on Software Engineering (ICSE), pp. 257–266. ACM (May 2013)
10. Polikarpova, N., Tschannen, J., Furia, C.A.: A fully verified container library. In: Bjørner, N., de Boer, F. (eds.) FM 2015. LNCS, vol. 9109, pp. 414–434. Springer, Heidelberg (2015)
11. Polikarpova, N., Tschannen, J., Furia, C.A., Meyer, B.: Flexible invariants through semantic collaboration. In: Jones, C., Pihlajasaari, P., Sun, J. (eds.) FM 2014. LNCS, vol. 8442, pp. 514–530. Springer, Heidelberg (2014)
12. Tschannen, J., Furia, C.A., Nordio, M.: AutoProof meets some verification challenges. International Journal on Software Tools for Technology Transfer, 1–11 (February 2014). Special section on the VerifyThis 2012 Verification Competition
13. Tschannen, J., Furia, C.A., Nordio, M., Meyer, B.: Usable verification of object-oriented programs by combining static and dynamic techniques. In: Barthe, G., Pardo, A., Schneider, G. (eds.) SEFM 2011. LNCS, vol. 7041, pp. 382–398. Springer, Heidelberg (2011)
14. Tschannen, J., Furia, C.A., Nordio, M., Meyer, B.: Automatic verification of advanced object-oriented features: the autoproof approach. In: Meyer, B., Nordio, M. (eds.) LASER 2011. LNCS, vol. 7682, pp. 133–155. Springer, Heidelberg (2012)

15. Tschannen, J., Furia, C.A., Nordio, M., Meyer, B.: Program checking with less hassle. In: Cohen, E., Rybalchenko, A. (eds.) VSTTE 2013. LNCS, vol. 8164, pp. 149–169. Springer, Heidelberg (2014)
16. Tschannen, J., Furia, C.A., Nordio, M., Polikarpova, N.: AutoProof: auto-active functional verification of object-oriented programs. In: Baier, C., Tinelli, C. (eds.) TACAS 2015. LNCS, vol. 9035, pp. 566–580. Springer, Heidelberg (2015)
17. Wei, Y., Furia, C.A., Kazmin, N., Meyer, B.: Inferring better contracts. In: Proceedings of the 33rd International Conference on Software Engineering (ICSE 2011), pp. 191–200. ACM (May 2011)
18. Wei, Y., Gebhardt, S., Meyer, B., Oriol, M.: Satisfying test preconditions through guided object selection. In: Third International Conference on Software Testing, Verification and Validation, ICST 2010, pp. 303–312. IEEE Computer Society (2010)
19. Wei, Y., Pei, Y., Furia, C.A., Silva, L.S., Buchholz, S., Meyer, B., Zeller, A.: Automated fixing of programs with contracts. In: Proceedings of the 19th International Symposium on Software Testing and Analysis, ISSTA 2010, pp. 61–72. ACM (July 2010)
20. Wei, Y., Roth, H., Furia, C.A., Pei, Y., Horton, A., Steindorfer, M., Nordio, M., Meyer, B.: Stateful testing: finding more errors in code and contracts. In: Proceedings of the 26th IEEE/ACM International Conference on Automated Software Engineering (ASE 2011), pp. 440–443. ACM (November 2011)

Mind the Gap: At the Crossroads of Design, Implementation, and Foundations

Einar Broch Johnsen

Department of Informatics, University of Oslo, Oslo, Norway
einarj@ifi.uio.no

To reduce complexity, general-purpose modeling languages strive for abstraction [4]. But what is the right level of abstraction? Design-oriented models capture the logical or physical organization of software, abstracting from their dynamic behavior. Foundational models capture core features in a way suitable for meta-theory, but rely on cumbersome encodings of other features. Specifications close to actual code get obfuscated by the low-level intricacies of specific implementations.

This talk reports on research on abstract behavioral specifications [3], aiming for a middle ground in the gap between design, implementation, and foundations. We consider executable, yet abstract models which are faithful to the control and data flow of concurrent and distributed object-oriented systems, yet abstract enough to facilitate formal verification [5]. We then consider how novel technologies such as virtualization and cloud computing reintroduce low-level concerns at the abstraction level of the models. Deployment decisions form an integral part of resource-aware, virtualized applications. We discuss how these technologies raise new challenges for model-based analysis [1,2].

References

1. Albert, E., de Boer, F.S., Hähnle, R., Johnsen, E.B., Schlatte, R., Tapia Tarifa, S.L., Wong, P.Y.H.: Formal modeling of resource management for cloud architectures: An industrial case study using Real-Time ABS. Journal of Service-Oriented Computing and Applications **8**(4), 323–339 (2014)
2. Hähnle, R., Johnsen, E.B.: Resource-aware applications for the cloud. IEEE Computer (2015, to appear)
3. Johnsen, E.B., Hähnle, R., Schäfer, J., Schlatte, R., Steffen, M.: ABS: a core language for abstract behavioral specification. In: Aichernig, B.K., de Boer, F.S., Bonsangue, M.M. (eds.) Formal Methods for Components and Objects. LNCS, vol. 6957, pp. 142–164. Springer, Heidelberg (2011)
4. Kramer, J.: Is abstraction the key to computing? CACM **50**(4), 36–42 (2007)
5. Wong, P.Y.H., Albert, E., Muschevici, R., Proença, J., Schäfer, J., Schlatte, R.: The ABS tool suite: modelling, executing and analysing distributed adaptable object-oriented systems. STTT **14**(5), 567–588 (2012)

Supported by the EU project FP7-610582 *Envisage: Engineering Virtualized Services.* http://www.envisage-project.eu

Reasoning About C Concurrency and Compilers

Francesco Zappa Nardelli

INRIA, Paris, France
francesco.zappa_nardelli@inria.fr

The C and C++ languages were originally designed without concurrency support, but the recent revision of the C and C++ standards introduced an intricate but precise semantics for threads; today's C and C++ compilers, whose optimisers were initially developed in absence of any well-defined concurrency memory model, are being extended to support this new concurrency standard. This is a fantastic opportunity to put at work all our tools to formalise, test, and reason about large scale semantics and software.

In this talk, after recalling the C and C++ memory models, we will explore in a theorem prover the correctness of compiler optimisations and present simple necessary conditions that can be used as a reference by compiler implementers. As an application, we will show how this theory enables building an automatic compiler fuzzer that hunts concurrency compiler bugs: subtle wrong code generation bugs which are observable only when the miscompiled functions interact with concurrent contexts.

Perhaps surprisingly, we will also show that by leveraging the semantics of low-level relaxed atomic accesses (which allows programmers to take full advantage of weakly-ordered memory operations), it is possible to build counterexamples to several common source-to-source program transformations (such as expression linearisation and roach motel reorderings) that modern compilers perform and that are deemed to be correct. We will evaluate a number of possible local fixes, some strengthening and some weakening the model, and perhaps conclude, that, currently, there is no really satisfactory proposal for the semantics of a general-purpose shared-memory concurrent programming language.

References

1. Batty, M., Owens, S., Sarkar, S., Sewell, P., Weber, T.: Mathematizing C++ concurrency. In: POPL 2011. http://doi.acm.org/10.1145/1926385.1926394
2. Morisset, R., Pawan, P., Nardelli, F.Z.: Compiler testing via a theory of sound optimisations in the C11/C++11 memory model. In: PLDI 2013. http://doi.acm.org/10.1145/2491956.2491967
3. Vafeiadis, V., Balabonski, T., Chakraborty, S., Morisset, R., Nardelli, F.Z.: Common compiler optimisations are invalid in the C11 memory model and what we can do about it. In: POPL 2015. http://doi.acm.org/10.1145/2676726.2676995

This talk is based on work done with Thibaut Balabonski, Soham Chakraborty, Robin Morisset, and Viktor Vafeiadis, and on discussions with Mark Batty and Peter Sewell. It is supported by the ANR grant WMC (ANR-11-JS02-011).

Contents

Scalable Incremental Test-Case Generation from Large Behavior Models

Bernhard K. Aichernig[1], Dejan Ničković[2], and Stefan Tiran[1,2]([✉])

[1] Institute for Software Technology, Graz University of Technology, Graz, Austria
{aichernig,stiran}@ist.tugraz.at
[2] Austrian Institute of Technology, Vienna, Austria
{Dejan.Nickovic,Stefan.Tiran.fl}@ait.ac.at

Abstract. Model-based testing is a popular black-box testing technology that enables automation of test generation and execution, while achieving a given coverage. The application of this technology to large and complex systems is still a challenging problem, due to the state-space explosion resulting from the size of specification models.

In this paper, we evaluate a test-case generation approach that tackles this complexity along two axes. Firstly, our approach relies on a synchronous specification language for test models, thus avoiding the problem of interleaving actions. Secondly, our specification language enables incremental test-case generation by providing support for compositional modeling, in which each requirement or view of the system is expressed as a separate partial model. The individual requirement models are then naturally combined by conjunction, which is incrementally computed during the generation of tests.

We apply our test-case generation technique to two large industrial case studies: (1) an electronic control unit (ECU) of an agricultural device; and (2) a railway interlocking system. We demonstrate the scalability of our approach by creating a series of test models with increasing complexity and report on the experimental results.

1 Introduction

Model-based testing is a promising technology that aims at reducing the effort in testing of complex systems and replacing the tedious, ad-hoc and error prone manual testing. Despite the multiple benefits resulting from the automation of both test-case generation and test-case execution, processing large test models remains a considerable challenge due to the state-space explosion problem.

In order to tackle this challenge, we proposed a compositional specification of test models that makes the testing activity more effective and facilitates incremental test-case generation [3]. We note that in model-based testing there are various possible test-selection mechanisms, which aim at different coverage criteria. Our approach is independent of the chosen test-selection mechanism and so we assume a so-called test purpose given from outside. A test purpose (test specification) describes a set of states within the test model to be reached. In

© Springer International Publishing Switzerland 2015
J.C. Blanchette and N. Kosmatov (Eds.): TAP 2015, LNCS 9154, pp. 1–18, 2015.
DOI: 10.1007/978-3-319-21215-9_1

our framework we represent a test case as sequence of input values together with the test model, which we use as test oracle. Figure 1 illustrates the test-case execution: the sequence of inputs is translated into concrete values, which can be sent to the system-under-test (SUT). The output values produced from the SUT are translated back into an abstract output sequence. A monitor takes both the abstract input and output sequence and uses the test model in order to decide the verdict, i.e. whether the SUT has passed the test.

The aim of test-case generation is to find a sequence of input values, which satisfies the test purpose on the test model. In our approach, the test model is structured into a conjunction of partial models $M_1 \ldots M_n$, each representing a specific aspect that the SUT must satisfy.

Instead of composing the partial models into one test model immediately, as illustrated in Figure 2 (a), we rather adopt an incremental approach to test generation. For a given test purpose, we first search for the required sequence of inputs on a partial model M_i only (TCG), resulting in a partial input sequence. We then invoke the test-case generator a second time, in order to extend the input sequence to the full model. In general the full test model can use more input variables than the partial view, which was picked in the first iteration. Even if the partial model M_i already contains all input variables, it has to be checked, whether the partial input sequence is still able to reach the test purpose on the full model. The incremental test-case generation (TCG_{inc}) is a search for an input sequence, reusing the valuations of input variables which already occurred in the partial input sequence.

This incremental test generation procedure was implemented using bounded model checking techniques based on the SMT solver Z3 [12]. A preliminary evaluation on a small example already suggested the potential benefits of such incremental test-case generation compared to the classical monolithic approach [3].

In this paper, we provide a comprehensive evaluation of our incremental test-case generation by applying it to two large industrial case studies: (1) an electronic control unit (ECU) of an agricultural device; and (2) a railway interlocking system. The first case study focuses on the control logic of a wheel-loader. Its main functionality is the conversion of deflection values of a joystick into electric currents that provide power to the electromagnetic valves, controlling the bucket of the wheel loader. The second case study considers the control logic of an interlocking system, which needs to establish safe, thus non-conflicting, train routes in the railway stations. In the process of conducting these case studies, we added another compositional feature to our framework - object-oriented models. Object-oriented modeling facilitates specification of complex systems that contain multiple instances of standard components. The size and complexity of the resulting test models allowed us to assess the scalability of our approach and its applicability to effective testing of real-world systems. We demonstrate the benefits of our incremental test-case generation techniques and report on experimental results.

Structure. In Section 2 we briefly recall the requirement interfaces modeling language and our incremental test-case generation procedure for such models.

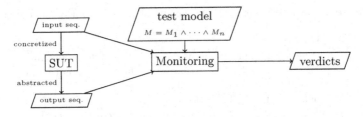

Fig. 1. Test-case execution

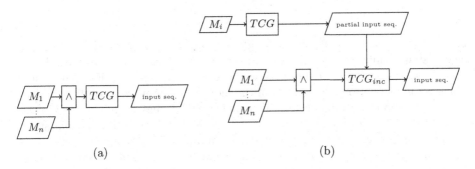

Fig. 2. Test-case generation: (a) monolithic; and (b) incremental

Section 3 and 4 present the wheel loader and the railway interlocking station case studies, respectively. In Section 5 we discuss the related work and Section 6 concludes the paper by giving hints on future work.

2 Preliminaries

In this section, we first shortly present *requirement interfaces* [3] as the specification language that we use to model the case studies and then recall the procedure that enables incremental generation of tests from such models. We finally discuss avoidance of vacuously reaching test purposes.

2.1 Requirement Interfaces

We first provide an informal presentation of requirement interfaces and illustrate the specification language with a bounded buffer example. The formal syntax and semantics of requirement interfaces are defined in previous work [3]. Requirement interfaces is a formalism for specification of synchronous data-flow systems. An N-bounded buffer can be seen as a synchronous reactive system whose behavior is specified with the informal requirements listed in Table 1.

The natural language requirements define the buffer's behavior as a set of dynamic relations between its variables. Variables are basic building blocks of requirement interfaces. They are partitioned into disjoint sets of *input, output*

Table 1. Natural language requirements of the behavior of the buffer

Req ID	Req Description
R1	enq triggers an enqueue operation when the buffer is not full.
R2	deq triggers a dequeue operation when the buffer is not empty.
R3	E signals that the buffer is empty.
R4	F signals that the buffer is full.
R5	Simultaneous enq and deq (or their simultaneous absence), an enq on the full buffer or a deq on the empty buffer have no effect.

and *hidden* variables. Output and hidden variables are controlled by the modeled system, while its external environment controls the input variables. Input and output variables are exposed to the external observers, while hidden variables are invisible from the outside of the modeled system. An N-buffer receives from its environment enqueue and dequeue requests, that we model as Boolean input variables enq and deq. The buffer updates accordingly its internal state, by increasing, decreasing or preserving the number of items that it stores. This internal state is not visible to external observers, hence we model it with a hidden integer variable k (bounded by N). In contrast, the buffer signals to the outside world when it is empty or full. We model this information with the Boolean output variables E and F, respectively.

The dynamic behavior of a requirement interface is defined by a set of rules that describe allowed transitions between its successive states. A transition is a pair consisting of a source and a target state. We use unprimed and primed variables to refer to source and target states respectively. More precisely, a rule in requirement interfaces, that we call a *contract*, is a pair consisting of an *assumption* about the external environment, and a *guarantee* that the modeled system is required to provide when the assumption hold. In essence, a contract either encodes a set of initial states or allowed transitions between states. Technically, assumptions and guarantees are predicates over primed and unprimed variables in the interface.[1] We say that a system conforms to a contract if whenever its environment satisfies the assumption predicate, it makes an update that satisfies the guarantee predicate. The system conforms to a requirement interface if it conforms to all of its contracts. We note that natural language requirements are typically translated to a contract. In requirement interfaces, we naturally associate one or more requirement identifiers to each contract, facilitating traceability of requirements in the model and the resulting test cases. Listing 1.1 shows the requirements interface formalization of the N buffer requirements.

---

[1] In this paper, we consider a definition of assumptions and guarantees that is relaxed with respect to our previous work [3], where assumptions and guarantees are not allowed to refer to primed output/hidden and primed input variables, respectively. This relaxation does not affect our incremental test-case generation approach.

Table 2. Natural language requirements of the power consumption of the buffer

Req ID	Req Description
RA	The power consumption equals zero when no enq/deq is requested.
RB	The power consumption is bounded to 2 units otherwise.

Listing 1.1. Formalized contracts of the behavior of the buffer

```
{R1} assume enq' and not deq' and k < N    guarantee  k' = k + 1
{R2} assume not enq' and deq' and k > 0    guarantee  k' = k - 1
{R3} assume true  guarantee  k' = 0 <-> E'
{R4} assume true  guarantee  k' = N <-> F'
{R5} assume enq' = deq' or enq' and F or deq' and E  guarantee  k' = k
```

Different requirements and views of a system, modeled as requirement interfaces, are naturally combined with the *conjunction* operation. Intuitively, a system that conforms to a conjunction of requirement interfaces must independently conform to each interface. In the N-buffer example, in addition to the behavioral view, we also consider its power consumption view. This non-functional view collects the requirements that define the power consumption of the buffer during different operations. The collected requirements are listed in Table 2.

The power consumption of the buffer depends on the enqueue and the dequeue requests, hence this extra-functional view shares the same input variables with the behavioral view. We model the actual power consumption with a bounded integer variable pc that we assume to be measurable and hence observable to the outside world. The contracts in the requirement interface that formalize the power consumption view of the N-buffer are shown in Listing 1.2.

Listing 1.2. Formalized contracts of the power consumption of the buffer.

```
{RA} assume not enq' and not deq'  guarantee  pc' = 0
{RB} assume enq' or deq'  guarantee  pc' <= 2
```

2.2 Incremental Test-Case Generation

In order to create a sequence of input values, which is the core part of our test case, we perform a bounded reachability analysis of the given test purpose on the transition relation associated with the test model. The test purpose is a predicate that defines a set of states that the tester wants to steer the system to. The transition relation ϕ of an interface is the conjunction of its contracts where a contract is represented as an implication from assumption to guarantee. The transition relation ϕ is unfolded by copying and replacing the variables with copies for each step, resulting in a series $\phi^0 \wedge \ldots \wedge \phi^k$. We denote by $[X \backslash X^i]$ the substitution of the variables with their respective copies of step i.

In our implementation we use the SMT solver Z3 in order tho check, whether the test purpose Π can be reached in A in at most k steps:

$$\mathbf{smt}(\phi^0 \wedge \ldots \wedge \phi^k \wedge \bigvee_{i \leq k} \Pi[X \backslash X^i])$$

The call **smt()** returns a pair, containing (1) a Boolean value stating whether the test purpose can actually be reached, and (2) a model containing a variable valuation for the underlying SMT problem in the case that the test purpose is reachable. If a model exists it can be mapped to a sequence of variable valuations of the modeled system, from which only the input variables are needed for the test-case execution.

Given the requirement interface for the behavioral view of the 2-bounded buffer, and the test purpose F, our test-case generation procedure gives the input sequence of size 3: $(\mathsf{enq}, \mathsf{deq}) \cdot (\mathsf{enq}, \neg\mathsf{deq}) \cdot (\mathsf{enq}, \neg\mathsf{deq})$.

Since the power consumption view does not add any input variables, this sequence could already be used in a test case together with the full model as oracle. However, it might happen that the input sequence, gained from a partial view only, does not lead to the test purpose in the full model anymore.

The aim of the incremental test-case generation algorithm is to add values from input variables which do not exist in the partial model and to check whether the partial input sequence is feasible on the full model.

Algorithm 1. Incremental TCG

Input: *partial model* M_{part}, *full model* M_{full}, *test purpose* Π, *exploration depth* k
Output: fail or $\sigma_{full} \in L(M_{full}) = X^0 \cdots X^k$ *such that* $\exists j : (X^{j-1}, X^j) \models \Pi$
1: $(sat, res) \leftarrow \mathbf{smt}(\phi^0_{M_{part}} \wedge \ldots \wedge \phi^k_{M_{part}} \wedge \bigvee_{i \leq k} \Pi[X \backslash X^i])$
2: **if** $\neg sat$ **then**
3:     **return fail**
4: **end if**
5: $in \leftarrow \pi(res)[X_{M_{part}, I}]$
6: $(sat, res) \leftarrow \mathbf{smt}(in = \pi(\sigma)[X_{M_{part}, I}] \wedge \phi^0_{M_{full}} \wedge \ldots \wedge \phi^k_{M_{full}} \wedge \bigvee_{i \leq k} \Pi[X \backslash X^i])$
7: **if** sat **then**
8:     **return** $\pi(res)[X_I \cup X_O]$
9: **else**
10:     **return fail**
11: **end if**

Algorithm 1 formally introduces our approach of incremental test-case generation using partial models. Input to the algorithm are the models M_{part} and M_{full}. The interface M_{part} is expected to be a partial view, containing all relevant contracts, which are necessary in order to reach one of the states described by Π in k steps. If the algorithm succeeds, it will return a trace σ_{full}, which can be executed on M_{full} and meets the purpose Π, otherwise it fails. In Line 1 a variable valuation encoding the trace leading to the test purpose within the partial view is determined and stored in the variable res. If no such valuation exists, the algorithm fails immediately in Line 3. Otherwise in Line 5, the part of the result containing the input valuations is extracted (projection π) and stored in the variable in. This is the partial input sequence used in order to guide the exploration in Line 6. More precisely, from the free variables σ the part containing input variables that are in common with the partial view $(\pi(\sigma)[X_{I,M_{part}}])$ are fixed with the values from the variable in.

As mentioned, preliminary results [3] suggest that the incremental test-case generation is more efficient than the monolithic approach and this hypothesis is evaluated in this paper on two industrial case studies.

2.3   Avoidance of Vacuously Reaching Test Purposes

The incremental approach to test-case generation that we described in Section 2.2 is based on the exploration of partial views of the system. However, in some cases the partial view may not contain enough information to guide the test-case generation towards a given test purpose. This situation results in the generation of input vectors that vacuously reach the test purpose in the partial model, but do not properly guide the SUT towards the desired goal.

Consider the N-buffer example from Section 2.1 and the test purpose F - we want to generate a test that leads the SUT to the state in which the buffer is full. If we generate such a test from a partial view that lacks one of the contracts formalizing requirements R_1, R_2, or R_5, the resulting test may reach the test purpose in a vacuous manner, because there exist input values for which the system is underspecified. This phenomenon is similar to spurious counter-examples in the counter-example guided abstraction refinement (CEGAR) techniques [10].

In order to avoid such spurious test cases, the test purpose can be directly extended with additional constraints that will help the test-case generator to choose meaningful input values staying inside the assumptions. This was crucial for the interlocking system case study, in which the decomposition into partial models removed some of the contracts handling aspects of an input variable, leaving some input reactions underspecified. This is unlike the cone of influence reduction technique [7], in which only those variables are removed, which do not affect the test purpose at all. In the future, we plan to replace this manual extension step by incorporating back-tracking techniques into our incremental test-case generation.

3   Wheel Loader Case Study

3.1   Use-Case Description

The first case-study focuses on an electronic control unit (ECU) of a wheel loader. This system implements the control of the bucket and bucket arm movement in a wheel loader. The controller processes inputs from a two-dimensional joystick in order to calculate appropriate control commands. In addition, the controller also provides error management functionality. Instead of an actual deflection, the joystick can report a fault by using some designated values. The ECU has to count the number of occurrences of the reported faults and switch to an error mode, in which the movements are stopped for safety reasons. When the controller is in the error mode and the joystick resumes producing valid inputs again, the ECU must recover and begin to move the bucket arm and the bucket according to the position of the joystick. Information about the internal error manager mode, the current position of the joystick as well as the current movements of the bucket arm and the bucket are shown to the user by sending references to predefined images in the user display.

3.2 Modeling

In this case study, we decompose our model of the ECU and consider three different aspects: (1) the error management view; (2) the control itself; and (3) the configuration view. As a result, our model of the ECU consists of three requirements interfaces. In total, the full model has 1 Boolean and 21 bounded integer variables and consists of 138 contracts. The variables are partitioned into 2 input, 7 output and 13 state variables.

The first requirement interface captures the error management behavior. It consists of 20 contracts describing how the ECU has to change its internal error manager state and which predefined picture has to be shown on the display. We illustrate 3 contracts from the error management view in Listing 1.3.

Listing 1.3. Subset of contracts in the error management view

```
{E1} assume   initialized and errorManagerState = 0 and joystick1' > 0 and
              joystick1' < 64000 and joystick2' > 0 and joystick2' < 64000
      guarantee errorManagerState' = 0 and un_valid_data_counter' = 0 and
              correction_counter' = correction_counter and
              systemStatusGraphic' = systemStatusGraphic
{E2} assume   initialized and errorManagerState = 0 and (joystick1' <= 0 or
              joystick1' >= 64000 or joystick2' <= 0 or joystick2' >= 64000)
      guarantee errorManagerState' = 1 and un_valid_data_counter' = 1 and
              correction_counter' = correction_counter and
              systemStatusGraphic' = systemStatusGraphic
{E3} assume   initialized and errorManagerState = 1 and (joystick1' > 0 and
              joystick1' < 64000 and joystick2' > 0 and joystick2' < 64000)
      guarantee errorManagerState' = 1 and un_valid_data_counter' =
              un_valid_data_counter and correction_counter' = correction_counter
              and systemStatusGraphic' = systemStatusGraphic
```

{E1} models the case where the ECU is initialized, its error manager has not encountered any recent fault (modeled as errorManagerState being equal to 0) and the values coming from the joystick (variables jostick1 and jostick2 that denote its 2 dimensions) are in the valid range of $(0, 64000)$. The associated guarantee states that the counter for recently reported faults (un_valid_data_counter) is reset, while the counter keeping track of how often the system has recovered (correction_counter) and the variable that contains the reference to the picture (systemStatusGraphic) do not change. {E2} models the reaction to an unexpected joystick value (joystick1 or joystick2 outside of the valid range) to the error management. In that case, the error management state is set to 1, the counter for recently reported faults is increased, while correction_counter and systemStatusGraphic do not change. {E3} describes the reaction to a valid joystick value, when the error management system is already in error management state 1. In that case, un_valid_data_counter, correction_counter and systemStatusGraphic do not change their value.

The second viewpoint captures the calculation of control values, based on the joystick inputs and the internal state of the system. It consists of 116 contracts. In practice, the input from the joystick is sensed and processed, resulting in the generation of an appropriate electric current that is applied to the bucket and the bucket arm. Because of physical limitations, the actual current must not differ to the one of the last step by a predefined bound. We model the resulting current with integer variables. Listing 1.4 shows 3 sample contracts from the second viewpoint.

Listing 1.4. Sample contracts describing the calculation of output values

```
{T1}  assume  initialized  and  joystick1' > 35339  and  joystick1' < 64000  and
             joystick2' < 64000   and  joystick2' > 0
      guarantee
targetEm1PortA' = (800 * (joystick1' - 35339)) div (64255 - 35339)
{T2}  assume  initialized  and  joystick1' > 0  and  joystick1' <= 35339  and
             joystick2' < 64000  and  joystick2' > 0
      guarantee  targetEm1PortA' = 0
{T3}  assume
initialized  and  (errorManagerState' = 0  or  errorManagerState' = 1)
             and  em1PortB = 0  and  targetEm1PortA' > (em1PortA + 50)
      guarantee  em1PortA' = em1PortA + 50
```

Table 3. Run-times in seconds for different configurations of the wheel loader

Config #	Depth	#$Vars$	t_{part}	t_{inc}	t_{mono}
1	39	861	2.0	3.6	16.8
2	43	945	2.0	3.4	47.7
3	44	966	1.6	2.8	31.9
4	47	1029	2.5	4.6	139.1
5	48	1050	2.1	3.9	45.3
6	49	1071	3.4	4.9	47.5
7	51	1113	3.3	4.8	52.2
8	52	1134	2.9	4.6	53.7
9	53	1155	3.0	4.8	252.4
10	56	1218	4.2	7.3	135.4
11	57	1239	6.1	7.8	33,810.4

The third viewpoint captures the configuration of the error management. It only consists of 2 contracts. The configuration viewpoint defines three parameters: (1) M denotes the maximum number of invalid joystick inputs that is allowed before the error management puts the system in a safe state by disabling bucket movements; (2) N denotes the number of consecutive valid joystick inputs needed to restore the system from its safe state and resume bucket movements; and K denotes the number of switches between the normal and the safe state before the system is shut down. Each specific choice for M, N and K gives a different instantiation of the system and determines the size of the underlying model.

3.3 Evaluation

In order to evaluate our incremental test-case generation approach, we first created a partial model that combined the error management and configuration but excluded the controller view. We also defined a test purpose for our partial view. We set up the following experiment consisting of applying three different approaches and compared them.

In the partial approach (*part*), we generated tests from the partial model and test purpose. The incremental approach (*inc*), consisted in using our incremental procedure to first generate tests from the partial model and the test purpose and then extend them with the constraints from the controller view. Finally, in the monolithic approach (*mono*), we combined all three partial models and only then derived tests for the same test purpose, using the monolithic test-case generation procedure. We compared the computation costs for generating tests with the incremental and the monolithic procedures. The experiment was conducted on a PC with a 3 GHz CPU and 8 GB RAM running Windows 7.

Table 3 shows the results of the experiment, which was conducted with 11 different configurations of the system. The complexity of each model instance is reflected by the depth, that is the length of the test case necessary to reach the test purpose, and the number of variables in the underlying SMT encoding of the test-case generation problem. Columns t_{part}, t_{inc} and t_{mono} show the time needed for the test generation using the partial, incremental and monolithic approaches, respectively.

It can be seen that the run-times for monolithic test-case generation do not increase strictly monotonic, but the trend is clear. At one point the run-time exceeds with over nine hours the reasonable time one is willing to wait for the generation of a single test case. The run-times of the incremental approach on the other hand increase very slow, never exceeding eight seconds.

4   Interlocking Case Study

4.1   Use-Case Description

The object of the second case study is the control logic of an interlocking system used in a railway station. Such a system controls and monitors elements like tracks, switches, and signals in order to establish safe train routes, which are not in conflict to each other. Inputs to the system come from so-called track supervision elements as well as the operator of the interlocking system. A track supervision element reports, whether a specific track element is occupied. This information is not only important in order to decide, when a specific train route can be set up, but it also allows the system to automatically dissolve a train route after a train has passed through. The operator can request the system to establish a train route between two signals, cancel an established train route, and manually move a switch to a specific position or lock a switch in a specific position. Outputs of the system are the position of the switches, the state of the signals as well as the usage of track elements within a train route. The requirements for the interlocking system were provided by Thales Austria GmbH.

4.2   Modeling

Unlike in the first case study, the requirements here usually refer to generic components, such as signals, switched and track elements, which are instantiated

Table 4. Mapping between classes of the model and corresponding variables

Class	Input	Output	Hidden
Track	occupied : $\mathbb{B}$	usage : $\mathbb{I}$	-
Switch	occupied : $\mathbb{B}$	usage, position : $\mathbb{I}$, locked, interlocked : $\mathbb{B}$	-
Signal	-	stop : $\mathbb{B}$	-
Train Route	-	-	state, sub_state : $\mathbb{I}$
Global	command : $\mathbb{B}$	not_permissive, cancel_log : $\mathbb{I}$	-

multiple times in a railway station. In addition, the layout of the railway station that defines the connection between track elements and switches and the position of the signals is also part of the model. Figure 3 shows the layout of the train station of size L. In this configuration there are three straight tracks (e.g. TCSSa, TCSSc, TCSSe) between each switch and the track element on which a train can stand (e.g. TCSS), while the other train passes. In order to increase the complexity of the model, we inserted another three track elements (e.g TCSSg, TCSSi, TCSSk) directly before TCSS and TCH resp. (twelve in total) and refer to the resulting model as model of size *XL*. We repeated this procedure in order to gain models of sizes *XXL*, *XXXL*, *XXXXL*, and *XXXXXL*, each containing twelve track elements more than the prior one. The fully instantiated models of size L and *XXXXXL* consist of 181 and 3323 contracts and use 85 and 205 variables respectively.

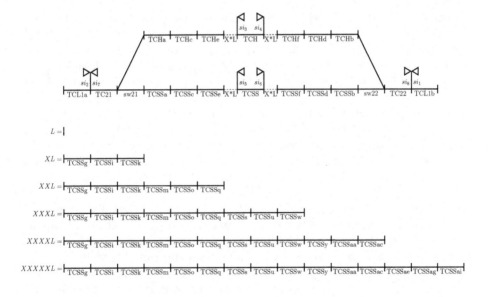

Fig. 3. Layout of the railway station

Variables. Table 4 shows how the variables of the behavior model correspond to the physical and logical entities of the interlocking system. Each track has an input variable occupied that denotes whether it is occupied and an output usage variable that describes how the track is used (see Figure 4 (b)). Switches have in addition to occupied and usage the variables position, locked and interlocked that encode the position of the switch, whether this position is locked by the operator or interlocked because its position is needed for a specific train route. Signals have the single output variable stop, which encodes whether or not a train is allowed to pass.

Train routes are logical entities of the interlocking system, grouping a set of physical elements arranged in a specific order. They are predefined by the OEM and can be in various states (modeled by state and sub-state variables) which are specified by the requirements document (see Figure 4 (a)). A train route is *idle* until it gets requested by the operator. It then goes to the *admissibility check* state in which the train route is either allowed or rejected. If the train route is admissible, it goes to the *set up* state, in which it stays until all switches are successfully set to their correct position and interlocked. Furthermore, all involved track supervision elements have to report that there is no train on any needed track element. The set up state is followed by the *signal clearing* state in which the signals are switched to show a "go" sign. After this is done, the train route goes to the *supervision* state in which it observes all involved track elements. As soon as the train has passed all other elements and stands in the so-called goal area, the train route is dissolved automatically. We note that whenever a phase is not successfully completed, the train route goes back to its *idle* state.

Similarly, tracks and switches have internal states encoded in their usage variable. The transition relation between these states is shown in Figure 4 (b). An element is *unused*, when it is not used in any train route. If a train route is established, it can be either *free* if the information from the track supervision elements confirm that there is no train standing on it, or it can be *not yet free* if for any reason this cannot be confirmed. The latter state switches to *free* as soon as the track supervision elements confirm that the element is now free. As soon as a train enters the specific element, this is again recognized by the track supervision element and the element switches to *occupied*. As soon as the train leaves the element, its usage is considered as *had been occupied* until the train route finally gets dissolved, which is done when the train has passed.

Global variables. The communication with the operator of the interlocking system is modeled with an additional input and two output variables. The input variable denotes the command that the operator is requesting. This includes commands for requesting to establish or to manually cancel a train route, to lock a switch or to manually change the position of a switch. The output variable not_permissive encodes whether the requested train route is admissible and the variable cancel_log is an output to a logging device, which keeps record of possibly hazardous commands from the operator.

The input variable command is an integer encoding an enumerative value: each combination of the command (e.g. *request train route, cancel train route,*

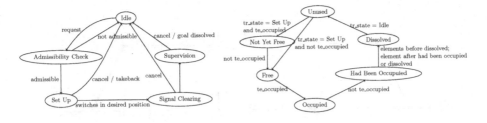

(a) States of a train route   (b) Usage of a track element

Fig. 4. State machines of the interlocking system

Table 5. Sample natural language requirements of the interlocking system

Req ID	Req Description
R161	A train route shall not be admissible, if any element in the selected route except the start element and the goal element is used in another train route.
R162	A train route shall not be admissible, if a switch in the route or its overlap is required in a position it does not have, and the switch is locked or interlocked.
R164	A train route shall not be admissible, if the goal element is locked for train routes.

change switch, ...) and the corresponding object (e.g. *tr_13*, *sw21*) is mapped to a specific value.

Parametrized contracts. Requirement interfaces do not provide native support for classes or other object-oriented data structures. During the development of this case study, we developed such an object-oriented support for modeling generic components which are then automatically instantiated. We used Scala, an object-oriented and functional programming language, to provide an easy and natural separation of the train station layout from its logic. Since our requirement interfaces testing tool is also written in Scala, it was possible to reuse the class hierarchy of the abstract syntax tree in order to encode a generic contract, which can be instantiated with every considered element. This approach is particularly well-suited for our incremental approach based on partial models - it facilitates instantiation of generic components for arbitrary layouts, but also enables generation of partial models that contain the meaningful subset of such instances. For instance, given a large railway station layout and a specific train route as a test purpose, our object-oriented approach allows to easily discard all tracks and switches that do not affect the train route and thus to considerably reduce the complexity of the (partial) model that is needed to be explored in order to generate the right test case.

Example. Table 5 shows three sample natural language requirements, which describe the behavior of the train routes. We first formalize this reoccurring kind of *refuse condition* into predicates, e.g. $\text{refuseCondition}_1(\text{tr}) =_{def}$
$exists(((\text{tracks}_{tr} \ \cup \ \text{switches}_{tr}) \backslash \text{goal}_{tr}), \neg \text{isUsage}(\text{elm}, \text{Unused}), \text{elm})$,   where

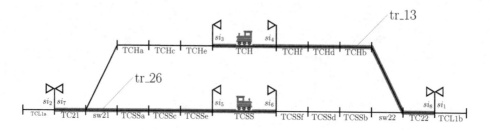

Fig. 5. Example of two train routes that can be established at the same time

"exists" is a shortcut for the existential quantification of the (bounded integer) free variable elm. The quantification is only visible in the meta model and flattened down to a disjunction in the resulting requirement interface. Variables tracks, switches, and goal are parametrized by the train route identifier. Applied to the function isUsage they map down to corresponding usage variable of the respective track element. Instantiated for the train route that starts at signal si_1 and ends at signal si_3 without any overlap, this expression compiles down to: $(((((\neg(\mathsf{TCHf\_usage} = Unused))) \vee (\neg(\mathsf{TCHd\_usage} = Unused))) \vee (\neg(\mathsf{TCSSb\_usage} = Unused))) \vee (\neg(\mathsf{sw22\_usage} = Unused))$ The predicates for R162 and R164 would be: $\mathsf{refuseCondition}_{tr}^2 =_{def} exists((\mathsf{switches}_{tr} \cup \mathsf{overlap}_{tr}), \mathsf{sw.position} \neq \mathsf{sw.position}(tr) \vee \mathsf{sw.locked} \vee \mathsf{sw.interlocked}, \mathsf{sw})$ and $\mathsf{refuseCondition}_{tr}^3 =_{def} \mathsf{end\_signal}_{tr}.\mathsf{locked}$ respectively.

These predicates can then be used in parametrized contracts, as shown in Listing 1.5.

Listing 1.5. Example of parametrized contracts

```
{R161}    assume    command' = request_tr ∧ isInState_tr(Admissibility Check)∧
                    refuseCondition^1_tr
          guarantee setState_tr(Idle) ∧ not_permitted' = tr
{R162}    assume    command' = request_tr ∧ isInState_tr(Admissibility Check)∧
                    refuseCondition^2_tr
          guarantee setState_tr(Idle) ∧ not_permitted' = tr
{R164}    assume    command' = request_tr ∧ isInState_tr(Admissibility Check)∧
                    refuseCondition^3_tr
          guarantee setState_tr(Idle) ∧ not_permitted' = tr
{R161,R162,R164}
          assume    command' = request_tr ∧ isInState_tr(Admissibility Check)∧
                    ¬(refuseCondition^1_tr ∨ refuseCondition^2_tr ∨ refurefuseCondition^3_tr
          guarantee setState_tr(Set Up) ∧ not_permitted' = -1
```

4.3   Test-Case Generation

As the test purpose we chose the state in which both train routes are about to be dissolved because a train has passed most of the tracks and stands on the last element (TCSS and TCH respectively). Figure 5 highlights the corresponding train routes. Using our notion this goal can be formalized as: $\mathsf{tr\_13\_state}' = Supervision \wedge \mathsf{tr\_26\_state}' = Supervision \wedge \mathsf{TCH\_usage}' = Had\ Been\ Occupied \wedge \mathsf{TCSS\_usage}' = Had\ Been\ Occupied.$

Table 6. Evaluation results for the interlocking system case study

Model size	# $vars_{part}$	# $vars_{full}$	t_{part}	t_{inc}	t_{mono}
L	720	1360	1.6	15.6	25.7
XL	1083	2071	4.3	39.3	94.2
XXL	1518	2926	10.4	87.3	316.2
XXXL	2025	3925	24.0	173.3	413.2
XXXXL	2604	5068	36.1	308.3	825.0
XXXXXL	3255	6355	63.1	480.8	5476.1

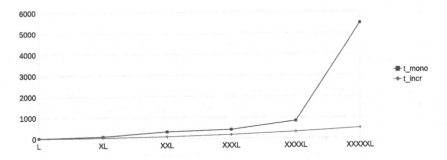

Fig. 6. Run-times in seconds for finding a trace

In order to guide the solver to assign meaningful values when processing the partial model, we extended the test purpose with additional constraints on the input variable of the form $\bigwedge_{obj}$ command $\neq$ operation$_{obj}$ where operation$_{obj}$ denotes some operation on an object obj, which is not considered by the partial model.

4.4 Evaluation

For the evaluation of the interlocking system case study, we defined an experimental setup similar to the one presented in Section 3.3. We applied the three test generation approaches, partial (*part*), incremental (*inc*) and monolithic (*mono*), to multiple model instances (L to XXXXXL), and compared the the computation costs to generate a test with each of the approaches. For each of the model instances, we expressed its complexity as the number of variables in the underlying SMT encoding of the test-case generation problem. Unlike in the first case study, the reason for the increasing number of variables is two-fold: firstly, a higher search depth is needed and therefore the transition relation is unfolded more often and secondly, due to the increased number of track elements the number of variables per step of the transition relation increases. Columns t_{part}, t_{inc} and t_{mono} show the time needed for the test generation using the partial, incremental and monolithic approaches, respectively.

Figure 6 visualizes the run-time comparison. The run-time for generating one test-case monolithically for the XXXXXL model again exceeds with over one hour any reasonable waiting time. Using the incremental approach for an equivalent test-case of the same model, generation only takes eight minutes, which is a considerable improvement. Significant performance improvement can also be seen on the next smaller model, where monolithic test-case generation takes about 14 minutes while the incremental test-case generation technique takes less than 6 minutes. On the smallest model L the incremental approach is with 15.6 seconds still almost twice as fast as the monolithic approach with 25.7 seconds.

5   Related Work

Incremental testing has been studied in various forms in the past.

In a recent work, we proposed decomposing the test model into partial models in order to facilitate test-case generation [1], and used the same wheel loader case study for evaluation. We also proposed a test-driven software development process, in which a series of partial test models was used in order to automatically derive test cases [4]. In contrast to this work, the modeling language in our former work [1,4] is UML, hence the underlying state space has all the interleavings of actions. In addition, the partial test cases generated from the UML model are not extended with the constraints from the other views.

Fraser and Wotawa [14] showed how to avoid generating duplicate test cases by incrementally extending existing ones to meet additional test purposes. In other previous work the performance improvements gained from incremental SMT solving [2] has been studied, ie. to leave common parts of the system description on the stack of the SMT solver. In the context of communicating extended finite state machines (CEFSMs), Bourhfir et al. [8] analyzed the dependency between components. Schwarzl and Peischl [17] propose a test-case generation for deterministic CEFSMs communicating via asynchronous messages. In their approach, the exploration of compound model paths respects the communication structure of its single components. They consider deterministic models which communicate via asynchronous messages and avoid interleavings by fixing the order of the messages. El-Fakih et al. [13] propose an incremental test-case generation approach that is similar to ours. They first generate a partial (internal) test case from a component model and then extend it to a full (external) test case that takes into account the component's context. In contrast to our work, both the component and the context are modeled as deterministic finite state machines.

Van der Bijl et. al [18] and Daca et. al [11] propose exploiting the structural properties of parallel composition in testing in order to infer properties of a system from testing its individual components. Incremental test-case generation based on the properties of the parallel composition was proposed in the context of real-time systems testing [16]. Arcaini and Gargantini [5] propose an approach to combine tests from subsystems given as sequential nets of Abstract State Machines. In a later work Arcaini et. al. [6] provide an automated abstraction technique for so-called Decomposable by Dependency Asynchronous Parallel

(DDAP) systems. In contrast to our work based on a synchronous system with a global clock, in their work modules communicate asynchronously such that only one system is active at the same time. Koo and Mishra [15] propose a method for decomposing both the model and the properties (which relate to the test purpose) of a synchronous test model.

In contrast to other requirement formalization approaches like $RSML^{-e}$ [9], we formalize requirements in order to build the transition relation instead of translating them to temporal properties to be checked.

6 Conclusion

In this paper, we applied our synchronous and incremental requirement-driven test-case generation technique to two large industrial case studies, from the transportation and the railway domains. We payed special attention to the scalability of our approach, and demonstrated its benefits, but also some limits.

We plan to address in the future the limits that we identified by conducting the case studies. The manual decomposition of the requirements document into partial models at the right level of abstraction remains the main bottleneck in applying such incremental techniques. We will provide additional support for the decomposition process by developing static dependency analysis between requirements. We also plan to extend our incremental technique to systems that communicate over asynchronous messages for applications such as telecommunication protocols in which the synchronous view is not sufficient.

Acknowledgments. We are grateful to the anonymous reviewers for their valuable and detailed feedback. The research leading to these results has received funding from the ARTEMIS Joint Undertaking under grant agreement N° 332830 and from the Austrian Research Promotion Agency (FFG) under grant agreement N° 838498 for the implementation of the project CRYSTAL, Critical System Engineering Acceleration. We want to thank Thales Austria GmbH for providing us with requirements for the railway interlocking case study and RE:Lab for providing the requirements for the wheel loader case study.

References

1. Aichernig, B.K., Brandl, H., Jöbstl, E., Krenn, W., Schlick, R., Tiran, S.: Killing strategies for model-based mutation testing. Software Testing, Verification and Reliability (Early view) (2014)
2. Aichernig, B.K., Jöbstl, E., Kegele, M.: Incremental refinement checking for test case generation. In: Veanes, M., Viganò, L. (eds.) TAP 2013. LNCS, vol. 7942, pp. 1–19. Springer, Heidelberg (2013)
3. Aichernig, B.K., Hörmaier, K., Lorber, F., Ničković, D., Tiran, S.: Require, test and trace IT. In: Núñez, M., Güdemann, M. (eds.) Formal Methods for Industrial Critical Systems. LNCS, vol. 9128, pp. 113–127. Springer, Heidelberg (2015)
4. Aichernig, B.K., Lorber, F., Tiran, S.: Formal test-driven development with verified test cases. In: MODELSWARD 2014, pp. 626–635. SCITEPRESS, Lisbon (January 2014)

5. Arcaini, P., Gargantini, A.: Test generation for sequential nets of abstract state machines with information passing. Science of Computer Programming **94**, Part 2(0), 93–108 (2014)

6. Arcaini, P., Gargantini, A., Riccobene, E.: An abstraction technique for testing decomposable systems by model checking. In: Seidl, M., Tillmann, N. (eds.) TAP 2014. LNCS, vol. 8570, pp. 36–52. Springer, Heidelberg (2014)

7. Berezin, S., Campos, S., Clarke, E.M.: Compositional reasoning in model checking. In: de Roever, W.-P., Langmaack, H., Pnueli, A. (eds.) COMPOS 1997. LNCS, vol. 1536, pp. 81–102. Springer, Heidelberg (1998)

8. Bourhfir, C., Dssouli, R., Aboulhamid, E., Rico, N.: A guided incremental test case generation procedure for conformance testing for CEFSM specified protocols. In: Testing of Communicating Systems. IFIP, vol. 3, pp. 279–294. Springer, Heidelberg (1998)

9. Choi, Y., Heimdahl, M.P.E.: Model checking RSML-e requirements. In: HASE, pp. 109–118. IEEE Computer Society (2002)

10. Clarke, E., Grumberg, O., Jha, S., Lu, Y., Veith, H.: Counterexample-guided abstraction refinement. In: Emerson, E.A., Sistla, A.P. (eds.) CAV 2000. LNCS, vol. 1855, pp. 154–169. Springer, Heidelberg (2000)

11. Daca, P., Henzinger, T.A., Krenn, W., Ničković, D.: Compositional specifications for ioco testing. Technical Report IST-2014-148-v2+1, IST Austria (2014). http://repository.ist.ac.at/152/1/main_tr.pdf (visited on: March 27, 2014)

12. de Moura, L., Bjørner, N.S.: Z3: an efficient SMT solver. In: Ramakrishnan, C.R., Rehof, J. (eds.) TACAS 2008. LNCS, vol. 4963, pp. 337–340. Springer, Heidelberg (2008)

13. El-Fakih, K., Petrenko, A., Yevtushenko, N.: FSM test translation through context. In: Uyar, M.U., Duale, A.Y., Fecko, M.A. (eds.) TestCom 2006. LNCS, vol. 3964, pp. 245–258. Springer, Heidelberg (2006)

14. Fraser, G., Wotawa, F.: Creating test-cases incrementally with model-checkers. In: GI Jahrestagung (2). LNI, vol. 110, pp. 381–386. GI (2007)

15. Koo, H.-M., Mishra, P.: Functional test generation using design and property decomposition techniques. ACM Trans. Embed. Comput. Syst. **8**(4), 32:1–32:33 (2009)

16. Krenn, W., Ničković, D., Tec, L.: Incremental language inclusion checking for networks of timed automata. In: Braberman, V., Fribourg, L. (eds.) FORMATS 2013. LNCS, vol. 8053, pp. 152–167. Springer, Heidelberg (2013)

17. Schwarzl, C., Peischl, B.: Test sequence generation from communicating UML state charts: An industrial application of symbolic transition systems. QSIC **2010**, 122–131 (2010)

18. van der Bijl, M., Rensink, A., Tretmans, J.: Compositional testing with ioco. In: Petrenko, A., Ulrich, A. (eds.) FATES 2003. LNCS, vol. 2931, pp. 86–100. Springer, Heidelberg (2004)

Test Case Generation for Concurrent Systems Using Event Structures

Konstantinos Athanasiou[1], Hernán Ponce-de-León[2](✉), and Stefan Schwoon[3]

[1] College of Computer and Information Science,
Northeastern University, Boston, USA
konathan@ccs.neu.edu

[2] Helsinki Institute for Information Technology HIIT and Department of Computer
Science and Engineering, School of Science, Aalto University, Espoo, Finland
hernan.poncedeleon@aalto.fi

[3] LSV (École Normale Supérieure de Cachan and CNRS), Cachan, France
schwoon@lsv.ens-cachan.fr

Abstract. This paper deals with the test-case generation problem for concurrent systems that are specified by true-concurrency models such as Petri nets. We show that using true-concurrency models reduces both the size and the number of test cases needed for achieving certain coverage criteria. We present a test-case generation algorithm based on Petri net unfoldings and a SAT encoding for solving controllability problems in test cases. Finally, we evaluate our algorithm against traditional test-case generation methods under interleaving semantics.

1 Introduction

The aim of testing is to execute a *system under test* (SUT) on a set of input data that was selected with the aim of finding discrepancies between the actual behavior of the SUT and its intended behavior as described by some specification. Model-based testing additionally requires a behavioral description of the SUT. One of the most popular formalisms studied in model-based testing is that of *input-output labeled transition systems* (IOLTS) where the correctness (or conformance) relation that the SUT must verify w.r.t. its specification is formalized by the **ioco** relation [1]. This relation has become a standard, and it is used as a basis in several testing theories for extended state-based models [2–5].

Model-based testing then consists of three steps: (1) exploring the specification to obtain a representation of relevant behaviours to test; (2) generating a suite of test cases from the mentioned representation; and (3) applying the tests to the SUT. This paper mainly deals with step (2) in the context of concurrent systems.

In the **ioco** theory, step (1) generates a *complete test graph* $\mathcal{G}$ describing the inputs the tester may propose and the outputs the system may produce,

---

K. Athanasiou—This research was done while the authors were part of LSV, supported by an INRIA internship and the TECSTES project.

© Springer International Publishing Switzerland 2015
J.C. Blanchette and N. Kosmatov (Eds.): TAP 2015, LNCS 9154, pp. 19–37, 2015.
DOI: 10.1007/978-3-319-21215-9_2

up to a depth that fulfills a given *test purpose*. Consider the example graph in Fig. 1 (a). It specifies that every tester should begin with input i_1, to which the system ought to respond by o_1. After this, there are two choices: the tester proposes either input i_2 or input i_3, to which the system should react accordingly. If the system shows an unexpected output or no output at all, it is deemed to be non-conformant.

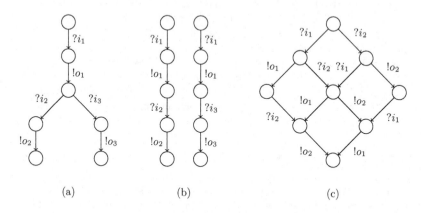

(a)   (b)   (c)

Fig. 1. Example of (a) a complete test graph; (b) the resulting test cases; (c) test graph for interleaving semantics of concurrent system

A *test case* is a subgraph of $\mathcal{G}$ that tells the tester which inputs to choose and which outputs to expect at which point during the test. For instance, no node may have two outgoing edges labelled by inputs. The suite of test cases corresponding to $\mathcal{G}$ is obtained during step (2), e.g., by using a backtracking strategy [6]. Fig. 1 (b) shows the two test cases resulting from the graph in (a).

Model-based testing of concurrent systems has been studied in the past [7–9], but mostly in the context of interleaving semantics which suffers from state-space explosion. For instance, consider a system with two independent components C_1, C_2, where input i_k in C_k should produce output o_k, for $k = 1, 2$. Applying **ioco**-conformance methods to the interleaving semantics of this system produces the test graph in Fig. 1 (c), which in turn produces four different test cases (see Example 4).

To avoid this problem, concurrent systems can be modelled by Petri nets, whose partial-order (or true-concurrency) semantics is given by its unfolding [10]. Some of the methods originally developed for Finite State Machines [11] have been adapted to k-bounded and safe Petri nets [12,13] while test-case generation for concurrent systems based on unfoldings has been studied in [14–16]. In particular, [16] proposed a suitable extension of **ioco** for testing concurrent systems, called **co-ioco**. In the latter, the test graph $\mathcal{G}$ is replaced by an *event structure* $\mathcal{E}$ characterizing the causal relations between inputs and outputs, and a concurrent (or global) test case becomes a prefix of $\mathcal{E}$ (with suitable properties). For instance, the example with two components C_1, C_2 leads to just one test case, where each component receives one input and produces one output. An abstract algorithm for obtaining the suite of test cases from $\mathcal{E}$ is proposed in [16], but it is not efficient since it enumerates linearizations of $\mathcal{E}$. Moreover, in some cases it can produce the same test case several times. Also, an actual implementation of these concepts was lacking so far.

In [14] and [17] finite event structures are constructed from the specification of the system and projected into the distributed components of the system; if the projection still contains concurrency, interleaving semantics are applied. Each path of the event structure represents a test case, but they do not give an explicit algorithm to compute them and argue that optimization techniques to minimize the number of test cases is out of the scope of the paper.

More recently, unfolding techniques have been applied to test multithreaded programs [18]; their setting is different to ours since they consider a white box implementation and construct an unfolding representing the flow of the program. The constructed unfolding represents symbolic executions to avoid the explosion causes by different inputs and a SMT solver is used to generate concrete test cases.

Contributions: test-case generation based on **co-ioco** thus consists of two tasks: (i) generating a suitable prefix of $\mathcal{E}$, and (ii) extracting test cases from it. In this paper we make the following contributions:

- As for task (i), we provide a concrete implementation for generating the above-mentioned event structure $\mathcal{E}$ for certain coverage criteria, as an extension of the tool MOLE [19].
- As for task (ii), we propose an improved algorithm for obtaining a test suite from $\mathcal{E}$ based on SAT-solving. The new algorithm is more efficient than [16] and does not produce the same test case several times.
- In practice, a system not only consists of inputs and outputs but also of silent transitions not observable by the tester. Naïvely adding silent events to the event structure would lead to huge test cases. We show how the test-case generation can handle silent transitions gracefully.
- Moreover, we implemented the above-mentioned components for test-case generation in a prototype tool called TOURS and report on experiments. Our experiments show that keeping concurrency explicitly in the test cases not only reduces their size by avoiding interleavings, but it also reduces the number of test executions to assure a certain coverage of the system.

The paper is organised as follows: Section 2 recalls background on Petri nets, unfoldings, and test cases; Section 3 presents our theoretical contributions towards test-case generation for **co-ioco**; Section 4 discusses our implementation and experiments; we conclude in Section 5.

2 Preliminaries

This section recalls previously known concepts used throughout the paper, such as Petri nets, event structures, and testing-related concepts. Since this paper focuses on test-case generation from a given event structure, we focus on event structures and present the other issues more concisely. A more detailed exposition of these subjects can be found in [16].

2.1 Petri Nets and Event Structures

We deal with concurrent, reactive systems modelled as Petri nets, where we differentiate between actions proposed by the tester (*inputs*), actions produced by the system (*outputs*) and internal (*silent*) actions. We assume familiarity of the reader with Petri nets and merely recall some basic facts.

A *Petri net* consists of two disjoint finite sets P and T representing *places* and *transitions* connected by *flow arcs*. A *marking* is a distribution of *tokens* over places. In what follows, we deal with *1-safe* nets where no reachable marking places more than one token into the same place; such Petri nets can in particular represent a collection of finite automata synchronizing on common actions. Thus, we represent a marking as the set of marked places. Transitions are labeled by a mapping $\lambda : T \rightarrow \mathcal{I}n \uplus \mathcal{O}ut \uplus \{\tau\}$ over input, output and silent actions. In the following, elements of $\mathcal{I}n$ are prefixed by '?' and elements of $\mathcal{O}ut$ by '!'.

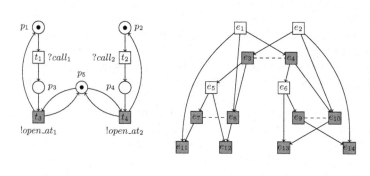

e	$\lambda(e)$	$\varphi(e)$
e_1	$?call_1$	t_1
e_2	$?call_2$	t_2
e_3	$!open\_at_2$	t_4
e_4	$!open\_at_1$	t_3
e_5	$?call_2$	t_2
e_6	$?call_1$	t_1
e_7	$!open\_at_2$	t_4
e_8	$!open\_at_1$	t_3
e_9	$!open\_at_1$	t_3
e_{10}	$!open\_at_2$	t_4
e_{11}	$!open\_at_1$	t_3
e_{12}	$!open\_at_2$	t_4
e_{13}	$!open\_at_1$	t_3
e_{14}	$!open\_at_2$	t_4

Fig. 2. A Petri net and its unfolding

Example 1 (Petri nets). Fig. 2 (left) shows a Petri net representing an elevator serving two floors. Places are shown as circles, transitions as boxes whose shading indicates the type of their label: inputs are shown in white, outputs in grey, and silent actions in light grey (see Fig. 5). From the initial marking $\{p_1, p_2, p_5\}$, the elevator can be called concurrently at both floors (transitions t_1 and t_2); both calls can be served sequentially (t_3 or t_4), i.e. the elevator cannot open its door at both floors at the same time. This is because both transitions compete for the token at place p_5.

It is well-known (see, e.g., [10]) that a Petri net can be *unfolded* into an acyclic, potentially infinite structure that represents the partial-order semantics of the net with its possible branching behaviours. Such an unfolding directly corresponds to an *event structure* [20] :

Definition 1. *An* event structure *is a tuple* $\mathcal{E} = (E, \leq, \#, \lambda)$ *where: (i) E is a set of* events; *(ii) $\leq \subseteq E \times E$ is a partial order (called* causality*) s.t. $\forall e \in E : |\langle e \rangle| < \infty$, where $\langle e \rangle = \{e' \in E \mid e' < e\}$; (iii) $\# \subseteq E \times E$ is an irreflexive symmetric relation (called* conflict*) satisfying the property of conflict heredity, i.e. $\forall e, e', e'' \in E : e \# e' \wedge e' \leq e'' \Rightarrow e \# e''$; (iv) the mapping $\lambda : E \to \mathcal{In} \uplus \mathcal{Out} \uplus \{\tau\}$ labels events.*

Causality represents dependence and conflict the inability of two actions to occur together. Conflicts that are not hereditary are called *immediate*; we write $e_1 \#^i e_2$ iff for any pair (e_1', e_2') with $e_1' \leq e_1$, $e_2' \leq e_2$, $e_1' \# e_2'$ implies $e_1' = e_1$ and $e_2' = e_2$. Likewise, we consider the *immediate causality* relation $\leq^i$, where $e \leq^i f$ iff $e \leq f$ and $e \leq g \leq f$ implies $e = g$ or $g = f$. In figures, events are represented by squares, immediate causality by arrows and immediate conflict by dashed lines. The sets of inputs, outputs and internal events are denoted respectively by $E^{\mathcal{In}} \triangleq \{e \in E \mid \lambda(e) \in \mathcal{In}\}$, $E^{\mathcal{Out}} \triangleq \{e \in E \mid \lambda(e) \in \mathcal{Out}\}$ and $E^\tau \triangleq \{e \in E \mid \lambda(e) = \tau\}$. Events that are neither related by causality nor by conflict are called concurrent, i.e. $e \mathbf{\,co\,} e' \Leftrightarrow \neg(e \leq e') \wedge \neg(e \# e') \wedge \neg(e' < e)$.

An event structure derived from the unfolding of a Petri net is equipped with a function $\varphi : E \to T$ that maps events back to the net, i.e. event e is an occurrence of transition t iff $\varphi(e) = t$.

Example 2 (Unfoldings). Fig. 2 (right) shows an initial part of the unfolding of the net on the left, where the labeling is given as a table. Events represent different instances of the transitions, indicated by $\varphi(e)$ in the table. The unfolding shows that both calls can be made concurrently, i.e. $e_1 \mathbf{\,co\,} e_2$ with $\lambda(e_1) = ?call_1$ and $\lambda(e_2) = ?call_2$, but they are served sequentially, for example $e_3 \leq e_8$ with $\lambda(e_3) = !open\_at_2$ and $\lambda(e_8) = !open\_at_1$.

In an event structure, the "state" of the system is represented by the events that have occurred so far. As causality represents precedence, such a computation must be causally closed. In addition, the computation must be conflict-free.

Definition 2. *A* configuration *of $\mathcal{E} = (E, \leq, \#, \lambda)$ is a set $C \subseteq E$ such that: (i) C is causally closed, i.e. $e \in C$ implies $\langle e \rangle \subseteq C$; and (ii) C is conflict-free, i.e. $e \in C$ and $e \# e'$ imply $e' \notin C$. The set of configurations of $\mathcal{E}$ is denoted $\mathcal{C}(\mathcal{E})$.*

For instance, $C_1 = \{e_1, e_2, e_3\}$ is a configuration, but $\{e_1, e_2, e_3, e_4\}$ is not as e_3 conflicts with e_4. W.r.t. the original Petri net, a finite configuration represents the set of transitions that fire in some finite execution. Let $Mark(C)$ denote the marking that arises from such a firing sequence, e.g. $Mark(C_1) = \{p_2, p_3, p_5\}$.

If $\mathcal{E}$ does not contain any events labelled by τ, we call $\mathcal{E}$ *deterministic* when its configurations can be uniquely determined from its action labels, i.e. if $C \in \mathcal{C}(\mathcal{E})$ and $C \uplus \{e_1\}, C \uplus \{e_2\} \in \mathcal{C}(\mathcal{E})$, then $\lambda(e_1) = \lambda(e_2)$ implies $e_1 = e_2$. We extend this to the case where $\mathcal{E}$ does include τ-labelled events: in that case, $\mathcal{E}$ is called deterministic if for all $C, C_1, C_2 \in \mathcal{C}(\mathcal{E})$ with $C_1, C_2 \supseteq C$, if e_1 resp. e_2 are the only non-τ-labelled events in $C_1 \setminus C$ resp. $C_2 \setminus C$, then $\lambda(e_1) = \lambda(e_2)$ implies $e_1 = e_2$.

2.2 Event Structures and Coverage Criteria

In general, the unfolding of a Petri net is infinite if the net contains a cycle of reachable markings. However, for many purposes, it suffices to study only a finite initial portion (a *prefix*) of the unfolding. With respect to testing, we are interested in finding a prefix that covers all behaviours relevant for a certain *coverage criterion* or *test purpose*. This relation was explored in [21], which proposes different criteria for truncating an unfolding w.r.t. certain coverage criteria. While the topic of coverage is somewhat orthogonal to the subject of this paper, we recall some well-known criteria:

- *all-states coverage*, i.e. every state (marking) of the specification must be covered at least once;
- *all-transition coverage*, i.e. every transition must be covered;
- *all-loops coverage*, i.e. every cycle is explored at least once.

We mention that the first two of these criteria correspond to the concept of *complete prefixes* known from the unfolding literature [10].

Definition 3. *A prefix $\mathcal{E}$ of the unfolding of a Petri net $\mathcal{N}$ is complete if for every reachable marking M of $\mathcal{N}$ there exists a configuration $C \in \mathcal{C}(\mathcal{E})$ such that: (1) $Mark(C) = M$ (i.e. M is represented in $\mathcal{E}$), and (2) for every transition t enabled in M there exists $C \uplus \{e\} \in \mathcal{C}(\mathcal{E})$ such that $\varphi(e) = t$.*

A prefix satisfying (1) but not necessarily (2) is also called *marking-complete*. For instance, the unfolding prefix in Fig. 2 (right) is complete; a prefix containing only events e_1 and e_2 would be marking-complete.

A marking-complete prefix assures all-states coverage, while a complete prefix additionally assures all-transitions coverage. A truncation method for all-loops coverage was developed in [21].

2.3 Test Cases

A test case is a specification of the tester's behavior during an experiment carried out on the system under test. A test suite is a set of test cases. During the experiment, the tester serves as an "environment" of the implementation. The tester controls the input actions and observes the output actions but does not control the latter. While the inputs made by the tester may depend on the previously observed outputs, the next input should always be uniquely determined, i.e. the tester must not have a choice between different inputs. Similarly, test cases do not contain choices between outputs and inputs, otherwise the implementation may produce an output without allowing the tester to propose the input. This

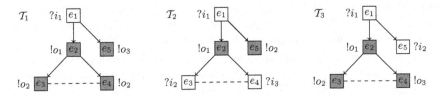

Fig. 3. Event structures as global test cases

property is called controllability [22]. These requirements also imply that the test case is required to be deterministic. Finally, we require the experiment to terminate, therefore the test case should be finite.

In the **ioco** theory, test cases are modeled by labeled transition systems with some structural assumptions [6]: *(i)* they have an acyclic and finite structure; *(ii)* they are deterministic; *(iii)* they contain only observable actions; *(iv)* there are no choices concerning inputs; and *(v)* they are output-complete (in every state of the test case where an output is enabled, the test case must handle all the possible outputs). We refer to such objects as *sequential test cases*.

For the **co-ioco** theory, designed to handle concurrent and distributed systems, [21] proposed a different type of test case, called *global test case*. Here, the tester has control over all components in the system and can observe them all. A global test case is represented by a finite, deterministic event structure; thus, inputs and outputs in different components may happen in parallel. In addition, immediate conflict between an input and any other event is forbidden. In contrast to **ioco**, we shall also allow for silent events in the specification, since this facilitates the work of the system designer. However, these silent events are irrelevant for conducting a test and are not permitted in global test cases; see also Section 3.2. Finally, since the test execution is not modeled by parallel composition[1] as in the case of **ioco**, we drop the output-complete assumption.

It is worth to notice that in practice, such global test cases are not meant to be actually executed globally. They would rather be projected onto the different processes of the distributed system to be executed locally; such local execution can be formalized as in the **ioco** case. However, a naive projection does not preserve information about concurrency; in order to make the observation of concurrency possible, further machinery is needed. An approach based on vector clocks has been proposed in [23].

Definition 4. A global test case *is a finite, deterministic event structure* $T = (E, \leq, \#, \lambda)$ *such that (i) all events are labelled by inputs or outputs, and (ii)* $(E^{\mathcal{I}n} \times E) \cap \#^i = \emptyset$.

Example 3 (Global test cases). Fig. 3 presents three event structures. T_1 is nondeterministic: from $\{e_1, e_2\}$ it is possible to perform $!o_2$ and reach both

---

[1] See [21] for details of the test execution in the concurrent setting.

$\{e_1, e_2, e_3\}$ or $\{e_1, e_2, e_4\}$; $\mathcal{T}_2$ has immediate conflict between actions $?i_2$ and $?i_3$. Thus neither $\mathcal{T}_1$ nor $\mathcal{T}_2$ is a global test case. However $\mathcal{T}_3$ is finite, deterministic, and without inputs in immediate conflict, i.e. it is a global test case.

In a global test case, events are allowed to happen in parallel. With respect to sequential test cases, this has two advantages: both the size and the number of test cases can be exponentially smaller than when concurrency is represented by interleavings. First, suppose that several outputs can happen concurrently. Then, a sequential test case must consider all their orderings, meaning that its size can be exponentially larger than the size of the corresponding global test case. Secondly, suppose that several inputs can happen concurrently. In **ioco** theory, concurrency between inputs is interpreted as a nondeterministic choice between the possible interleavings, a choice that needs to be solved to avoid uncontrollability. Thus, an **ioco**-based test suite may require an exponentially larger number of test cases than in **co-ioco** to cover the same specification.

Example 4 (Global vs. sequential test cases). Consider a process calculus notation where "$\|$" is parallel composition, "$;$" sequentialization and "$+$" choices. For a specification $(i_1; o_1 \| i_2; o_2)$ (which is deterministic and has no choices), the test suite $\mathcal{TS}_1 = \{i_1; o_1 \| i_2; o_2\}$ contains one single test case to cover all the behaviors. By contrast, if interleaving semantics is used, then the test suite $\mathcal{TS}_2$ obtained by the **ioco** algorithms contains four sequential test cases:

$$\mathcal{TS}_2 = \left\{ \begin{array}{c} ?i_1; !o_1; ?i_2; !o_2 \\ ?i_2; !o_2; ?i_1; !o_1 \\ ?i_1; ?i_2; (!o_1; !o_2 + !o_2; !o_1) \\ ?i_2; ?i_1; (!o_1; !o_2 + !o_2; !o_1) \end{array} \right\}$$

3 Constructing Global Test Cases

In this section, we present a new methodology of generating test cases for **co-ioco**-conformance that offers two advantages over the methods previously presented in [16]: *(i)* it is more efficient in practice (it avoids enumerating linearizations of the causality relation); and *(ii)* it avoids generating the same test case several times.

We recall that model-based testing consists of several steps: in the first step, one obtains a representation of the behaviours that are relevant w.r.t. a given coverage criterion. In the case of **co-ioco**, this representation is an event structure $\mathcal{E}$, more precisely an unfolding prefix of the Petri net representing the specification. In a second step, which is the subject of this section, one uses $\mathcal{E}$ to obtain a suite of test cases. Since the choice of a coverage criterion is orthogonal to our subject, we henceforth assume that $\mathcal{E}$ is given. Our task then is to extract all global test cases from $\mathcal{E}$. We make the technical assumption that $\mathcal{E}$ is deterministic; note that analogous assumptions about the complete test graph are made in **ioco** settings.

A first algorithm for this purpose was presented in [16]. The algorithm takes as an input a linearization $\mathcal{L}$ of the causality relation and adds events to the

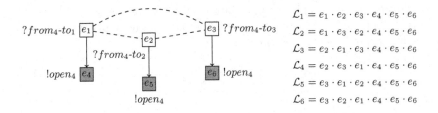

$$\mathcal{L}_1 = e_1 \cdot e_2 \cdot e_3 \cdot e_4 \cdot e_5 \cdot e_6$$
$$\mathcal{L}_2 = e_1 \cdot e_3 \cdot e_2 \cdot e_4 \cdot e_5 \cdot e_6$$
$$\mathcal{L}_3 = e_2 \cdot e_1 \cdot e_3 \cdot e_4 \cdot e_5 \cdot e_6$$
$$\mathcal{L}_4 = e_2 \cdot e_3 \cdot e_1 \cdot e_4 \cdot e_5 \cdot e_6$$
$$\mathcal{L}_5 = e_3 \cdot e_1 \cdot e_2 \cdot e_4 \cdot e_5 \cdot e_6$$
$$\mathcal{L}_6 = e_3 \cdot e_2 \cdot e_1 \cdot e_4 \cdot e_5 \cdot e_6$$

Fig. 4. A first approach for test case generation

test case following the order of $\mathcal{L}$ whenever they do not introduce controllability problems. To obtain different test cases, the algorithm needs to be run with different linearizations. Even if using these linearizations seems to reduce the advantages of using true concurrency models, this method is only exponential on the number of immediate conflicts between inputs, which is usually very small compared with the number of all possible interleavings. However this method still has a drawback: it generates several times the same test case whenever several inputs are pairwise in immediate conflict.

Example 5 (A first approach for test case generation). Consider the event structure of Fig. 4 which represents the controller of an elevator in the 4th floor. When calling the elevator, the user indicates which floor he wants to reach. Whatever his choice, eventually the elevator arrives at the 4th floor and opens its door. According to [16], linearizations $\mathcal{L}_1$ - $\mathcal{L}_6$ are needed to construct a test suite covering the specification. If events are added one by one to the test case following these linearizations whenever they do not introduce controllability problems, $\mathcal{L}_1$ and $\mathcal{L}_2$ construct the same test case since once e_1 is added, neither e_2 nor e_3 (nor their futures) are added. This problem comes from the fact that the conflict relation consider pairs of events, but once an event is selected, the order of every other event which is in immediate conflict with it becomes irrelevant.

3.1   Encoding Test Cases by SAT

In order to solve controllability problems and avoid constructing the same test case several times as mentioned in Example 5, we propose a new, non-redundant characterization of global test cases. This characterization can be encoded in propositional logic, hence we will be able to employ a SAT solver to obtain the global test cases. Given a finite event structure, we use a SAT variable φ_e for each event e and construct a formula whose satisfying assignments correspond to global test cases. A solution assigning 1 to variable φ_e means that event e belongs to the test case, while assignment 0 means that it does not.

As test cases need to preserve causality from the specification, whenever the condition of an event is true, the conditions of its immediate causal predecessors (and, by transitivity, all indirect precedessors) should also be true:

$$\forall e, f \in E : \bigwedge_{f \leq^i e} \varphi_e \Rightarrow \varphi_f \tag{1}$$

In addition, for each pair of immediate conflicts involving an input, at most one of them belongs to the test case (remember that immediate conflict between outputs is accepted). This is encoded as:

$$\forall e \in E, f \in E^{In} : \bigwedge_{f \#^i e} \neg \varphi_e \vee \neg \varphi_f \qquad (2)$$

We intend the test suite to cover the whole prefix, therefore the test cases should be maximal in the sense that adding any event should violate (1) or (2). An event of the prefix does not belong to the test case only if *(i)* neither does one of its immediate predecessors, or *(ii)* it is in immediate conflict with an input of the test case. We encoded this by the SAT formula

$$\forall e, f \in E, g \in E^{In} : \neg \varphi_e \Rightarrow \left(\bigvee_{f \leq^i e} \neg \varphi_f \vee \bigvee_{g \#^i e} \varphi_g \right) \qquad (3)$$

Global test cases are encoded by the conjunction of (1), (2) and (3).

Example 6 (Avoiding redundancy by the SAT encoding). Consider the event structure of Fig. 4. The SAT formula of this event structure is

$$\text{AMO}(\varphi_{e_1}, \varphi_{e_2}, \varphi_{e_3}) \wedge (\varphi_{e_1} \vee \varphi_{e_2} \vee \varphi_{e_3}) \wedge (\varphi_{e_1} \Leftrightarrow \varphi_{e_4}) \wedge (\varphi_{e_2} \Leftrightarrow \varphi_{e_5}) \wedge (\varphi_{e_3} \Leftrightarrow \varphi_{e_6})$$

where $\text{AMO}(x_1, \ldots, x_n)$ is satisfied iff at most one of $x_1, \ldots, x_n$ is satisfied. The formula has three solutions representing the test cases $e_1; e_4, e_2; e_5$ and $e_3; e_6$ which cover the whole specification and avoid the redundancy seen in Example 5.

3.2   Removing Silent Events

It is natural for a system specification to include silent events, e.g. to express that two components in the system synchronize without producing an output observable by the tester. In this case, such a silent event also forms part of $\mathcal{E}$, and the test cases identified by the formula in Section 3.1 are not yet guaranteed to satisfy condition *(i)* of Definition 4. In this section we show how to remove internal events from $\mathcal{E}$ while preserving the causality and conflict relations for the remaining events.

The data structure that we use to represent an event structure does not keep explicit information of the whole causality and conflict relation, but only information about the immediate relations. We associate each event e with the following sets: P_e and S_e consisting of the immediate predecessors and successors of e respectively, and C_e consisting of events e' such that $e \#^i e'$. Algorithm 1 updates the sets P_e and S_e so that the causality relation between the remaining events is preserved (lines 2–5). Also, it propagates the immediate conflict relation of the silent event to all its immediate successors (line 8). Function NOTINCONFLICT is responsible for checking whether two events are already in (not necessarily immediate) conflict.

Algorithm 1. Removal of Silent Events

```
1: for each e in Eᵀ do
2:      for each p in Pₑ do
3:          Sₚ := Sₚ ∪ Sₑ \ {e}
4:      for each s in Sₑ do
5:          Pₛ := Pₛ ∪ Pₑ \ {e}
6:          for each c in Cₑ do
7:              if NotInConflict(s, c) then
8:                  Cₛ := Cₛ ∪ {c};  C_c := C_c ∪ {s}
9:      for each c in Cₑ do
10:         C_c := C_c \ {e}
11:     E := E \ {e}
```

The non-immediate causality and conflict relations are not stored per se but are computed from the sets S_e, P_e and C_e. For any pair of events $e_i, e_j \in E$, the relation $e_i \leq e_j$ can be computed starting from S_i and recursively traversing its successors until e_j is found, meaning that there is a path from e_i to e_j with arcs in $\bigcup \{ S_k \mid e_i \leq e_k \}$. The relation $e_i \# e_j$ can be computed by checking that there exist events $e_k \in C_l$ and $e_l \in C_k$, i.e. $e_k \#^i e_l$, such that $e_k \leq e_i$ and $e_l \leq e_j$. We show that both relations are preserved after removing the silent events of $\mathcal{E}$.

Proposition 1. *Let $\mathcal{E}$ be an event structure and $\mathcal{E}'$ be the resulting event structure after applying Algorithm 1. For every pair of observable events e_i, e_j, we have $e_i \leq_{\mathcal{E}} e_j$ iff $e_i \leq_{\mathcal{E}'} e_j$.*

Proof. Suppose $e_i \leq_{\mathcal{E}} e_j$, then there exists a path from e_i to e_j in $\mathcal{E}$. Suppose that Algorithm 1 removes an event e in the path. Since line 3 sets $S_p := S_p \cup S_e \setminus \{e\}$, the path still exists after removing e: any event reachable from e can be reached from p now. This invariant holds after removing every internal event and therefore the result holds. The counterpart is immediate since causalities are not added, only some immediate ones are removed. □

Proposition 2. *Let $\mathcal{E}$ be an event structure and $\mathcal{E}'$ be the resulting event structure after applying Algorithm 1. For every pair of observable events e_i, e_j, we have $e_i \#_{\mathcal{E}} e_j$ iff $e_i \#_{\mathcal{E}'} e_j$.*

Proof. Whenever an immediate conflict $e \#^i e'$ is removed (while removing event e), for every successor s of e, either s and e' are already in conflict (this is checked by NotInConflict), or the new direct conflict $s \#^i e'$ is added (line 8). Since conflict is inherited w.r.t causality, all the conflicts remain represented. The counterpart is immediate since immediate conflicts are only added whenever the events were not already in conflict. □

Algorithm 1 does not take in account whether two events are already causally related when it updates S_e and P_e (lines 2–5), potentially leading to redundant

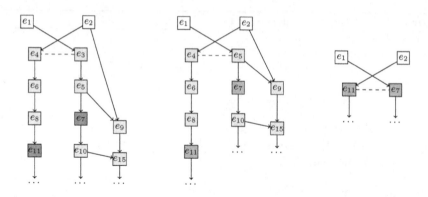

Fig. 5. Removing silent events

(non immediate) relations getting stored. Such redundant relations can be eliminated: we temporarily remove e_i and e_j from P_j and S_i respectively. If e_j is still reachable from e_i, then the information was redundant and can be permanently removed.

Example 7 (Removing Silent Events). Fig. 5 shows how Algorithm 1 works: the structure in the middle is obtained by removing event e_3 from the original prefix while the final result of the algorithm is shown on the right. In the original event structure (left) we have $S_1 = P_5 = C_4 = \{e_3\}$ and $P_3 = \{e_1\}, S_3 = \{e_5\}, C_3 = \{e_4\}$. The structure in the middle is obtained as follows: line 3 updates S_1 to $\{e_5\}$ and line 5 sets $P_5 = \{e_1\}$; since e_5 and e_4 are not in conflict yet, line 8 adds e_4 to C_5 and e_5 to C_4; finally e_3 is removed from C_4 (line 10).

Consider that some events are removed from the prefix in the middle in the following order: e_3, e_5, e_{10}, e_9. Whenever e_5 is removed, its immediate conflict with e_4 is propagated to both e_7 and e_9, however, when e_9 is eliminated, the conflict does not need to be propagated since e_4 and e_{15} are already in (non-immediate) conflict: we have $e_4 \#^i e_7$ and $e_7 \leq e_{15}$. Such situations are handled by the NOT-INCONFLICT function.

4   Experiments

We implemented a prototype tool called TOURS (Testing On Unfolded Reactive Systems) for **co-ioco**-based test-case generation. TOURS is based on the MOLE unfolding tool [19] with the following main additions:

- variable cut-off criteria, including all-loops coverage by the criterion of [21];
- implementation of the algorithms presented in Section 3;
- computation of the immediate conflict and immediate predecessor relation.

TOURS computes a first over-approximation of $\leq^i$ by inserting all pairs (e, f) such that f consumes a token produced by e. Redundant pairs are then eliminated in the same way as in Section 3.2. The immediate-conflict relation $\#^i$ is obtained by considering all event pairs (e, f) that compete directly for a token, and testing whether there exists a configuration that can be extended with e and with f, but not with both. The latter is a simple variant of a subroutine frequently used by MOLE. TOURS is publicly available under

http://www.lsv.ens-cachan.fr/~ponce/tours

The rest of this section presents experimental results based on two families of examples: a parametric version of the elevator, where we also consider internal behaviors, and an example (called Diamonds) showing how our approach deals with immediate conflict between inputs.

4.1   The Examples

The Elevator Example: we extend the elevator example of Section 2 for several floors and elevators, and we also model its internal behavior. The example is modeled as a network of automata synchronizing on shared actions which can be equivalently captured by a Petri net; we obtain a finite prefix of its unfolding and construct test cases with the SAT encoding using the TOURS prototype.

The system consists of the following components, represented by the automata of Fig. 6 for two floors and one elevator:

Floors: each floor consists of a button that can be pressed to call an elevator. The floor is in an *idle* state where the elevator can be called ($?call_i$), and afterwards sends the call to the controllers of every elevator e_j ($e_j\text{-}takes\text{-}call_i$) followed by a synchronization action that the door of elevator e_j has been opened at that floor ($e_j\text{-}opened\text{-}at\text{-}f_i$), returning to the *idle* state. Once the elevator is called, it cannot be called again until it returns to the idle state since the $?call_i$ actions are not enabled in the remaining states.

Controllers of elevators: the controller of each elevator e_j starts at an *idle* state and can take a call from any floor f_i. From there the controller can either move the elevator to the corresponding floor ($e_j\text{-}go\text{-}to\text{-}f_i$) or acknowledge that the elevator is already at that floor ($e_j\text{-}at\text{-}f_i$).

Elevators: each elevator starts at some floor, i.e. state at_i. From this state it can tell its controller that it is already on the floor, or it can move to another floor. When the elevator is at floor f_i, it opens the door ($!open_{j\text{-}i}$) and acknowledges this action to the corresponding floor.

This system is given as an input to the unfolding algorithm (using the all-loops criterion). TOURS returns a prefix whose observable behavior (after removal of silent actions) is shown in Fig. 2 (right). This prefix contains no immediate conflict between inputs, therefore the SAT encoding has a unique solution: the entire prefix. Thus, our method generates exactly one test case in this example.

Intuitively, the specification of the elevator is that every call at any floor ought to be served eventually (i.e., the door opens at that floor) in any correct implementation; infinite many calls are possible only if infinite many opens happens since

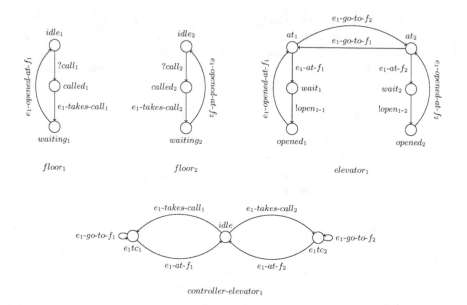

Fig. 6. Network of automata of the elevator example with one elevator and two floors

the $?call_i$ actions are not allowed at every state. Consider the test case of Fig. 2 (right) and the $?call_2$ action represented by event e_2. This call is followed by an $!open_2$ action in any maximal configuration. Event e_3 corresponds to the scenario where the call is immediately served; e_{10} reflects the fact that the elevator can be called concurrently from another floor ($?call_1$) and that that call can be served first ($e_4 \leq e_{10}$); e_{14} shows that two calls from the first floor (e_1 and e_6) can be served before serving the call from the second floor. The latter shows that there are no priorities between serving different floors; however all the calls are eventually served. A similar analysis can be made for the other call actions.

The example can easily be parametrized to add floors and elevators. If a new floor f_i is added, in addition to adding a new automaton for the floor with transitions e_j-$takes$-$call_i$ for each elevator e_j, the existing automata representing elevators and controllers need to be extended: a new state $e_j tc_i$ is added to the controller of every elevator e_j with transitions

$$idle \xrightarrow{e_j\text{-}takes\text{-}call_i} e_j tc_i \qquad e_j tc_i \xrightarrow{e_j\text{-}go\text{-}to\text{-}f_i} e_j tc_i \qquad e_j tc_i \xrightarrow{e_j\text{-}at\text{-}f_i} idle$$

Furthermore, the states $at_i, wait_i$ and $opened_i$ are added to the elevator e_j with transitions

$$at_i \xrightarrow{e_j\text{-}at\text{-}f_i} wait_i \qquad wait_i \xrightarrow{!open_{j\text{-}i}} opened_i \qquad opened_i \xrightarrow{e_j\text{-}opened\text{-}at\text{-}f_i} at_i$$

and for each floor $k < i$ all the possible movements between them and the new floor are added, i.e.

$$at_k \xrightarrow{e_j\text{-}go\text{-}to\text{-}f_i} at_i \qquad at_i \xrightarrow{e_j\text{-}go\text{-}to\text{-}f_k} at_k$$

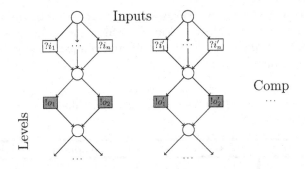

Fig. 7. The diamonds example

If a new elevator is added, two automata (representing the elevator itself and its controller) are added, and for every floor f_i we add the possibility that the new elevator e_j serves its call, i.e. we add transitions

$$called_i \xrightarrow{e_j\text{-}takes\text{-}call_i} waiting_i$$

The Diamonds Example: We present another example (see Fig. 7) that possesses several global test cases. The example consists on several **components** where the user has a number of choices (**inputs**), after which the system can produce several outputs. This behavior can be repeated several times depending on the **levels** of the components. We run the experiments using different parameters for the components, the inputs and the levels as shown in Table 2.

4.2   The Experimental Setup

In order to make a fair comparison of the algorithms presented in this article and the algorithms of the **ioco** theory, we need to use the same test selection method. Available tools such as TGV [6] or JtorX [24] use test purposes rather than a testing criterion. We therefore proceed as follows to compare with **ioco**: *(i)* the Petri net is translated into its reachability graph; *(ii)* since **co-ioco** coincides with **ioco** in the absence of concurrent events, we apply TOURS to the reachability graph.

In the **ioco** setting, using the all-loops criterion led to test graphs of large size even for simple examples, making it impractical to compute all the test cases. For more meaningful comparisons to be possible, we run the experiments using the original cut-off criterion of MOLE which assures all-transitions and all-states coverage.

4.3   Results

Tables 1 and 2 report the number of events in the unfolding prefix obtained by our method, the number of global test cases (event structures), the number of transitions in an under-approximation[2] of the complete test graph and the number of

---

[2] This graph is not output-complete.

sequential test cases (labeled transition systems) for the two examples introduced in the last section. The unfolding tool and the SAT encoding consider internal events, while the sizes displayed on the prefix and complete test graph columns only consider observable events.

Table 1. The elevator example results

Floors	Elevators	Prefix	Global Tests	Test Graph	Sequential Tests
2	1	11	1	95	14
2	2	29	1	3929	X_{SAT}
3	1	43	1	2299	X_{SAT}
3	2	220	1	3911179	X_{SAT}
3	3	1231	1	X_{unf}	X_{unf}
4	1	219	1	X_{unf}	X_{unf}
4	2	1853	1	X_{unf}	X_{unf}
4	3	17033	1	X_{unf}	X_{unf}

Table 2. The diamonds example results

Comp	Inputs	Levels	Prefix	Global Tests	Test Graph	Sequential Tests
2	1	3	19	1	307	98
2	2	3	37	16	613	794
2	3	3	55	49	919	2938
3	1	1	7	1	133	21
3	1	2	13	1	853	125
3	2	2	25	27	1705	13255

We can easily observe the exponential explosion in the number of events when interleavings are used. In addition we see that irrespectively of how many floors or elevators are added in the elevator example, the obtained global test case is always unique since the example does not introduce conflict between input events. In contrast, the number of sequential test cases increases in the interleaving setting since concurrency is transformed into conflict. The diamonds example introduces conflicts between inputs generating several global test cases, however the number of tests can still be exponentially smaller than in the sequential case.

The $\boldsymbol{X}_{unf}$ symbol indicates that the unfolding tool was not able to obtain a finite prefix (complete test graph), while the $\boldsymbol{X}_{SAT}$ symbol indicates that the SAT solver was not able to find solutions (for more than 3 floors and 2 elevators, we were not able to run the SAT solver with interleaving semantics since the unfolding had not finished).

The unfolding of the Petri net for 3 floors - 2 elevators example using interleaving semantics (when internal actions are considered) contains 15353982 events, showing that the unfolding tool can handle very big examples. Since causality is transitive and conflict is inherited w.r.t causal dependence, the SAT encoding can be improved by just considering observable events. However immediate causality and immediate conflict between only observable events need to be computed as explained in Section 3.2 increasing again the computational time of the method. We are currently working on the implementation to achieve a better performance by just considering observable events.

5   Conclusion

This paper shows the advantages of using true-concurrency models to describe the behavior of test cases in concurrent systems. We have shown how to split a finite prefix of the specification's unfolding into a test suite even in the presence of internal actions. Finally, the results of this article have been implemented in the prototype tool TOURS and run on several examples showing the advantages of our method compared with traditional **ioco** test-case generation algorithms.

The obtained global test cases are not meant to be actually executed, they would rather be projected onto the different processes of the distributed system to be executed locally. In order to make the observation of concurrency possible, further machinery is needed [23]. We will study the concretization of the generated abstract test cases into inputs that can be given to the actual system under test to allow the automatic execution of test cases and thus completely automate the testing procedure. A possible approach is to consider labeling actions as a symbolic representation of the input and output domain and apply SMT for the concretization.

Future work also includes a tighter integration of the test-case generation part of TOURS with the unfolding component to improve its performance.

References

1. Tretmans, J.: Model based testing with labelled transition systems. In: Hierons, R.M., Bowen, J.P., Harman, M. (eds.) FORTEST. LNCS, vol. 4949, pp. 1–38. Springer, Heidelberg (2008)
2. Heerink, L., Tretmans, J.: Refusal testing for classes of transition systems with inputs and outputs. In: Proc. FORTE. IFIP, vol. 107, pp. 23–38 (1997)

3. Jéron, T.: Symbolic model-based test selection. Electronic Notes in Theoretical Computer Science **240**, 167–184 (2009)
4. Krichen, M., Tripakis, S.: Conformance testing for real-time systems. Formal Methods in System Design **34**(3), 238–304 (2009)
5. Hierons, R.M., Merayo, M.G., Núñez, M.: Implementation relations for the distributed test architecture. In: Suzuki, K., Higashino, T., Ulrich, A., Hasegawa, T. (eds.) TestCom/FATES 2008. LNCS, vol. 5047, pp. 200–215. Springer, Heidelberg (2008)
6. Jard, C., Jéron, T.: TGV: theory, principles and algorithms. International Journal on Software Tools for Technology Transfer **7**(4), 297–315 (2005)
7. Hennessy, M.: Algebraic theory of processes. MIT Press series in the foundations of computing. MIT Press (1988)
8. Peleska, J., Siegel, M.: From testing theory to test driver implementation. In: Gaudel, M.-C., Wing, J.M. (eds.) FME 1996. LNCS, vol. 1051, pp. 538–556. Springer, Heidelberg (1996)
9. Schneider, S.: Concurrent and Real Time Systems: The CSP Approach, 1st edn. John Wiley & Sons Inc., New York (1999)
10. Esparza, J., Römer, S., Vogler, W.: An improvement of McMillan's unfolding algorithm. Formal Methods in System Design **20**(3), 285–310 (2002)
11. Lee, D., Yannakakis, M.: Principles and methods of testing finite state machines - A survey. Proceedings of the IEEE **84**, 1090–1123 (1996)
12. Jourdan, G., von Bochmann, G.: On testing 1-safe petri nets. In: TASE 2009, Third IEEE International Symposium on Theoretical Aspects of Software Engineering, July 29–31, 2009, Tianjin, China, pp. 275–281 (2009)
13. von Bochmann, G., Jourdan, G.: Testing k-safe petri nets. In: Testing of Softwareand Communication Systems, 21st IFIP WG 6.1 International Conference, TESTCOM 2009 and 9th International Workshop, FATES 2009, November 2–4, Eindhoven, The Netherlands, pp. 33–48 (2009)
14. Jard, C.: Synthesis of distributed testers from true-concurrency models of reactive systems. Information & Software Technology **45**(12), 805–814 (2003)
15. Ulrich, A., König, H.: Specification-based testing of concurrent systems. In: Proc. FORTE. IFIP Conference Proceedings, vol. 107, pp. 7–22 (1997)
16. Ponce de León, H., Haar, S., Longuet, D.: Model-based testing for concurrent systems with labeled event structures. STVR **24**(7), 558–590 (2014)
17. Henniger, O.: On test case generation from asynchronously communicating state machines. In: International Workshop on Testing Communicating Systems. IFIP Conference Proceedings, pp. 255–271. Springer (1997)
18. Kähkönen, K., Saarikivi, O., Heljanko, K.: Using unfoldings in automated testing of multithreaded programs. In: IEEE/ACM International Conference on Automated Software Engineering, ASE 2012, September 3–7, Essen, Germany, pp. 150–159 (2012)
19. Schwoon, S.: The MOLE unfolding tool. http://www.lsv.ens-cachan.fr/~schwoon/tools/mole/
20. Nielsen, M., Plotkin, G.D., Winskel, G.: Petri nets, event structures and domains, part I. Theoretical Computer Science **13**, 85–108 (1981)

21. Ponce de León, H., Haar, S., Longuet, D.: Unfolding-Based test selection for concurrent conformance. In: Yenigün, H., Yilmaz, C., Ulrich, A. (eds.) ICTSS 2013. LNCS, vol. 8254, pp. 98–113. Springer, Heidelberg (2013)
22. Jéron, T., Morel, P.: Test generation derived from model-checking. In: Halbwachs, N., Peled, D.A. (eds.) CAV 1999. LNCS, vol. 1633, pp. 108–121. Springer, Heidelberg (1999)
23. Ponce-de-León, H., Haar, S., Longuet, D.: Distributed testing of concurrent systems: vector clocks to the rescue. In: Ciobanu, G., Méry, D. (eds.) ICTAC 2014. LNCS, vol. 8687, pp. 369–387. Springer, Heidelberg (2014)
24. Belinfante, A.: JTorX: a tool for on-line model-driven test derivation and execution. In: Esparza, J., Majumdar, R. (eds.) TACAS 2010. LNCS, vol. 6015, pp. 266–270. Springer, Heidelberg (2010)

Fast Model-Based Fault Localisation with Test Suites

Geoff Birch[1]([✉]), Bernd Fischer[2], and Michael R. Poppleton[1]

[1] University of Southampton, Southampton SO17 1BJ, UK
{gb2g10,mrp}@ecs.soton.ac.uk
[2] Stellenbosch University, Stellenbosch 7602, Matieland, South Africa
bfischer@cs.sun.ac.za

Abstract. Fault localisation, i.e. the identification of program locations that cause errors, takes significant effort and cost. We describe a fast model-based fault localisation algorithm which, given a test suite, uses symbolic execution methods to fully automatically identify a small subset of program locations where genuine program repairs exist. Our algorithm iterates over failing test cases and collects locations where an assignment change can repair exhibited faulty behaviour. Our main contribution is an improved search through the test suite, reducing the effort for the symbolic execution of the models and leading to speed-ups of more than two orders of magnitude over the previously published implementation by Griesmayer et al.

We implemented our algorithm for C programs, using the KLEE symbolic execution engine, and demonstrate its effectiveness on the Siemens TCAS variants. Its performance is in line with recent alternative model-based fault localisation techniques, but narrows the location set further without rejecting any genuine repair locations where faults can be fixed by changing a single assignment.

Keywords: Automated debugging · Fault localisation · Symbolic execution

1 Introduction

Fault localisation, i.e. the identification of program locations that can cause erroneous state transitions which eventually lead to observed program failures, is a critical component of the debugging cycle. Since it puts a significant time [26, 27] and expertise burden [1,34] on programmers, a variety of different automated fault localisation methods have been proposed [4,6,11,13,14,17,29–31].

We describe a fast model-based fault localisation algorithm which, given a test suite, uses symbolic execution methods to fully automatically identify a small subset of program locations within which (under a single fault assumption) a genuine program repair exists. Our main contribution is an improved search through the test suite that drastically reduces the effort for the symbolic execution of the models.

© Springer International Publishing Switzerland 2015
J.C. Blanchette and N. Kosmatov (Eds.): TAP 2015, LNCS 9154, pp. 38–57, 2015.
DOI: 10.1007/978-3-319-21215-9_3

Model-based fault localisation [28] (sometimes also called model-based debugging [7]) is the application of model-based diagnosis methods [18] to programs. It involves three main steps: (*i*) the construction of a logical model from the original program; (*ii*) the symbolic analysis of this model; and (*iii*) mapping any faults found in the model back to program locations. One approach to model-based fault localisation is to transform the program so that a symbolic program verification tool can be reused for all three steps. For example, Griesmayer [11] describes a method in which the model (in form of a logical satisfiability problem) is derived by running the CBMC model checker over the transformed program, and analysed by means of a SAT solver. The transformation "inverts" the program's specification (cf. section 2, producing failures where the original program would complete and blocking paths where the original program would fail), and replaces each assignment by conditional assignment with either the original value or an unconstrained symbolic value, depending on the value of a toggle variable. The actual localisation can then be reduced to extracting the possible values of the toggle variable from the satisfying assignments that the SAT solver returns.

However, Griesmayer's technique requires detailed specifications to achieve acceptable precision—the weaker the specification, the more program locations are flagged as potential faults. Unfortunately, such detailed specifications rarely exist in practice. What *does* commonly exist, though, are extensive unit test suites, in particular in the context of modern test-driven design approaches. Griesmayer has shown that his technique can be extended to work with (failing) test cases, but the published results [11] are prohibitively slow. The bad performance is caused by Griesmayer's naïve search algorithm, which simply iterates over all test cases and runs an unoptimized "full width" search over all possible locations for each test case (cf. section 2 for more details). However, the more locations the solver needs to explore the longer each analysis takes. Moreover, the algorithm contains no optimizations to deal with test cases that generate intractable problems for the solver. Approximating model-based fault localisation approaches for test suites, such as Jose and Majumdar [17] (cf. section 6), can run faster but can also miss a true fault location when evaluating a test case.

Our approach addresses these shortcomings, which leads to typical speed-ups of more than two orders of magnitude compared to Griesmayer's results, and yields a performance in line with current approximation techniques such as [17]. It still iterates over the failing test cases and runs a Griesmayer-style localisation task for each individual test case, but maintains a *whitelist* of still viable fault locations which is narrowed down as the localisation tasks return. The algorithm manages individual localisation tasks via a task pool to take advantage of the underlying multi-core hardware, and dispatches the tasks in batches to percolate improvements in whitelist narrowing generationally. Tasks that fail to complete in a dynamically adjusted time are terminated and if the whitelist is smaller, resubmitted at the tail of the iteration, where they may become tractable. This early termination/resubmission increases the speed with which we can process larger test suites, without harming the localisation performance, as they typically have more redundant (for localisation purposes) test cases. It also prevents a loss of completeness in the results that model-based approaches can provide, within the limits of the symbolic analyser's accuracy.

Our approach is compatible with the modern test-driven design approach of specification by unit test suite. It inherits the typical strength of dynamic analysis, in that no prior knowledge of the program under test is required beyond test cases being flagged as passing or failing. We implemented our algorithm in a tool with the use of ESBMC [9] or KLEE [3] symbolic analysers, and thus Z3 [23] as underlying solver, and with PyCParser [2] handling the program transformations to encode the specification and other model constraints. The algorithm inherits the underlying behaviour, in respect of method calls, unrolling loops, and so on, of the symbolic analyser used. We demonstrate this algorithm on the defective TCAS program variants from the Siemens [15] repository.

2   Model-Based Fault Localisation

Model-based fault localisation techniques are derived from the extension of model-based diagnosis [18,28], used to reason about digital circuits, into the software domain.

A common process for model-based fault localisation uses static analysis on a model that is generated from a transformed input program using the language specifications. This transformation is provided by a checker tool that converts the program code into one or more logic expressions which analyses the symbolic execution of the system symbolically. A solver is invoked that can evaluate the logic expressions. This returns constraint satisfiability results for the expressions.

This symbolic analysis may be accelerated with the use of built-in theories to compactly reason over the logic expression [25]. The symbolic analyser uses these results to generate traces of specification violating execution paths (counterexamples), if any exist. Some methods operate directly on the satisfiability result for the logic expression, for example exploring common omissions when using a maximum satisfiability solver [17]. Programs can be modified, e.g. augmented with additional predicates, to generate more information from the data in the failing traces.

Griesmayer [11] described a technique where a specified input C program is reconfigured to use an "inverted" version of the specification. This inversion is applied to the C source code before the model is generated by the CBMC model checker, which then analyses the model using a SAT solver. Each potentially failing assert-statement is replaced by blocking assume-statement with the same argument. Failing assert(0)-statements are inserted before the program's terminal nodes to force the generation of new counterexamples. The purpose of this inversion is to provide the inverted output. Hence, traces that originally returned counterexamples due to specification failure do no longer, and traces that satisfy the specification now generate counterexamples. The exploration becomes one searching for a trace to the exit point that satisfies the initial specifications. Thus, in the simple inverted program an exiting trace will not be found for a failing test case.

To enable the search for potential fault locations on this now inverted program, an unsigned int global toggle variable, __toggle, is added that allows any one location to run alternative code. In the program body this toggle is made symbolic and constrained to the range of locations being explored (in our example 39 locations). In a KLEE-style API this would be achieved by the calls:

```
klee_make_symbolic(&__toggle); klee_assume(__toggle < 39);
```

Assignments in the source program are modified to become conditional assignments that flip to an unconstrained symbolic value, __sym, when toggled. Hence, if we assume that var = a + b; is the third assignment in the program, the translation yields:

```
var = ((__toggle == 2)? __sym : a + b);
```

The generated counterexamples from this new model provide the toggle values that identify candidate assignment locations as sites of possible repair. The technique described by Griesmayer requires that the input programs have detailed specifications. In practice, these typically do not exist. Griesmayer demonstrated [11] an extension to this technique using a test suite as specification. A failing test case is encoded into the input program and then inverted. The results for each toggle value therefore identify candidate repairs for that failing test case. Any assignment that was identified by all failing test cases becomes a location flagged as being the site of a potential repair. The localisation process effectively generates a look-up table at each flagged location that will repair all failing test cases. For each failing test case, the value of the alternative assignments, __sym, can be different and will be reported for each location flagged by this process. The flagging process means the chosen __sym value leads to the end of the program without failure of the original specification. All passing test cases define their own correct values for the assignment. So this look-up table is a genuine repair for the full test suite.

This approach, where each test case is treated as an independent specification and all results are collected independently, results in prohibitively slow execution time. Using test suites demonstrates a strength of dynamic analysis: no prior knowledge of the program beyond flagged test cases as correct or incorrect is required. But the published results indicated that the run-time cost was too high using the common localisation performance measure of the Siemens TCAS [15] variants.

3 The Algorithm

We propose a fast algorithm which optimises the search of the test suite and viable repair locations to bring this process into line with current performance expectations and without compromising the completeness of the results this technique allows. Each test case in the suite comprises an input string, which becomes the argument vector, and a desired output string from an oracle version of the program variant. We discuss this algorithm design with respect to the C programming language but it can be applied to any language with suitable support for symbolic analysers.

We transform an input C program using an extended Griesmayer inversion process (see subsection 3.1). This is handed to a worker task (see subsection 3.2) with a whitelist of locations to search and a single failing test case. The returned set from this worker is a narrowed whitelist of locations that the test case flagged as being a potential repair. We manage this process using the main tool loop (see subsection 3.3). In the algorithms below we denote C programs as C and (after transformation) D and E. Individual failing test cases are f from the non-empty queue F. The refining whitelist of locations is L, which is renamed to K during narrowing inside Algorithm 1. In the Process Manager algorithm, P is the worker pool manager.

We provide two main contributions with this algorithm design. First, the reduction in symbolic execution work via the use of a narrowing process of whitelisting locations searched. Second, the management of cases where the time to return a narrowed whitelist is significantly beyond the mean time for a failing test case. This later case can be due to either an intractable model representation or poor narrowing compared to other unexplored failing test cases. This management is designed to provide a more consistent completion time over a range of different localisation searches. This aims to avoid slowdown from the highest cost branches of the search rather than focussing on providing an optimal search when all branches are cheap to search.

3.1   Program Transformation into Model

The program under analysis is transformed in two stages. First, an initial generic transformation *ApplyGenericTransforms* is applied once, as described in subsection 3.3. This includes the Griesmayer inversion, as outlined in section 2, and some accommodation of test case input and output data as inline specification. In the second stage *ApplySpecificTransforms* is applied, as described in subsection 3.2, for each subsequent test case processed. This implements any whitelist narrowing possible at this iteration via the toggle; for ESBMC it also includes some test-case-specific input data encoding into the program text.

The previously discussed Griesmayer inversion is always applied during the generic stage, *ApplyGenericTransforms*. Also at this stage, we automatically encode the test case specification into the input program, avoiding the need to manually hard-code the inputs into the program. The input and output of C programs are defined by the passed program arguments, `argv`, and the standard inputs and standard outputs. To encode the desired output we widen `argv` to also accept the desired output as an extra string value. This can be compared in the transformed program against modified stdout commands, replacing calls to e.g. `printf` with comparisons that increment a pointer to the desired output when it matches the previous output of the `printf`. Assertions inserted before the program's terminal nodes, which confirm the pointer to the desired output has reached the end of the string, will complete this encoding of the specification.

An optimisation of this is used for simple programs, such as TCAS, that only require a single value to be checked for output specification compliance. Rather than encode the output as a string that is walked, it can be handled in the same way most input variables are. A call to `printf("%d", val);` can be replaced with `assert(val == atoi(argv[X]));` for X being the last value of the now-widened input vector.

Program transformations can extend the number of assignments visible for repair, for example by treating any return statement that returns more than a single variable as an assignment to a temporary variable that is then returned. If returns are always considered to be implicit assignments then localisation is expanded from assignment locations to also include all return statements, as our tool does. `return (y * z);` becomes `return ((__toggle == 3)? __sym : y * z);` for symbolic value `__sym` at the fourth assignment in the program.

During the specific stage, i.e. *ApplySpecificTransforms*, the whitelist of locations must be applied to narrow the range of toggles being searched. We do this by adding assumptions of the form `klee_assume(__toggle != 11);` to the program body for any values to be omitted from this search (blocking the twelfth assignment in this example).

For ESBMC there is no way to populate `argv` in the program simulation, so the `argv` values need to be hard-coded into the transformed program before handing to the symbolic analyser. As this is linked to the specific test case, this can only be done at the specific stage. KLEE provides a POSIX implementation for program I/O during simulation. This allows the test case input to be fed into the standard `argv` parameters and removes the requirement for this specific stage transform.

3.2 The Test Case Search Algorithm

Algorithm 1 outlines a single task, which defaults to being deployed to a single core via the pool manager discussed in subsection 3.3. When *AddTask* is called on lines 5 and 20 of Algorithm 2 by the manager then an instance of this single unit of work is queued into the worker pool. These tasks run independently until they return their narrowed list of locations, K, on line 7 or are ejected by the pool manager. Each task takes an input program which has already been transformed by the generic stage, a single failing test case, and a whitelist of locations that are indicated by their associated toggle values.

Input: Program D; Failing Test Case f; Location Set L
Output: Fault Location Set K
1: E = ApplySpecificTransforms(D, L, f);
2: $CounterExamples$ = CallModelCheckerOnInput(E, f)
3: K = [];
4: **for** c in $CounterExamples$ **do**
5:     **if** c.UnconditionalAssertionFailure() **then**
6:         K.Add(ExtractLocationValue(c));
7: **return** K;

Algorithm 1. Test Case Search Worker Algorithm

ApplySpecificTransforms is discussed in subsection 3.1. The final transformed program is generated, ready for submission to the symbolic analyser. The toggle values are restricted to the whitelist and, in the case of ESBMC, the test case is hard-coded into the source code.

CallModelCheckerOnInput passes the transformed program to the model checker. For ESBMC the failing test case has been encoded into the source code (in *ApplySpecificTransforms*) but KLEE still requires this information. KLEE, using the POSIX runtime environment model, is passed the argument vector (extended to contain the desired output) during the simulation of the program execution.

The call to *CallModelCheckerOnInput* returns the counterexamples for this failing test case, which are a set of traces that result in the raising of specification failure when simulating the execution of the transformed program. The traces are parsed into a format that holds the failure type and the associated assignment to `__toggle` and `__sym`. In the case of ESMBC, this process is iterative as only one counterexample is generated by each instantiation of the symbolic analyser. For ESBMC, a loop that modifies the input program to further narrow the toggle values explored allows the symbolic analyser to run repeatedly until no new toggle value is generated. This, executed inside the call to *CallModelCheckerOnInput* in Algorithm 1, generates a full list of toggle values associated with repairs for this failing test case. KLEE does this loop automatically within a single call.

On lines 3 – 6 the old whitelist is replaced with the new list of toggle values returned by the counterexamples, generated by the symbolic analyser execution. This narrowing checks the counterexample type to ensure the assertion raised is the `assert(0);` added before the program's terminal nodes.

The time it takes to process this task is not predictable with any degree of certainty. The core operation of calling the solver inside the symbolic analyser is a logical satisfiability problem, which is NP complete [8]. This type of SAT problem has been shown [5] to not provide predictable tractability. This unpredictability of the time it takes to process each logic expression in the symbolic analyser is the core issue that our algorithm must cope with. Each counterexample generated has a corresponding solver stage and there are an unknown number of counterexamples multiplying this unknown per-instantiation processing time.

Each counterexample generated increases processing time and so a significantly narrowed whitelist, which blocks off many counterexamples, is highly beneficial. We manage uncertainty via the pool manager and ensure that narrowing results are percolated to new tasks as soon as possible.

3.3   The Pool Manager Algorithm

The main tool loop, which manages the process pool and task scheduling, generates an output set of viable repair locations (lines 21 and 16 of Algorithm 2). The input is an untransformed C program and a non-empty queue of failing test cases, each of which comprises an input string and a correct output string. To provide our evaluation of this tool with generalization validity, the queue must

Input: Program C; Failing Test Case Queue $F \neq []$
Output: Fault Location Set L

1: $(D, L) = $ ApplyGenericTransforms(C);
2: $VisibleCores = $ Min(Len(F), $OS.VisibleCores$);
3: $P = $ EstablishWorkerPool($VisibleCores$);
4: **for** 1 .. $VisibleCores$ **do**
5:     P.AddTask(D, Dequeue(F), L);
6: $WithoutImprovement = 0$;
7: **while** P.HasOpenWorkers() **do**
8:     Sleep($TickTimerMS$);
9:     **if** P.HasCompletedTasks() **then**
10:        Sleep(0.25 * P.GetFastestCompletedTaskTime());
11:        **for** w in P.GetCompletedTasks() **do**
12:            $Lnew = w$.Locations $\cap$ L;
13:            **if** $Lnew == L$ **then** $WithoutImprovement$++;
14:            **else** $WithoutImprovement = 0$;
15:            $L = Lnew$;
16:        **if** $WithoutImprovement > 15$ **then return** L;
17:        F.Enqueue(P.ReturnTCsForIncompleteTasks());
18:        **for** w in P.GetAllTasks(); **do**
19:            P.RemoveTask(w);
20:            **if** Len(F) > 0 **then** P.AddTask(D, Dequeue(F), L);
21: **return** L;

Algorithm 2. Pool Manager Algorithm

be an unordered list. This is because the optimised search varies in performance based on the test case order, as discussed in section 4.

The tool applies the generic transform stage discussed in subsection 3.1 during line 1's *ApplyGenericTransforms*. This parsing of the source file, as it walks all the fault locations being searched to apply the assignment transform, is also used to generate the initial whitelist of all toggle values that correlate to a localisation.

A worker pool is established on line 3, which provides the interaction point for all calls involving workers and the tasks they are executing or schedule for future execution. The tool queries the operating system to establish the multiprocessing pool is as wide as the exposed CPU core count, unless there are fewer failing test cases than available cores (line 2). The use of the worker pool is to avoid a single intractable task from stalling the entire search. This is most efficiently achieved on modern multi-core consumer hardware by dedicating one core to each worker. A similar pool could be managed on a single-core processor using the OS scheduler to manage the tasks, with the added overhead of regularly swapping the current process.

Each worker will process an independent task (i.e. Algorithm 1) which takes the transformed program from line 1, a failing test case, and the current whitelist. This will eventually deplete the test case queue. Lines 4 and 5 push an initial batch of tasks to the pool system, which will use the un-narrowed whitelist created on line 1. Batching tasks with a multiprocessing implementation increases throughput, even with an algorithm dependent on the pruning of the search space for efficiency. Critically, this prevents one slow task, whose individual contribution is not required for the search, from completely stalling the full search. A typical four-core CPU executing highly variable return-time tasks with probability p intractable outliers in the task queue will only stall the entire process when all cores are filled with intractable outliers at once. This probability of p^4 is a significant improvement, especially for this process where stalled tasks may become tractable later due to whitelist narrowing of the search space.

The main tool loop starts on line 7 of Algorithm 2. The loop exits when the pool manager is not holding any completed tasks (waiting for their return value to be processed), no tasks are in flight, and no tasks are queued waiting to be started.

The pool manager thread sleeps to allow the pool's workers to monopolise the CPU, periodically waking to check if any tasks have completed with *HasCompletedTasks*. When at least one completed task is ready for retiring from the pool, the main thread waits for other tasks to complete. This waits a maximum of 125% of the time the fastest task completed with (line 10). This allows slower tasks with valuable narrowing results to complete and be added to the narrowing before the next generation of tasks is dispatched. The completed tasks after this timeout are iterated on lines 11 – 15. To prepare for the next generation of tasks to be dispatched, a new whitelist is created that includes all narrowing returned from the completed tasks during this generation.

A counter, *WithoutImprovement*, is incremented if the returned narrowing does not prune the existing set. This will eventually trigger an early termination clause (line 16) when the narrowing process has stalled for many failing test cases in a row. This provides enhanced time performance with larger failing test case sets, without harming the narrowing performance, as the larger sets have more redundant (for narrowing) test cases.

Any task which has been flagged as failing to complete in a time consistent with the others, missing the 125% dynamically assessed expected time, is queried on line 17. The failing test case it failed to complete is added back to the tail of the queue. If the whitelist is smaller when this task comes back up then it can be rescheduled, with the reduced search space increasing the likelihood of a fast completion time. Test cases are flagged as repeats so they are not enqueued a third time if they failed to complete a second time. This protects against intractable tasks which will not provide narrowing data. All of the tasks from a generation will have now been processed, so they are ejected from the pool (line 19). The next batch of tasks is despatched to the pool (line 20) with the newly narrowed whitelist, if there are still failing test cases in the queue.

This generational search process, with percolated combined narrowing, limits the explored search space to relevant branches where a find is still viable and reduces the symbolic execution work for the solver. Some tasks may still be intractable so, to prevent them slipping through any cracks in this process, a global timer that must be configured to denote what is an "unreasonable" processing time is established that ejects tasks that fail to complete in that time. This will only be triggered if all active workers are stalled with intractable problems but does require configuration of what is an unacceptable wait.

Scheduling this task pool over a standard consumer multi-core CPU with these guards against search stalls and early rejection of superfluous searches provides significant performance improvements, as indicated by our preliminary results.

4   Preliminary Experimental Results

4.1   Experimental Setup

We demonstrate the time and localisation performance of our tool on the Siemens test suite's TCAS program and test universe taken from the Software-artifact Infrastructure Repository (SIR) [10]. TCAS is a 173 line C program from which 41 variants have been generated by seeding (injecting) faults. Of these, 33 variants have been seeded with a single fault and exhibit at least one failing output with the test suite of 1608 test cases. These provide meaningful interpretation when comparing the performance of localisers with a single-fault assumption. For the single-fault variants, we maintain time performance within the same order of magnitude as the current model-based fault localisation state of the art, Jose and Majumdar. We guarantee returning the location of the injected fault in every failing case, which Jose and Majumdar cannot. For 31 of the 33 single-fault variants we improve on the localisation performance of Jose and Majumdar's results.

In Table 1 and Table 2 the headings refer to the following data sources and test platforms: Griesmayer's original data [11, §4, Table1, p. 104] (**G**) uses CBMC on a 2.8GHz Pentium 4; our naïve reimplementation of Griesmayer's algorithm (**N**) uses ESBMC v1.17 on a 3GHz Core2Duo E8400; our new algorithm using ESBMC (**E**) and KLEE (**K**) as back-end both ran on a 3.1GHz Core i5-2400, with the ESBMC [9] v1.21 and KLEE [3] (for LLVM 3.4) symbolic analysers; and Jose and Majumdar's results (**J**) reconstructed from data provided [17, §6, Table1, p. 443] using MSUnCORE on a 3.16GHz Core2Duo. Boldface entries in the table represent the best performance, underlined entries indicate failure to return the injected repair for all failing test cases. In Table 1 the Jose and Majumdar time data has been calculated by taking the number of executions per test case and multiplying by the reported average time to complete a single execution of a failing test case.

We shuffle the test suite to randomise the order of the failing test cases when invoking our tool. This prevents the performance reported by our current tool only reflecting the time performance when provided with the default test case order. The time performance reported is the average of ten runs.

Table 1. Seconds to Return Location Set for Test Suite. Griesmayer's original data [11, Table 1, p. 104] (**G**). Naïve reimplementation of Griesmayer's algorithm (**N**). New algorithm using ESBMC (**E**) and KLEE (**K**) as back-end. Jose and Majumdar's results [17, Table1, p. 443] (**J**).

	G	N	E	K	J		G	N	E	K	J		G	N	E	K	J
v1	2953	1442	9.0	4.5	**2.1**	v14	594	101	3.2	**1.4**	1.4	v26	311	114	3.4	2.1	**1.2**
v2	836	678	3.7	**3.2**	4.7	v16	1263	746	8.8	**3.9**	7.3	v27	153	107	3.3	2.3	**1.1**
v3	423	240	6.7	3.6	<u>**2.2**</u>	v17	1300	365	5.6	3.6	**3.4**	v28	642	711	**2.0**	2.7	<u>6.1</u>
v4	576	307	7.5	2.9	**2.7**	v18	499	188	3.7	**3.0**	3.6	v29	224	112	2.9	3.4	<u>**1.7**</u>
v5	159	106	3.2	2.3	**1.2**	v19	691	193	5.4	3.4	**2.1**	v30	939	508	3.9	**2.8**	3.7
v6	253	134	4.9	2.8	**1.3**	v20	748	196	7.4	4.3	**2.2**	v34	1906	790	4.9	**3.0**	7.7
v7	743	359	5.9	3.9	**2.6**	v21	585	197	6.7	3.7	**1.7**	v35	1069	711	**2.3**	2.8	<u>4.6</u>
v8	26	10	1.7	1.4	**0.1**	v22	223	42	2.8	2.6	**0.6**	v36	877	219	**2.1**	2.4	3.0
v9	114	72	2.0	2.1	**0.8**	v23	885	189	4.2	**2.8**	<u>4.2</u>	v37	822	729	**3.7**	4.1	3.7
v12	1664	727	5.0	**3.4**	<u>11.5</u>	v24	254	71	3.3	2.1	**0.6**	v39	66	8	1.0	1.5	**0.3**
v13	149	43	1.9	1.1	**0.3**	v25	68	8	1.0	1.5	**0.2**	v41	956	309	8.0	4.2	**2.4**

4.2 Run Time Performance

Griesmayer provided results on TCAS using state of the art (for the time) model checking tools (CBMC) but indicated the design had not been optimised, saying "we do not concentrate on performance" [11, §4.1, p. 105]. We reimplemented this naïve process as described in Griesmayer's paper. This is running on more modern hardware and updated to use the current, CBMC-derived, SMT symbolic analyser ESBMC. We implemented automatic specification encoding into the tool to hard-code test cases. This tool iterates over all failing test cases, waiting for the symbolic analyser to return all flagged locations. The tool then returns the common locations flagged by all the failing test cases.

The average halving, at most six-fold, decrease in completion time from Griesmayer's results (696 seconds average) to our naïve reimplementation (325 seconds average) in Table 1 shows some performance increase is derived from using a modern symbolic analyser on modern hardware. But, for example, variant 1 moving from over 49 minutes to over 24 minutes to return a location set is not viable compared to the 2.1 seconds of Jose and Majumdar or comparable with our optimised algorithm when also using ESBMC, at 9 seconds.

We have implemented our algorithm as tools interfacing with ESBMC or KLEE. As discussed in section 3, this is designed to maximise consistency and avoid worst case processing time, as well as reducing the symbolic execution burden to improve times. We provide run time numbers for our algorithm using an ESBMC and KLEE back-end in Table 1. This indicates that using KLEE is often somewhat faster, compared to the ESBMC back-end, but the use of KLEE as the symbolic analyser is not a major factor in the orders of magnitude time performance gap between the naïve reimplementation of Griesmayer and our algorithm with a KLEE back-end.

We maintain time performance within the same order of magnitude as the current model-based fault localisation state of the art, as presented by Jose and Majumdar, throughout the singe fault TCAS variants, marginally beating their

Table 2. Percentage of Lines of Code Returned by Localisation; see Table 1 for legend

	G	N	K	J		G	N	K	J		G	N	K	J
v1	8.7	10.4	**7.5**	8.6	v14	**2.3**	2.9	2.9	8.1	v26	4.6	6.9	**4.0**	9.2
v2	**2.9**	**2.9**	**2.9**	4.6	v16	8.7	10.4	**7.5**	9.2	v27	4.0	8.1	**3.5**	10.9
v3	**4.0**	8.7	5.2	<u>9.8</u>	v17	2.3	**1.7**	2.3	9.2	v28	1.2	1.2	1.2	<u>5.7</u>
v4	8.7	11.0	**8.1**	9.2	v18	**2.3**	**2.3**	**2.3**	6.9	v29	**1.7**	2.3	2.3	<u>5.7</u>
v5	4.0	8.1	**3.5**	8.6	v19	2.3	**1.7**	2.3	9.2	v30	**2.3**	2.9	2.9	5.7
v6	7.5	11.0	**6.9**	8.6	v20	8.7	12.1	**8.1**	9.2	v34	4.0	5.8	**3.5**	8.6
v7	2.3	**1.7**	2.3	9.2	v21	8.7	12.7	**8.1**	8.6	v35	1.2	1.2	1.2	<u>5.7</u>
v8	11.0	16.8	10.4	**8.6**	v22	4.6	**4.0**	4.6	5.7	v36	1.2	1.2	1.7	2.9
v9	5.2	**4.6**	**4.6**	5.2	v23	5.2	**4.6**	**4.6**	<u>6.3</u>	v37	2.9	**1.7**	2.3	8.6
v12	**4.0**	4.6	**4.0**	<u>9.2</u>	v24	8.7	11.0	**7.5**	8.6	v39	4.6	**3.5**	4.0	6.9
v13	**5.2**	9.2	**5.2**	9.2	v25	4.6	**3.5**	4.0	6.9	v41	**8.7**	12.7	9.2	**8.6**

times in ten of the 33 variants. Our tool, using the KLEE back-end, averages a completion time of 2.87 seconds per TCAS variant, compared to an average of 2.80 seconds in Jose and Majumdar's results. The ability of KLEE to scale to larger input programs offsets the few instances where it does not lead our tool's results compared to the ESBMC back-end.

These preliminary results support our claim that a Griesmayer-derived model-based localisation technique can be modified to be fast, comparable to the current alternatives. Using intelligent pruning of the search space to min-imise the symbolic execution load while minimising the disruption of a slow or intractable search node is facilitated by a multiprocess design that takes advan-tage of modern consumer processor architectures.

4.3   Localisation Performance

The scope of the localisation of a tool quantifies which locations are being searched by the process and flagged as a potential fault. Different localisation scopes for each technique's implementation means their localisation performance is not precisely comparable. The results published by Griesmayer only explore the 34 explicit assignments in the TCAS variants, which increases the localisa-tion performance we would expect to see in Table 2 as there cannot be more than 20% of the total lines of code returned. Our naïve reimplementation has an expanded scope that finds implicit assignments within the source code, expand-ing the potential locations returned to 43 assignments, or 25% of the source lines. This accounts for the weak, for Griesmayer-derived, localisation perfor-mance. The localisation results for our algorithm using the ESBMC back-end are omitted, but were noted to fall in line with the original Griesmayer results and our current numbers with KLEE. Our current tool, using a KLEE back-end, does not apply all implicit assignment transforms implemented in our naïve reimplementation, only implementing the transforms described in subsection 3.1. This reduces the assignments tracked to 39, or 23% of the source lines.

We can conceptualise the Griesmayer-derived searches as building a look-up table for each assignment location returned that, if complete, repairs all failing test cases. Passing test cases already have a known correct value for their assignments. Any location flagged by a failing test cases will have, in the __sym value extractable from the counterexample, the assignment which repairs that trace and so test case. It is thusly possible, for locations flagged by all failing test cases, to construct a complete look-up table at that assignment location that ensures every test case now has a specification-complying trace, i.e. a genuine repair exists at that location. In our results, the injected repair is always included in the locations returned. But, with this conceptualisation of the process, the other locations are not false positives but additional locations where a genuine repair will allow the test suite to pass, to the limits of the symbolic analyser's accuracy.

All our results confirm roughly comparable localisation performance between the various Griesmayer-derived methods, after accounting for the differences in localisation spaces. Any performance regression in localisation performance, when comparing the original Griesmayer results with our Griesmayer-derived localisation results, is most likely the result of searching a wider assignment space. Localisation performance improvements are likely to have resulted from more modern symbolic analysers providing a more accurate exploration of the input C program, exploring new potential traces. Exact localisation performance, while a common metric for comparison on TCAS and in general, is slightly defocussed as a primary metric here. Evaluating the difference between Griesmayer-derived techniques, as they all operate to generate this family of locations with look-up table justification, is to penalise a tool for returning justified fault candidates; while not the injected fault location, they are locations with a repair.

Jose and Majumdar, with an approach based on mapping MAX-SAT clauses back to source code, cannot be directly compared in terms of potential C code coverage. The mapping of the MAX-SAT output, from logic clauses in the maximum satisfiable result to source locations, can flag locations other than assignments. However, the granularity of this mapping is not clear. Some of the lack of competitive localisation performance in some variants shown in Table 2 for Jose and Majumdar, when compared to Griesmayer or our algorithm can be explained by this different scope of potentially returned locations, where additional genuine repairs are being suggested outside of assignment modifications.

When comparing the localisation performances, even without being apples to apples, this is ultimately comparing sets of proposed fault sites where human developers must search for a genuine repair, possibly the injected one. Our current tool is typically ahead in this metric, sometimes by a significant percentage. In the two variants where our tool performs worse, v41 returns a set of locations only one larger than those returned by Jose and Majumdar, and v8 returns a set three locations larger.

When comparing the localisation performance of these tools, we must consider that there is an injected fault location for each of the single-fault variants of TCAS. For all the Griesmayer-derived techniques then the injected fault location (the location where a variant was seeded with a fault) is always included in the returned list of locations. Due to the technique's design (where a location is only returned if it is common between all individual failing test cases), this means that this injected location will also be returned when only given a single failing test case from any of the test suites and on any of the single-fault variants. Any subset of the test suite that contains at least one failing test case will, for all Griesmayer-derived tools, flag the injected fault location.

The results from Jose and Majumdar cannot make a similar claim. To account for some failing test cases not indicating the injected fault location, their final set is based on the most commonly indicated locations, not locations that are always flagged by every failing test case. Their results for each full test suite do flag the injected fault location for TCAS as most common. But they indicate that there exist subsets of the failing test cases for which they would not flag the injected fault in the case of six single-fault variants (underlined in the tables).

4.4   Limitations

In subsection 4.3 we have already discussed issues with making direct localisation performance comparisons. The single-fault assumption that underpins our model prevents any meaningful localisation performance on the seven TCAS variants which contain multiple injected faults, where positive localisation results would be derived from blind chance. The performance of a single-fault localiser will be faster than more extensive searches that include k-fault analysis. However, the single-fault assumption is common in fault localisation techniques.

The fault-seeded variants of the small Siemens program we are testing on are not a representative sample of C programs and the faults they contain. The TCAS variants explored all contain injected faults inserted at return expressions or assignments. Our results may not generalise to other C programs. Our focus on a subset of programs, and use of real world code which is atypical in the heavy use of global variables, may obscure comparative analysis of performance against other tools with different program features. Performance on relatively small, loop-free programs like TCAS does not provide guidance into how this process scales to large programs with more complicated control flow. This issue is common to all tools which demonstrate their localisation effectiveness on the TCAS variants.

We can use any (C99 comprehending, supporting assume functionality) symbolic analyser to process our generated C code but our results are linked to either KLEE or ESBMC. Any issues related to those tools may affect our results, if not our methods/process. No high performance symbolic analyser of C can perfectly transform an input program into an exact representation according to the full C specifications. The lack of exact specification compliance by the various widely used (optimising) C compilers also makes such an impracticable achievement undesirable. Real compiled code does not perfectly map to a strict adherence to a single, deterministic interpretation of the C specifications.

Familiarity with the specific problem being solved (the small Siemens program) could have subconsciously influenced our research direction towards a process that is unfairly high performing for this specific problem and does not adequately generalise to C code. To minimise this risk, our choice of time-out, sleep delay, and early termination values have not been tuned or selected for optimising with respect to the test suite; that would compromise our preliminary results.

5   Extensions

We currently present results where the known correct output is provided with the test case input in the test suite. This is encoded as the assertion that the correct output is generated by the program to comply with the specification for that test case. This can be weakened if a test case only specifies that the output does *not* take a given value, i.e. for input x, the output is *not* y. This weakened specification only requires the assertion that the known incorrect output is not generated. These two types of test cases can be mixed, providing a test suite with both known correct outputs and known wrong outputs for failing test cases. They would require two separate transformed programs that encoded this difference (at the generic stage). This would be a small extension for a tool that can, separately, operate on both types of failing test case. Weaker specifications would be far less restrictive on the locations where a potential repair could exist, as any location where the final output could be nudged to no longer generate the same value would be flagged. This may limit the value of localising with such a weak specification.

As described in subsection 3.1, the current tool's transformation process modifies return statements when the returned expression is more than a single variable. This allows localisation to an implicit assignment hidden by any return statement not creating a temporary variable for the returned value. We can extend this to other locations where an assignment is implicit, with a process similar to Single Assignment C transformations. This can be expanded in many ways to inspect for fault classes outside of assignments. For example, the search for spurious statements, i.e. looking for superfluous lines of code that can be safely removed. That is, we remove a statement that enables the failing test cases to pass and not regress passing test cases. Rather than inserting the toggle into the right hand side of an assignment, the entire statement can be made optional by the toggle test `if(loc != [LOC_VAL])original_statement;`. The location, when toggled, would explore how the program functioned without that statement. This sort of fault class exploration provides narrowing of the whitelist of locations when exploring passing test cases, a feature not seen in the modified assignments currently employed. This is not providing a widening of the program functionality with symbolic values but a mutation of the program when a location is activated by the toggle. These more extensive modifications to location searches outside of assignments can be done in combination with current searches or independently.

The currently discussed algorithm uses a single toggle value to activate a single location to perform the alternative assignment of a symbolic value. If multiple toggles were used with (`__toggle1 == 3 || __toggle2 == 3`) conditions activating the modified locations, then the search would be able to produce localisations searching for multiple faults (up to the number of toggles inserted and chained in the or-conditions). This extension was proposed as an extension in the Griesmayer paper [11]. This would increase the solver cost due to additional non-determinism and would also increase the total combination of counterexamples returned. It may be severely limited to small input programs to retain tractability but is a theoretical extension of this process to a k-fault assumption.

The scalability limitations of our current approach will be quantified by exploring the tool's performance on larger, more complex input programs and production code samples. The transition from ESBMC to KLEE as the back-end and a concolic execution approach facilitates this expansion of the scope of input C programs.

6   Related Work

Localisation by examining counterexample traces, test cases, or other output from static and dynamic analysis tools is an active area of research [4,6,11,13, 14,17,29–31].

Griesmayer et al. [11] have first applied model-based diagnosis methods to software. Our work follows the same lines; see section 2 for a more detailed discussion. Griesmayer et al. [12] improve the original implementation to achieve times roughly comparable to our own initial re-implementation (see section 4 for details). They also expand the possible fault locations to non-assignments (e.g. expressions in control flow guards), which could easily be applied to our approach as well, although the higher number of locations considered can lead to more complicated solver problems and thus higher run times.

Königshofer and Bloem [19,20] have developed the foREnSiC system which includes a Griesmayer-style localisation. They have applied this to TCAS as well, but published results only for a few variants; here localisation times are more than an order magnitude slower (around 120 seconds) than our results. Königshofer et al. [21] report slightly improved times (around 37 seconds) but had to annotate all functions with contracts, and so do no longer work from test suites alone.

Griesmayer's approach has also been applied to hardware designs in SystemC [22], often combined with different solver technologies such as QBF [32] or unsatisfiable cores [33]. Our results indicate that "plain old SAT/SMT" is still sufficient, but these technologies could be considered as alternatives in our approach as well.

Jose and Majumdar [17] convert an input C program to a maximum Boolean satisfiability problem which is analysed with MAX-SAT solver. However, because it returns the complement of the maximal subset of clauses that can be true for each single test case, their approach can omit genuine repair locations. It therefore relies on summing the results of the different test cases, providing a ranking of most to least commonly flagged locations. This is the approach, and so inherits the strengths/weaknesses, of many heuristic-based fault localisation techniques. As discussed in section 4, our approach provides comparable localisation times but a higher precision.

Spectrum-based fault localisation techniques, compared in [24,35,36], operate by examining passing and failing test cases separately. They assume that faults are more likely to be exercised by failing test cases and less likely to be exercised by passing test cases. The statements in a program can then be ranked based on the different weighting techniques. The analysis of the performance of these approaches is typically based on several scoring formulas that roughly correspond to how much of a program must be explored, given an ordered list of locations as tool output, before the genuine fault is found. The best-known example of this technique is the Tarantula tool [31] with TCAS results provided earlier [16]. Tarantula provides over 50% of runs on various of the Siemens small programs (including TCAS) with a localisation performance that puts the genuine fault location in the top 10% of lines returned. But this performance is inconsistent and 7% of these runs fail to narrow the localisation list so that the genuine fault location is in the top 80% of locations.

State of the art spectrum-based fault localisation methods have recently been compared using different theoretical frameworks [24,36]. Several methods have been identified as optimal under these frameworks; there is also empirical data over various of the Siemens small programs. While Tarantula is not optimal [36], it is also not far behind the state of the art for TCAS. In empirical results [24, Table XI, p. 11:23], the only method identified as optimal under that paper's framework ranked the injected fault location on average at the 17th returned location (9.9%) over all TCAS variants. Tarantula returned the injected fault location at an average location between the 18th and 19th ranked location (10.8%).

This is significantly below the worst performance of the symbolic model checking approaches detailed in Table 2. The spectrum-based reporting metrics provide the average rank, as a percentage, in a ranked list of all lines of code. The symbolic model checking results report the total unranked lines flagged as suspicious, as a percentage of total lines of code. To compare these results, we must convert the unranked sets in Table 2 to ranked lists from which to derive averages. Randomly ranking all the returned lines above a list that randomly ranks all the lines not returned provides this conversion. The injected fault location, when it is returned as part of the unranked set, will, on average, be in the middle of the ranked returned lines. Using this conversion, the KLEE average result (4.6%) over the TCAS single defect variants is equivalent to returning the injected fault location at the 4th ranked location (2.3%). As noted in subsection 4.3, the different localisation scopes involved with each technique mean these results are not directly comparable. A spectrum-based approach will not only localise to assignment locations and TCAS is not ideally suited to providing these approaches with easily differentiable statements.

Delta Debugging [37] is a family of approaches that involve splitting up a large set of changes to find the minimal set that flip the program behaviour from correctly functioning to exhibiting a failure. This has variously been used to minimise inputs and traces but was later extended to source code exploration. The principle applied here [6] is to look at passing and failing traces and minimise the differences between them to isolate the failing components. This is reminiscent of a binary search, looking for interesting subset behaviour to narrow down variables that correlate with failure. However, this does require the existence of at least one passing trace and the localisation performance of Delta Debugging on the small Siemens programs [6] is worse than Tarantula's [16] results.

7 Conclusions

Our main contribution in this paper is an improved search through the test suite, reducing the effort for the symbolic execution of the model. Our results show Griesmayer's technique works in comparable time to the state of the art when driven with our optimised algorithm. This algorithm outperforms the naive reimplementation of the technique and the technique's originally published implementation by more than two orders of magnitude.

We generate genuine lists of repair locations as specified by test cases for any repair that could be expressed as a look-up table for the right-hand side of an assignment, within the limits of symbolic analyser accuracy. Our time performance is in line with recent alternative model-based fault localisation techniques, but narrows the location set further without rejecting any genuine repair locations where faults can be fixed by changing a single assignment. This is more consistent than the localisation performance of other techniques and does so without compromising the narrowing extent, which might be done to avoid the false negatives shown in the competition.

References

1. Ahmadzadeh, M., Elliman, D., Higgins, C.: An analysis of patterns of debugging among novice computer science students. In: SIGCSE, pp. 84–88 (2005)
2. Bendersky, E.: Pycparser: C parser and AST generator written in Python (2012). https://github.com/eliben/pycparser
3. Cadar, C., Ganesh, V., Pawlowski, P.M., Dill, D.L., Engler, D.R.: EXE: Automatically Generating Inputs of Death. ACM Trans. Inf. Syst. Secur. **12**(2), 10A (2008)
4. Chandra, S., Torlak, E., Barman, S., Bodik, R.: Angelic debugging. In: ICSE, pp. 121–130 (2011)
5. Cheeseman, P., Kanefsky, B., Taylor, W.M.: Where the really hard problems are. In: IJCAI, pp. 331–337 (1991)
6. Cleve, H., Zeller, A.: Locating causes of program failures. In: ICSE, pp. 342–351 (2005)
7. Console, L., Friedrich, G., Dupre, D.T.: Model-based diagnosis meets error diagnosis in logic programs. In: Fritzson, P.A. (ed.) AADEBUG 1993. LNCS, vol. 749, pp. 85–87. Springer, Heidelberg (1993)
8. Cook, S.A.: The complexity of theorem-proving procedures. In: Proc. ACM Symposium on Theory of Computing, pp. 151–158 (1971)
9. Cordeiro, L., Fischer, B., Marques-Silva, J.: SMT-Based Bounded Model Checking for Embedded ANSI-C Software. IEEE Trans. Softw. Engg. **38**(4), 957–974 (2012)

56   G. Birch et al.

10. Do, H., Elbaum, S., Rothermel, G.: Supporting Controlled Experimentation with Testing Techniques. Empirical Softw. Engg., 405–435 (2005)
11. Griesmayer, A., Staber, S., Bloem, R.: Automated Fault Localization for C Programs. Electronic Notes in Theoretical Computer Science, 95–111 (2007)
12. Griesmayer, A., Staber, S., Bloem, R.: Fault localization using a model checker. Softw. Test. Verif. Reliab. **20**(2), 149–173 (2010)
13. Groce, A., Chaki, S., Kroening, D., Strichman, O.: Error explanation with distance metrics. Int. J. Softw. Tools Technol. Transf. **8**(3), 229–247 (2006)
14. Groce, A., Visser, W.: What Went Wrong: Explaining Counterexamples. In: Ball, T., Rajamani, S.K. (eds.) SPIN 2003. LNCS, vol. 2648, pp. 121–135. Springer, Heidelberg (2003)
15. Hutchins, M., Foster, H., Goradia, T., Ostrand, T.: Experiments on the effectiveness of dataflow- and control-flow-based test adequacy criteria. In: ICSE, pp. 191–200 (1994)
16. Jones, J.A., Harrold, M.J.: Empirical Evaluation of the Tarantula Automatic Fault-localization Technique. In: ASE, pp. 273–282 (2005)
17. Jose, M., Majumdar, R.: Cause Clue Clauses: Error Localization Using Maximum Satisfiability. SIGPLAN Not **46**(6), 437–446 (2011)
18. de Kleer, J., Williams, B.: Diagnosing multiple faults. Artificial Intelligence **32**(1), 97–130 (1987)
19. Konighofer, R., Bloem, R.: Automated error localization and correction for imperative programs. In: FMCAD, pp. 91–100 (2011)
20. Könighofer, R., Bloem, R.: Repair with On-The-Fly Program Analysis. In: Biere, A., Nahir, A., Vos, T. (eds.) HVC. LNCS, vol. 7857, pp. 56–71. Springer, Heidelberg (2013)
21. Könighofer, R., Toegl, R., Bloem, R.: Automatic Error Localization for Software Using Deductive Verification. In: Yahav, E. (ed.) HVC 2014. LNCS, vol. 8855, pp. 92–98. Springer, Heidelberg (2014)
22. Le, H.M., Grosse, D., Drechsler, R.: Automatic TLM Fault Localization for SystemC. Trans. Comp.-Aided Des. Integ. Cir. Sys. 31(8), 1249–1262 (2012)
23. de Moura, L., Bjørner, N.S.: Z3: An Efficient SMT Solver. In: Ramakrishnan, C.R., Rehof, J. (eds.) TACAS 2008. LNCS, vol. 4963, pp. 337–340. Springer, Heidelberg (2008)
24. Naish, L., Lee, H.J., Ramamohanarao, K.: A Model for Spectra-based Software Diagnosis. ACM Trans. Softw. Eng. Methodol. **20**(3), 11A (2011)
25. Nelson, G., Oppen, D.C.: Simplification by Cooperating Decision Procedures. ACM Trans. Program. Lang. Syst., 245–257 (1979)
26. Nguyen, H.D.T., Qi, D., Roychoudhury, A., Chandra, S.: SemFix: program repair via semantic analysis. In: ICSE, pp. 772–781 (2013)
27. Pham, H.: Software reliability. Springer (2000)
28. Reiter, R.: A theory of diagnosis from first principles. Artificial Intelligence **32**(1), 57–95 (1987)
29. Renieres, M., Reiss, S.P.: Fault localization with nearest neighbor queries. In: ASE, pp. 30–39 (2003)
30. Sahoo, S.K., Criswell, J., Geigle, C., Adve, V.: Using likely invariants for automated software fault localization. In: ASPLOS, pp. 139–152 (2013)
31. Santelices, R., Jones, J.A., Yu, Y., Harrold, M.J.: Lightweight fault-localization using multiple coverage types. In: ICSE, pp. 56–66 (2009)
32. Staber, S., Bloem, R.: Fault Localization and Correction with QBF. In: Marques-Silva, J., Sakallah, K.A. (eds.) SAT 2007. LNCS, vol. 4501, pp. 355–368. Springer, Heidelberg (2007)

33. Sülflow, A., Fey, G., Bloem, R., Drechsler, R.: Debugging design errors by using unsatisfiable cores. In: MBMV, pp. 159–168 (2008)

34. Vessey, I.: Expertise in debugging computer programs: A process analysis. International Journal of Man-Machine Studies **23**(5), 459–494 (1985)

35. Wong, W.E., Debroy, V.: A survey of software fault localization. Tech. Rep. UTDCS-45-09, Uni. of Texas at Dallas (2009)

36. Xie, X., Chen, T.Y., Kuo, F.C., Xu, B.: A Theoretical Analysis of the Risk Evaluation Formulas for Spectrum-based Fault Localization. ACM Trans. Softw. Eng. Methodol. **22**(4), 31A (2013)

37. Zeller, A.: Yesterday, my program worked. Today, it does not. Why? SIGSOFT Softw. Eng. Notes **24**(6), 253–267 (1999)

Case Study: Automatic Test Case Generation for a Secure Cache Implementation

Roderick Bloem, Daniel Hein, Franz Röck$^{(\boxtimes)}$, and Richard Schumi

Institute for Applied Information Processing and Communications (IAIK),
Graz University of Technology, Graz, Austria
franz.roeck@iaik.tugraz.at

Abstract. While many approaches for automatic test case generation have been proposed over the years, it is often difficult to predict which of them may work well on concrete problems. In this paper, we therefore present a case study in automatic, model-based test case generation: We implemented several graph-based methods that compute test cases with a model checker using trap properties, and evaluate these methods on a Secure Block Device implementation. We compare the number of generated test cases, the required generation time and the achieved code coverage. Our conclusions are twofold: First, automatic test case generation is feasible and beneficial for this case study, and even found a real bug in the implementation. Second, simple coverage methods on the model may already yield test suites of sufficient quality.

Keywords: Automatic test case generation · Model-based testing · Model checking · Trap properties

1 Introduction

Testing is the most prevalent method to discover errors in software. As part of the software development process, engineers invest significant time and effort to construct a test suite that exercises the program intensively. This burden can be lessened by methods to automatically generate test cases that provide some form of systematic coverage of the behavior of the software.

Model-based testing is a method to generate test cases from a *model* of the software [24]. Model-based testing is particularly attractive when the model is available as a part of a system's specification, for instance, for certification purposes. In this case, the model functions both as a source for test cases and as a *test oracle* that decides whether the software behaves correctly. The main challenge is then to derive test cases from the model that when combined form a high-quality test suite [4]. For models that are given as graphs, the typical approach is to generate test cases that provide a certain *coverage* of the model,

This work was supported by the Austrian Research Promotion Agency (FFG) through projects NewP@ss (835917) and TARGET (845633) and by the European Commission through project IMMORTAL(644905).

J.C. Blanchette and N. Kosmatov (Eds.): TAP 2015, LNCS 9154, pp. 58–75, 2015.
DOI: 10.1007/978-3-319-21215-9_4

such as visiting all nodes or all edges. As described below, we can combine this notion with logic-based coverage conditions on the predicates on the edges of the graph.

We can provide such test cases using a model checker [10], which can provide witnesses of executions that reach a certain part of the graph [17]. The test cases thus derived are abstract and are subsequently mapped to concrete test cases by a *test adapter*.

In this paper we put the theory of test case generation with model checkers into practice. We have developed a tool that generates an abstract test suite from a model using a model checker. We have applied our tool in a case study to a real world implementation of a cache used in a Secure Block Device (SBD). We have provided the tool with a model of the cache and we evaluate the resulting test suite in terms of the time required to generate the abstract test cases and the code coverage achieved by the test suite. We also evaluate different graph-based and logic-based coverage criteria. Our results show that test case generation with a model checker is feasible for a real world implementation with a model of reasonable size. The resulting test suite achieves sufficient line coverage on the source code and is able to find a bug that is hard to find manually.

The rest of this paper is structured as follows. In Section 2 we will cover related research. Section 3 introduces some background information. Section 4 presents our realization of test case generation using a model checker. Section 5 presents results of our tool applied on our case study. Finally, Section 6 draws conclusions and gives ideas for future work.

2   Related Work

The idea of generating test cases based on formal specifications was presented by Bernot et al. in [3]. Since then, a lot of research has been done in this field, including [11,14,18,22]. Many formal modeling languages use state machines and automatic test case generation techniques focus on methods to extract high quality test cases from these graphs.

Graph coverage criteria require certain parts of the graph to be covered by test cases: node coverage and edge coverage require each node (edge) to be visited by a test case, and path coverage requires a visit to every path in the graph (or to every path of a certain length). Test generation can now be treated as reachability problem and be solved using a model checker [16]. Additionally, logic coverage criteria such as Active Clause Coverage, as presented in [2], can be used to make sure that the logical predicates on the edges in the graph are properly exercised.

The abstraction level of the model has the most influence on the quality of the test suite. While a very abstract model will induce relatively few test cases that may not explore the behaviour of an implementation very well, a very detailed model may not be amenable to model checking [7].

Fraser et al. present a survey of the principles of model-based testing using model checkers [16]. They show that a model checker can generate a test suite from *trap properties* that claim that coverage criteria can not be met. The counterexamples to these trap properties then meet the coverage criteria. We put some of the proposed techniques in practice and evaluate their applicability on a real implementation.

Tools for test case generation are divided into online and offline tools. Those that generate offline tests are often more intricate as they do not rely on immediate feedback from the System Under Test (SUT).

Mutation-based testing [13, 21] is a related method in which a model is modified in different ways and test cases are generated that show the difference in behaviour between the original model and the modified models.

While graph-based generated test suites should produce fairly high code coverage if the models are relatively detailed, achieving full code coverage is hard. Other tools directly analyze the source code to obtain a test suite with high coverage, but lack the advantage that the model can be used as a specification. (See for instance, [5, 23].)

3   Background

This chapter gives some background information. A brief overview of the coverage criteria implemented in the tool is given. Trap properties and the used model checking tool NuSMV are explained.

A graph of a specification is an illustration of states represented as nodes and transitions, represented as edges, from one state to the other. Edges may have guards expressing under which condition the edge is taken. Test case generation techniques focus on those components and coverage criteria require to cover the one, the other, or both.

3.1   Model Checking

The tool we use for model checking is NuSMV [9]. NuSMVs modeling language allows defining a finite state machine. A model consists of states and input variables, and of transitions defining how an input leads from one state to the next state. The rules on the transitions can be complex logical decisions. We use the state machines of every single variable as graphs for our tool, assuming that every variable is initialized. The transition guards in these state machines are a conjunction of the next statements of the variable to reach the next state.

Properties that are checked on the model can be specified using Linear Temporal Logic (LTL) or Computational Tree Logic (CTL). In LTL it is possible to define paths referring to the future, for example, a formula ϕ will always be true, or a variable b will become true in the next state if a is true now. Those logics allow precise specification of properties which a model checker can then check on the model.

3.2   Trap Properties

A popular approach in order to create a test case which covers specific parts of the model is to create trap properties [17]. A trap property is a property that formulates a claim that is expected not to hold. The claim is expressed as a formula stating that the target component is never visited. This trap property will then result in a counterexample when being model checked. The resulting counterexample is a trace, leading to the desired component that is expected to be covered by the test case. The same method can be used with witnesses instead of counterexamples. For witnesses the property has to be formulated in its normal form claiming that the property is expected to hold. For example, to generate a witness for $node_x$, the formula has to express that there exists a path on which $node_x$ is visited.

The resulting counterexamples contain the expected traces and can, therefore, be used as an oracle. The output of the SUT and the expected value of the counterexample are compared. If the values match, the test passes. If the values do not match, the test fails.

3.3   Node Coverage

Node coverage is a basic graph coverage criterion. The idea is to visit every node in the graph at least once. While this can be achieved in the best case with a single test case, the maximum number of non redundant test cases equals the number of nodes in the graph. The advantage of node coverage is that the number of test cases is reasonable small as the number of states in models is usually manageable. Node coverage can be seen as an analogous to statement coverage on the source code. The main drawback of the resulting test suite is that branches might not be covered, as the designated state is already covered by another test case and therefore no test case for a different branch leading to the same state is generated.

To generate a test suite containing a test case for every node in our model, a trap property is formulated for every node claiming that the node can not be reached. A more formal description of trap properties generating counterexample traces that satisfy node coverage is $\forall node \exists t \in \tau : G(\neg node)$, where $node$ is a single node in the graph and t is a single test case of the test suite τ. In our NuSMV model, the number of states per variable corresponds to the number of possible values this variable can take. The total number of nodes to cover is therefore the sum of the individual states per variable.

3.4   Edge Coverage

Whereas for node coverage all nodes have to be visited, for edge coverage all edges have to be visited. Whenever all edges are covered, all nodes are covered, i.e., edge coverage subsumes node coverage. In the best case, the test suite is a single test case. In the worst case the size of the test suite corresponds to the number of edges in the graph. Edge coverage can be seen as the equivalent to branch coverage on the source code.

To construct trap properties for edge coverage the same principle is applied as for node coverage. It is claimed that it is impossible to reach the destination node of the target edge from the source node of the target edge with a satisfied edge guard. A more formal description of trap properties achieving edge coverage is $\forall j \exists t \in \tau : G(edge_j\_src \wedge edge_j\_guard \rightarrow X(\neg edge_j\_dst))$, where $j \in J$ with J being the set of edges in the graph, $edge_j$ is a single edge in the graph, t is a single test case of the whole test suite τ, $edge_j\_src$ is the source node of $edge_j$, $edge_j\_guard$ the transition guard of $edge_j$ and $edge_j\_dst$ the destination node of $edge_j$.

3.5 Path Coverage

To achieve full path coverage, all paths in the graph have to be taken. Path coverage of paths with length up to 2 is called edge pair coverage [1]. As every existing edge is part of at least one path, path coverage subsumes edge coverage. However, the number of test cases explodes, with increasing size and complexity of the model. This can make path coverage already infeasible for models without loops. A model containing loops requires an infinite number of test cases, i.e., complete path coverage is impossible for models with loops.

k-path Coverage. A variant of full path coverage is k-path coverage that only requires to cover paths up to length k. To generate a test suite satisfying path coverage for paths of a fixed length k, the approach is basically the same as for edge coverage. Let $q \in Q$ represent a state of our set of states and $e_i \in E$ represent the transition from our set of transitions leading from q_{i-1} to q_i and let q_0 be the initial state. To cover the path $\pi = q_0 e_1 q_1 e_2 ... e_k q_k$ of length k, the trap property has to require that the trace follows π up to e_k and then the trap property has to claim that the path can not reach q_k. A more formal description of trap properties for path coverage is $\forall \pi \in \Pi_k \exists t \in \tau : q_0 \wedge e_1 \wedge X(q_1 \wedge e_2 \wedge X(.. \wedge X(q_{k-1} \wedge e_k \wedge X(\neg q_k))..)..)$.

3.6 Other Graph-Based Coverage Criteria

Many more graph coverage criteria exist, focusing on different aspects [1]. Criteria like the "all-du-paths" coverage criterion, which are focusing on data flow, may require that a test suite contains a test for every def-use path. Various weaker data flow coverage criteria require fewer paths to be covered [19].

3.7 Logic-Based Coverage Criteria

Graph-based coverage criteria only focus on graph components, they treat all edges the same. Those criteria do not consider that some transition guards might consist of complex logic expressions. Therefore, logic-based coverage criteria can

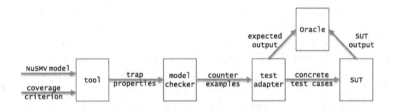

Fig. 1. Flow of the test case generation process

be used in combination with graph-based coverage criteria to generate test cases taking the complexity of the transition guards into account as well. To cover logical expressions, various coverage criteria exist [2]. They start with simple decision coverage and increase complexity to Correlated Active Clause Coverage (CACC), which, for specifications, is the analog to masking Modified Condition Decision Coverage (MCDC) on source code. Whereas decision coverage only requires that the whole condition evaluates once to true once to false, MCDC requires test cases for every single condition within the whole guard, each of them independently affecting the whole decisions outcome [8]. This complex coverage criterion is used especially in safety standards for airborne systems or automotive industry for source code coverage. The whole decision is tested in more detail, as every single condition in the whole decision is tested individually and has to have an influence on the outcome of the decision.

4   Test Case Generation

In this section we present the generation of concrete test cases from the model. The goal is to cover the model according to a given criterion. To achieve this, our tool automatically generates trap properties. Those trap properties will force the model checker to create traces such that the desired parts of the graph are covered. A test adapter finally maps the values of these traces to actual input values of the SUT. To check if the SUT behaves as expected according to the model, the test adapter has to observe and compare the output values of the SUT to the values of the according trace.

Figure 1 illustrates the test case generation and execution:

1. Our tool parses the model and generates trap properties according to the desired coverage criterion.
2. The model checker produces counterexamples based on the trap properties. These counterexamples are traces through the model that pass the desired component(s).
3. A test adapter translates the abstract test cases, i.e., the counterexamples, to concrete test cases according to a given mapping.
4. Test cases are executed on the SUT.
5. The oracle verifies if the behaviour of the SUT is ok.

Whereas test case generation is independent of the SUT and on a higher level of abstraction, the test adapter requires detailed knowledge about the interfaces of the SUT. Moreover, the user has to define a mapping from the abstract variables of the model to the SUT. Variables of the model can be divided into three groups: input, output and internal variables. Input variables determine the inputs to the SUT. The values of the output variables are the expected responses from the SUT, i.e., they are the test oracle such that a decision can be taken if the test passed or failed. Internal variables are all variables that are neither input nor output variables. They can usually not be observed if the SUT is treated as a blackbox and, therefore, they can not be mapped.

The test case generation and execution approach works as follows. The NuSMV model is given as an input to our tool. All variables that are not explicitly tagged as input or output for the test adapter will be treated as internal variables which can neither be controlled by us nor observed from the SUT.

The tool automatically generates the trap properties required to achieve the coverage desired by the user. To do this, the tool iterates through all nodes/edges it attempts to cover and generates a trap property for every component that can be either a node, an edge or a path.

4.1   Combination of Graph-Based and Logic-Based Criteria

There are two options to generate counterexamples that satisfy not only graph-based coverage metrics but also logic coverage criteria for transition guards like CACC. One is to express the CACC criterion within the LTL property for the graph-based criterion. The other is to let an SMT solver determine a variable assignment which then can be included in the property. The model checker is then forced to use the dedicated variable assignment to produce the counterexample. We decided to implement the second approach as this approach divides the problem and shifts part of the problem to the SMT solver in a first step. Due to the variable assignment produced by the SMT solver, the trap property becomes more specific. The external tool we used for getting the variable assignment is described in the paper by Bloem et al. in [6]. This tool takes a Boolean formula, in our case the guard of the edge, as input. For every variable appearance in the formula it derives the two corresponding test cases that satisfy the CACC criterion. In the first test case the variable evaluates to true and in the second the variable evaluates to false. In both test cases the variable determines the result of the formula. The resulting assignment is included in the trap property.

4.2   Abstract Test Case Generation

The trap properties that are produced according to the chosen criterion are together sent with the model to a NuSMV process. For every trap property that fails – as expected – a counterexample is generated. This counterexample represents the trace through the model which is the actual abstract test case. Invalid trap properties, those which do not fail, do not need to be handled separately, as the model checker will just not create any counterexample but state that they are valid. These invalid trap properties can occur, if paths are constructed that are infeasible or if variable assignments are chosen for a certain state that are impossible in this specific state, as the tool deriving the variable assignment has no knowledge on limitations to reach that state. A comparison of the number of trap properties to the number of counterexamples indicates how successful the test case generation has been, because only the resulting counterexamples can be translated to concrete test cases that form the final test suite.

4.3   Test Adapter

To run the test suite on the SUT, the test adapter reads the counterexamples generated by the model checker and extracts the input and output values for every step based on the mapping provided by the user. The input values are handed to the SUT step by step as required from the counterexample. The output values of the SUT are evaluated by the test adapter and compared to the values from the counterexample. A test case run is successful if the values of all output variables match the observed values from the SUT. Whenever an output value does not match the expected value, an exception is raised as the SUT does not behave as expected.

5   Experimental Results

In Section 5.1 we will first evaluate our tool on the well known triangle problem. Then we will apply it in section 5.2 in our case study on the cache implementation of a SBD. We run our experiments on a Mac OS X 10.9.5 with an Intel Core i5 @2.6 GHz and 8 GB RAM. The achieved code coverage in our case study is measured using gcov. For the triangle problem we used EclEmma. We assume that a line coverage of 90% is satisfying.

5.1   The Triangle Problem

To evaluate our tool on a small problem, we used the well known triangle problem [20]. Three numbers, representing the three side lengths of a triangle, are given as input. The system decides based on the side lengths what type of triangle is formed. If all side lengths are equal, an equilateral triangle is formed. A triangle that has two sides of equal length is called isosceles. If all three sides are of unequal length, a scalene triangle is formed. No triangle can be formed, if one or more side lengths are zero. The NuSMV model consists of four nodes which express the four types of a triangle. Edges between these nodes contain the requirements to the side lengths when taking a transition from one triangle type to the other triangle type.

Our tool automatically generated test suites achieving node coverage, edge coverage and path coverage of lengths one, two and three. The resulting code coverage achieved by the derived test suites is presented in Table 1. Whereas

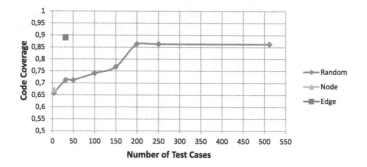

Fig. 2. Achieved line coverage on the triangle implementation

Table 1. Test cases generated

coverage criterion	test cases	line coverage	branch coverage
Node	4	67.1%	50.0%
Edge	32	89.0%	94.4%
Path Length 1	8	86.3%	88.9%
Path Length 2	64	89.0%	94.4%
Path Length 3	512	89.0%	94.4%

the test suite satisfying node coverage contains only four test cases and has a rather low code coverage, the test suite satisfying edge coverage with 32 test cases achieves a line coverage of 89%. In a comparison to a test suite containing random generated numbers (values between 0 and 100) for every side length, Figure 2 illustrates the advantage of the test case generation approach with a model checker over the random testing approach. While random testing required 200 test cases to achieve a line coverage of 86.3%, the test suite generated by the model checker satisfying edge coverage achieved a line coverage of 89% at a size of 32 test cases.

5.2 Case Study: Secure Block Device Cache[1]

The Secure Block Device Cache. We applied our test case generation tool to the block cache of the Secure Block Device (SBD), a software component for secure persistent data storage. The SBD uses symmetric cryptography to guarantee data integrity and data confidentiality, including data freshness, while retaining fast and scalable random access to the securely stored data, by splitting the data into blocks of fixed size. To achieve its security goals the SBD uses a client selectable authenticated encryption scheme in conjunction with a hash tree. Thus, the SBD reduces the problem of protecting the confidentiality and integrity of arbitrary amounts of data at rest to protecting a single cryptographic

---

[1] Additional information: http://www.student.tugraz.at/franz.roeck/TAP2015/

key and the hash tree root hash. Technically, the SBD is a C library that supports any back-end interface that is compatible to the Portable Operating System Interface (POSIX) `pread` and `pwrite` C standard functions.

When the SBD writes data to the back-end interface, this data is encrypted and integrity protected. Conversely, when the SBD reads data it has to reverse the encryption and verify the data integrity. Both ways, this is computationally more costly than simply reading and writing unprocessed data. To minimize these costs the SBD uses a block cache software component. The block cache retains a configurable number of data blocks[1] in unencrypted an unprotected form for quick access in RAM.

To actually achieve the SBD's security goals of data confidentiality and integrity the cryptographic mechanism requires additional overhead data per block. Specifically, it needs a cryptographic nonce and an authentication tag. The cryptographic nonce guarantees the uniqueness of every encrypted block, thus preventing statistical attacks, whereas the authentication tag authenticates the data integrity of a single block. The cryptographic nonce and the authentication tag are public values and do not need to be kept confidential. However, these values need to be protected against modification.

The SBD bundles cryptographic nonces and authentication tags for a specific number of data blocks in a special block type called a management block. These management blocks are stored in the persistent data storage back-end, where they are interleaved with the blocks containing actual input data. On writing, management blocks are integrity protected and the corresponding authentication tag is stored in a hash tree that guarantees overall data integrity. The hash tree root hash is the only value that needs to be stored in a secure memory, where secure means it is protected against unauthorized modification. Management blocks are not encrypted.

As management blocks contain data pertinent to a range of data blocks, the cache component gives them preferential treatment over pure data blocks. Also, to read and write a specific data block, the corresponding management block needs to be in the cache. This is an invariant that must hold for the SBD to work, and the cache has partial responsibility for ensuring it.

An additional peculiarity of the SBD block cache is its eviction strategy. Instead of the commonly used approach based on Least Recently Used (LRU) lists, we use an approximation of this concept. LRU list orders the blocks by their time of use, where the head of the list is the least recently used element and the tail of the list is the most recently used element. The approach we use approximates this behaviour. The main difference is that instead of moving the most recently used element to the tail of a list, we just swap its position with its less recently used neighbour. Here, this operation is called *bumping* the block. Management blocks get a preferential treatment that ensures that a management block is always considered more recently used than its most recently used corresponding data block. This process is done lazily, that is, it is enforced every time a management block is about to be evicted, and it also ensures the above invariant.

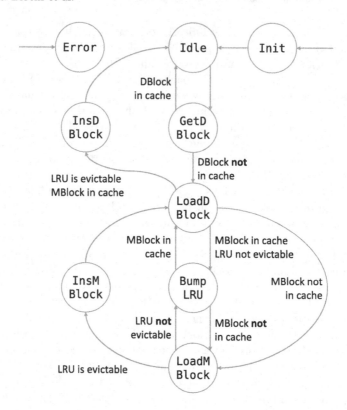

Fig. 3. Model of the cache control logic when accessing a block

The block cache component provides a very simple interface towards the SBD. The interface comprises a call back to the SBD for writing a dirty block before evicting it from the cache, a call back predicate function to test if given management block is responsible for a given data block, and a request data block function. The request data block function either provides access to the requested block data, if it is cached, or a free cache slot. The SBD can use the free cache slot for storing the block data it now reads from the persistent data storage back-end. Before the data is stored in the free cache slot, the SBD also decrypts it and verifies its integrity.

The Model. In a first step, we created a NuSMV model for requesting a data block (DBlock) from the cache. A data block is either already in the cache, or it has to be loaded, put into the cache and then returned to the caller. The model is depicted in Figure 3[2]. Whenever a data block is requested from the cache, the cache controller first checks if the data block is already in the cache (GetDBlock). If it is, it is *bumped* and returned to the caller. If it is **not** in the cache, the cache controller has to check if the corresponding management block (MBlock) is in

---

[2] We have simplified the model for clarity. For the full model see http://www.student. tugraz.at/franz.roeck/TAP2015/

the cache (`LoadDBlock`). If the management block is **not** in the cache, then the cache controller will try to load it (`LoadMBlock`). To load the management block the cache controller first tries to evict the LRU element from the cache. If the LRU element can be evicted, the cache controller evicts it and loads the management block. In our cache it can happen that the LRU element **cannot** be evicted (`BumpLRU`). This happens only if the LRU element is a management block (M_{LRU}). Here we differentiate two cases. Either there is at least one corresponding data block for M_{LRU} in the cache, or M_{LRU} corresponds to the data block that was requested by the caller. In the first case, we bump M_{LRU} until it is more recently used than its most recently used corresponding data block. In the second case, we make it the most recently used element. Once the management block is in cache, the cache controller will load the data block. Again, the cache controller will try to evict the LRU element. If it can be evicted, the cache controller loads the data block and returns it to the caller. If the LRU element **cannot** be evicted the cache controller goes into state `BumpLRU` until a cache slot is freed, and then proceeds to load the data block and return it.

To test our implementation, we used a cache size of four cache lines. We believe a larger cache will just increase complexity, but not add any additional value for the evaluation. Without formal proof, here is the outline of our argument. The cache maintains the invariant that for every data block in the cache the corresponding management block is also in the cache. This invariant is maintained by the `BumpLRU` state, which frees up a cache slot for inserting either a management (`InsertMBlock`) or a data block (`InsertDBlock`). Here the next state of the cache depends on the LRU element, and if it is a management block (M_{LRU}), also on the most recently used data block. We argue that we can model all relevant cases with only four cache slots and that the M_{LRU} case with a corresponding data block is the most complex configuration. If the LRU element is a data block, or a management block without corresponding data block it is evicted. In the M_{LRU} with corresponding data block case the M_{LRU} gets bumped until it holds a position that is more recently used than its most recently used data block. We argue that if we increase the cache size of our model, we only increase the number of bumps. Furthermore, we argue that after a finite number of consecutive visits to `BumpLRU` there will always be LRU element that can be evicted, either because it is a data block, or a management block without corresponding data blocks.

Our cache model consists of four state machines modeling each individual cache slot. The state machines are copies of each other with minor modifications for the corner slots to take into account that they only have a single neighbour and that blocks are evicted or inserted in the least recently used slot. The current state represents what kind of block the cache slot currently holds. With a cache size of four there can be at most three data blocks and one management block, or three management blocks and one data block in the cache. Therefore, the state machines in our model have six states. Let us denote the states representing the cache slot holding a data block as `Dx`, `Dy` and `Dz`, and the states for the corresponding management blocks as `Mx`, `My` and `Mz`. Figure 4 depicts a simplified

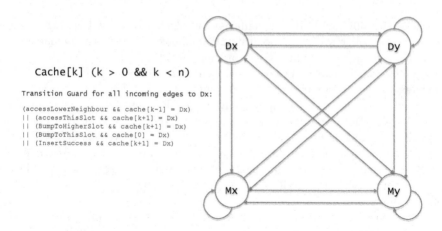

Fig. 4. Cache slot model with two different block types

state machine for a single cache slot with the cache size being expressed as n. For ease of presentation only two different data blocks (Dx, Dy) and their management blocks (Mx, My) are shown. The transitions model the conditions under which the content of the cache slot changes. The transition guard is identical for all incoming edges of a single state. The content changes (i) if the slot or the lower neighbour is accessed or (ii) if the least recently used slot gets bumped to this slot or a higher slot. If a new block is inserted successfully, it results in bumping it to the most recently used slot as well. In case none of the guards is satisfied, the state machine stays in its previous state. To keep the model readable only the label of the transition guard for incoming edges of Dx is included in the figure. This figure makes it obvious that the number of possible transitions and cache setups explodes even for small cache sizes.

Experimental Setup. We evaluate the test suites based on the time required to generate the test suite and the achieved code coverage, line coverage, and branch coverage. The generation time that includes the time for model checking will give an idea on how reasonable it is, to use the one or the other coverage criterion in practice. The code coverage measure gives a hint on the quality of the test suite, but depends heavily on the modeled details. All test suites were generated on the same computer to keep the generation time comparable. Additionally, we will list the generated counterexamples per coverage criterion to get an idea of the resulting test suite size. Although the size of a test suite does not determine its quality, test suites should have a manageable size. Smaller test suites, with fewer redundant test cases are preferable. Moreover, we will use an old version of the SBD implementation containing a bug that was hard to find by manual inspection. We implemented a test adapter to translate the generated abstract counterexamples to concrete test cases.

The general modus operandi of the test adapter is as follows. First the test adapter initializes the cache, and ensures a consistent state. Specifically, the test adapter makes sure that for each data block the corresponding management block is also in the cache. Next, the test adapter creates source code that implements the test cases. The test cases use the interface of the cache (the SUT) to implement their tests. The cache interface consists of functions to request a single cache block and to import or dump the whole cache content. The functions for importing and dumping the cache content are essential for cache initialization and observation.

Specifically, our test adapter reads the initial cache setup from the counterexample and initializes the secure cache as required, by using the import function. The initial setup specifies which data and management blocks to put into specific cache slots. Then the test adapter will translate the rest of the counterexample. Whenever a block is requested in the counterexample, the test adapter maps it to the function that requests this block. In every step after the request block function call, the test adapter compares the cache content of the SUT to the cache content specified by the counterexample. If the SUT cache content differs from the counterexample, the test case fails. This generated source code can then be executed on the SUT.

Results. We applied the tool on the model composed of the cache control logic (see Figure 3) and the cache slot logic (see Figure 4) creating different test suites. The summarized results can be seen in Table 2. Basic node coverage took $\approx$ two and a half minutes from model parsing until the counterexamples were created. Counterexamples were created for every node but the error node. The error node can never be reached if the model covers all possibilities. The test suite for basic node coverage covers a significant part of the source code (see Table 3). It contains 45 test cases and achieves 87% line coverage on the SUT.

To generate a test suite satisfying edge coverage on the model, the tool derived 530 trap properties from which 357 counterexamples were produced. The large number of trap properties without counterexamples is due to edges that can never be taken. These edges are default edges going to the error node, and also edges which are not taken due to restrictions during the initialization process which limit transitions in the cache slot model. Those restrictions ensure that the cache setup is valid at the beginning of the test, as all test cases start with a filled cache. The total generation time was $\approx$ 18 minutes. Taking the increased number of generated test cases into account the time required to generate a single test case increased only slightly compared to the generation time of the test suite for node coverage. While the resulting test suite contains more than seven times the number of test cases than the test suite created for node coverage, the gain in code coverage is insignificant. Line coverage could only be improved from 87.1% to 89.52%.

The state space of our model consists of 46 states. We used our tool to generate a test suite covering all paths of length two. The tool produced 15,629 trap properties. Due to model restrictions that allow transitions only if certain conditions are satisfied, most of the generated paths are infeasible paths and did not result in a counterexample.

Test suite generation took ≈ 27.5 hours. The generated test suite consisted of 451 counterexamples. As Fraser et al. [15] have shown using the proper model checker and the proper technique for the right kind of model can significantly reduce the time required for model checking.

The final test suite we generated with our tool had to satisfy edge coverage on the model and CACC on the guards. It took ≈ 110 minutes to create 1,328 test cases from 7,584 trap properties. While this test suite has far more trap properties than the edge coverage criterion, the generation time didn't explode as it did for path coverage. The time needed to generate a single test case is significantly smaller in comparison. This is due to the different approach we used for CACC. As we use the SMT solver Z3 [12] to get a variable assignment for variables of the guard, the search space for the model checker is reduced, hence the speed up. Although the edge coverage with CACC test suite is three times the size of the edge coverage test suite, it did not improve the code coverage. Line coverage and branch coverage stayed at the same values as for normal edge coverage.

Table 2. Test case generation characteristics

| Coverage criterion | Trap properties | | | |
| | Total | Valid | Invalid | Runtime |
	#	#	#	[s]
Node	46	45	1	3m 13s
Edge	530	357	173	18m 39s
Path Length 2	15,629	451	15,178	27h 31m
Edge with CACC	7,584	1,328	6,256	1h 49m

Table 3. Code Coverage

Coverage criterion	test cases	line coverage	branch coverage
Node	45	87.1%	58.14%
Edge	357	89.52%	59.30%
Path Length 2	357	89.52%	59.30%
Edge with CACC	924	89.52%	59.30%

Besides evaluating code coverage, we also used the automatically generated test suites to evaluate which of them is able to discover a real bug in the SBD implementation. While implementing the SBD Cache, a hard to find bug occurred. After an arduous[3] search the bug was manually discovered and fixed. However, it required a lot of time to analyze the data and control flow to find it. The bug was triggered when a data block was requested and the corresponding management block was the LRU element. When a management block is the LRU element and there are no corresponding data block cached, then this block is evicted. However, the new data block being requested depended on this management block. Thus deleting this management block introduced an error. We "patched" the latest version of the SBD Cache code reintroducing the bug, and then we subjected it to the generated test suites. Already the test suite satisfying node coverage was able to detect this bug. The counterexample, from which test that detected the bug was created, also helps the developer to understand the error.

6   Conclusion and Future Work

In this paper, we have presented a case study that evaluates existing methods for automatic test case generation using model checkers and trap properties. We implemented a tool to automatically generate the trap properties when given a formal model in NuSMV format and a coverage criterion. Our tool can derive test suites for node coverage, edge coverage and path coverage and also offers the option to apply logic coverage criteria like Correlated Active Clause Coverage (CACC) on the transition guards in combination.

The case study consists of the cache component of a Secure Block Device (SBD). Our tool produced test suites for all coverage criteria and we evaluated the required time for generation and the achieved code coverage. For our case study, simple node coverage already achieved a high line and branch coverage on the source code. As we did not have any complex guards on the transitions, applying CACC on the guards in combination to standard graph coverage did not add any value. While the test case generation time increased significantly, no gain in source code coverage was observed. We found a real life bug in the SBD cache with the simple node coverage test suite. This illustrates that simple coverage criteria like node coverage may already yield test suites of sufficient quality to discover bugs that are hard to find manually.

In the future, we plan to enhance the tool with further trap property generation methods that limit the search space for the model checker and therefore reduce the overall time for test suite generation. We plan to do this by having additional calculations via SMT-solver as we did already for the CACC generation in this implementation. Another possible enhancement is creating a smaller test suite. One counterexample might just be a subset of another counterexample and, therefore, no additional test case is necessary.

---

[3] It was a holiday. In August. With breathtaking weather. Did we mention that our offices have no air conditioning?

References

1. Ammann, P., Offutt, J.: Introduction to Software Testing, 1st edn. Cambridge University Press, New York (2008)
2. Ammann, P., Offutt, J., Huang, H.: Coverage criteria for logical expressions. In: 14th International Symposium on Software Reliability Engineering: ISSRE 2003, pp. 99–107. IEEE (2003)
3. Bernot, G., Gaudel, M.C., Marre, B.: Software testing based on formal specifications: a theory and a tool. Softw. Eng. J. **6**(6), 387–405 (1991). http://dx.doi.org/10.1049/sej.1991.0040
4. Beyer, D., Chlipala, A.J., Henzinger, T.A., Jhala, R., Majumdar, R.: Generating tests from counterexamples. In: Proceedings of the 26th International Conference on Software Engineering, ICSE 2004, pp. 326–335. IEEE Computer Society, Washington, DC (2004). http://dl.acm.org/citation.cfm?id=998675.999437
5. Bloem, R., Könighofer, R., Röck, F., Tautschnig, M.: Automating test-suite augmentation. In: 2014 14th International Conference on Quality Software, October 2–3, Allen, TX, USA, pp. 67–72 (2014). http://dx.doi.org/10.1109/QSIC.2014.40
6. Bloem, R.P., Greimel, K., Könighofer, R., Röck, F.: Model-based MCDC testing of complex decisions for the java card applet firewall. In: VALID Proceedings, IARIA, Ed., pp. 1–6 (2013)
7. Brooks, R.J., Tobias, A.M.: Choosing the best model: Level of detail, complexity, and model performance. Mathematical and Computer Modelling **24**(4), 1–14 (1996)
8. Chilenski, J.J.: An investigation of three forms of the modified condition decision coverage (MCDC) criterion. Tech. Rep., DTIC Document (2001)
9. Cimatti, A., Clarke, E., Giunchiglia, E., Giunchiglia, F., Pistore, M., Roveri, M., Sebastiani, R., Tacchella, A.: NuSMV 2: an opensource tool for symbolic model checking. In: Brinksma, E., Larsen, K.G. (eds.) CAV 2002. LNCS, vol. 2404, pp. 359–364. Springer, Heidelberg (2002)
10. Clarke, E.M., Grumberg, O., Peled, D.: Model checking. MIT Press (2001). http://books.google.de/books?id=Nmc4wEaLXFEC
11. Dalal, S.R., Jain, A., Karunanithi, N., Leaton, J.M., Lott, C.M., Patton, G.C., Horowitz, B.M.: Model-based testing in practice. In: Proceedings of the 21st International Conference on Software Engineering, ICSE 1999, pp. 285–294. ACM, New York (1999). http://doi.acm.org/10.1145/302405.302640
12. de Moura, L., Bjørner, N.S.: Z3: an efficient SMT solver. In: Ramakrishnan, C.R., Rehof, J. (eds.) TACAS 2008. LNCS, vol. 4963, pp. 337–340. Springer, Heidelberg (2008)
13. DeMillo, R.A., Lipton, R.J., Sayward, F.G.: Hints on test data selection: Help for the practicing programmer. Computer **11**(4), 34–41 (1978). http://dx.doi.org/10.1109/C-M.1978.218136
14. Dick, J., Faivre, A.: Automating the generation and sequencing of test cases from model-based specifications. In: Larsen, P.G., Wing, J.M. (eds.) FME 1993. LNCS, vol. 670, pp. 268–284. Springer, Heidelberg (1993)
15. Fraser, G., Gargantini, A.: An evaluation of model checkers for specification based test case generation. In: ICST 2009, Second International Conference on Software Testing Verification and Validation, April 1–4, Denver, Colorado, USA, pp. 41–50 (2009). http://dx.doi.org/10.1109/ICST.2009.33
16. Fraser, G., Wotawa, F., Ammann, P.E.: Testing with model checkers: A survey. Softw. Test. Verif. Reliab. **19**(3), 215–261 (2009). http://dx.doi.org/10.1002/stvr.v19:3

17. Gargantini, A., Heitmeyer, C.: Using model checking to generate tests from requirements specifications. SIGSOFT Softw. Eng. Notes **24**(6), 146–162 (1999). http://doi.acm.org/10.1145/318774.318939

18. Gaudel, M.-C.: Testing can be formal, too. In: Mosses, P.D., Nielsen, M. (eds.) CAAP 1995, FASE 1995, and TAPSOFT 1995. LNCS, vol. 915, pp. 82–96. Springer, Heidelberg (1995)

19. Hong, H.S., Lee, I., Sokolsky, O., Ural, H.: A temporal logic based theory of test coverage and generation. In: Katoen, J.-P., Stevens, P. (eds.) TACAS 2002. LNCS, vol. 2280, pp. 327–341. Springer, Heidelberg (2002). http://dl.acm.org/citation.cfm?id=646486.694621

20. Jorgensen, P.C.: Software testing - a craftsman's approach, 3rd edn. Taylor & Francis (2008)

21. Offutt, A.J., Untch, R.H.: Mutation, : Uniting the orthogonal. In: Wong, W.E. (ed.) Mutation Testing for the New Century, pp. 34–44. Kluwer Academic Publishers (2000)

22. Offutt, J., Liu, S., Abdurazik, A., Ammann, P.: Generating test data from state-based specifications. Software Testing, Verification and Reliability **13**, 25–53 (2003)

23. Sen, K., Marinov, D., Agha, G.: CUTE: a concolic unit testing engine for C. In: Wermelinger, M., Gall, H.C. (eds.) Proceedings of the 10th European Software Engineering Conference held jointly with 13th ACM SIGSOFT International Symposium on Foundations of Software Engineering, September 5–9, pp. 263–272. ACM, Lisbon (2005). http://doi.acm.org/10.1145/1081706.1081750

24. Utting, M., Pretschner, A., Legeard, B.: A taxonomy of model-based testing approaches. Softw. Test. Verif. Reliab. **22**(5), 297–312 (2012). http://dx.doi.org/10.1002/stvr.456

Verifying Code Generation Tools
for the B-Method Using Tests: A Case Study

Anamaria M. Moreira[2], Cleverton Hentz[1], David Déharbe[1],
Ernesto C.B. de Matos[1(✉)], João B. Souza Neto[1], and Valério de Medeiros Jr.[1]

[1] Federal University of Rio Grande do Norte, Natal, Brazil
{chentz,ernestocid,jbsneto,valerio}@ppgsc.ufrn.br,
david@dimap.ufrn.br
[2] Federal University of Rio de Janeiro, Rio de Janeiro, Brazil
anamaria@dcc.ufrj.br

Abstract. In this paper, we present a case study where two code generators for the B-Method were validated using software testing techniques. Our testing strategy is a combination of Grammar-Based Testing (GBT) and Model-Based Testing (MBT) techniques. The strategy consists of two steps. In the first step, grammar-based coverage criteria are used to generate a wide and meaningful set of test input models to validate the parsing capabilities of the code generators. In the second step, a MBT tool is used to validate the correctness of the output produced by these tools. The MBT tool generates a set of tests based on the same input model used by the code generation tools. The generated code is considered correct (consistent with the input model) if it passes this set of tests. Using this testing strategy, we were able to find problems in both code generation tools with moderate effort.

Keywords: Model-Based Testing · Grammar-Based Testing · B-Method · Code generation

1 Introduction

Verifying a compiler or a code generator is a complex task. There are several ways to tackle this problem, most of them use formal verification or software testing techniques. Formal verification is usually the more complex and time-consuming approach. Previous work has shown that formally proving the correctness of a compiler may take years of work [14]. Because of that, many choose to rely on software testing.

Testing a compiler or code generation tool usually involves the verification of two different aspects. First, a set of input artefacts must provide a good coverage of the possible inputs of the tool and be used to check if it is able to produce code for a wide range of inputs. Second, the behaviour of the generated code must be verified against the one of the source artefact to check for correctness.

J.C. Blanchette and N. Kosmatov (Eds.): TAP 2015, LNCS 9154, pp. 76–91, 2015.
DOI: 10.1007/978-3-319-21215-9_5

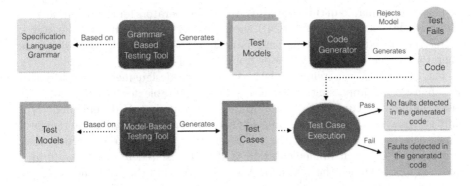

Fig. 1. The testing strategy to test the code generators

This paper presents a case study where two code generation tools were verified using a testing approach. An overview of the testing strategy that we used is presented in Figure 1. The strategy applies two different test case generation paradigms: Model-Based Testing and Grammar-Based Testing. Both lines of the applied testing strategy are supported by tools that generate the tests automatically.

On one hand, the Grammar-Based Testing part of our strategy aims to evaluate if the code generation tools can handle their entire input language (the language in which the input models for the code generators are written). It is responsible for the generation of input models that should exercise the whole grammar of the input language. How thoroughly this grammar is exercised depends on the grammar-based coverage criteria used, the more traditional being terminal coverage and production coverage [2]. However, given the complexity of code generators, more demanding criteria, such as context-dependent branch coverage [11] may be applied to increase thoroughness.

The MBT part, on the other hand, serves as an oracle to evaluate the correctness of the code generated by the code generation tools. The ideal oracle would formally verify the existence of some kind of refinement relation between the generated program and the input model. But, automatically verifying this correctness is undecidable in general, and manually checking the generated code is time-consuming and error prone. Therefore, the same set of models in the input language of the code generation tools is used as input for the code generators and the MBT tool. The MBT tool generates test cases based on each one of these input models. These test cases are in turn used to check if each program generated by the code generator tool has the behaviour specified by the corresponding source model. They serve as the basis for an oracle definition in the test process of the code generators, as they are used to evaluate the result of the code generation process for each input model. Again, the rigour of the coverage criteria applied for MBT test generation directly influences the confidence one can have on the final results.

The tools evaluated in this case study are code generators for the B-Method [1]. The first code generator verified is C4B, the C code generator included in the Atelier B IDE (Integrated Development Environment)[1]. The second is b2llvm [4], a code generator to generate LLVM [13] code from B models.[2]

The B-Method is a refinement-based software design method with a single language encompassing abstract constructs suitable for specification and classic imperative constructs for computer programming. B development typically starts with a specification, in a so-called *machine*, followed by incremental refinements to an *implementation*, where only imperative-like constructs may be employed [3]. Such implementation is then translated to source code in a programming language (here, C or LLVM). The steps in the B-Method are verified using certified theorem proving technologies. However, ultimately, the final refinement must be translated to a conventional programming language, and the result of this translation must be subsequently compiled for the target platform. These last two steps, carried out by our target code generators and platform specific compilers, do not benefit from the same mathematical rigour and their verification is out of the scope of the B-Method. Ideally, one would like to have a formal proof of correctness of the code generators, and have a complete formal process, but there are some obstacles to this solution, such as the lack of common formalization framework for the semantics of the source and target programming languages. Tests are then employed as an alternative for their verification.

Besides the proposed testing strategy, we believe that this work also contributed to the validation of the code generation tools evaluated in our case study. During the case study, we were able to find problems in both code generation tools, such as the generation of faulty code and the lack of support for some constructs used by the code generator's inputs.

The remainder of this paper provides more details about our testing strategy and the case study, and is organized as follows: Section 2 presents related work; Section 3 gives a brief introduction to the B-Method and its notation and presents C4B and b2llvm, the target tools of our case study; Section 4 presents the testing strategy proposed for the case study and Section 5 presents details about the case study execution and the obtained results; ultimately, Section 6 concludes with final discussions and future work.

2   Related Work

Research on verification of compilers and code generators follows different paths, which may be based on formal verification or testing. They may also have different objectives, like trying to verify the tool itself or to validate each of the outputs produced by the tool on the fly.

Formal verification focuses on techniques that prove a compiler or code generator to be correct for every input program or model [5]. It is the most rigorous

---

[1] Atelier B website: http://www.atelierb.eu/en/.

[2] LLVM is an active open-source compiler infrastructure used by many compiling tool chains, that is a complete collection of compiler and related binary programs.

approach and demands experience, and specialised knowledge to specify and to prove language semantics and translation rules. Formal verification up to assembly level also requires much effort and is a time-consuming activity. In [14] the authors developed 50,000 lines of Coq[3] specifications to do that; the cost was estimated to 4 person-years (specialists in the field). This approach is suitable for well-established languages and mature compiler technologies.

Test case generation based on grammars produces test programs or models for a compiler or code generator based on the grammar of the source language [8,9]. It focuses on the first aspect of our testing strategy presented on Figure 1. The test programs or models are derived systematically from the grammar of the source language. Their main objective is to exercise the compiler or code generator with a wide range of inputs, testing all the different constructs supported by the source language. In [10] a survey about techniques for testing compilers was presented, and the first parser test generation algorithm was proposed by Purdom [18]. Grammar-based testing is a traditional way to test a grammar-related software and in general it presents positive results [7,9,12], making it a reasonable choice for testing any software in which valid inputs are described by a grammar. However, it usually lacks the focus on complex semantic issues related to code generation.

Translation validation shows the correct translation of individual programs or models[17]. In this approach, outputs produced by the code generator under test are individually checked for correctness. The objective here is to verify if the generated code was translated correctly from a specific input model. This specific term is frequently used in situations where, instead of validating the tool *a priori*, validation is carried out each time the compiler or code generator is used (on the fly validation). In [21] a methodology for the translation validation of optimizing compilers is presented. In this approach, a correspondence between the source and target code is formally proved using a specific intermediate representation (IR). Similarly, the chaining of the MBT part of our testing approach in the end of the B-Method process could also be used as an alternative to formal verification in the implementation of an on the fly translation validation approach.

Translation validation can also be used in the context of the verification of the code generator, acting as an approach to test the code generator itself. In this case, different levels of rigour can be used in the translation validation, either formally verifying the correctness of each specific output or using some kind of verification by testing as we did in our case studies. In any case, this means that we need a good test set (input models for the code generator) that fully exercises the code generating functionalities.

Another approach that uses the concept of Tracts to test model transformations is presented in [6]. In this approach, a set of OCL constraints to the models (source and target) and the transformation are defined. Then, a set of source models is automatically generated from these constraints, and it is used to test the transformation. Finally, the results are checked against the constraints

---

[3] Coq project website: https://coq.inria.fr/

defined for the transformation. This approach was adapted in [20] for testing model to text transformations, with applications, for instance, to test an UML to Java transformation. This approach focuses both on the generation of semantically significant inputs and on the validation of the corresponding outputs, requiring for that the specification of test specific constraints.

The work presented herein applies *test case generation based on grammars* and *translation validation*. It applies grammar-based testing criteria to derive a good coverage of the source model language, and MBT to verify "functional equivalence" between a model and the generated code. This equivalence happens when the model simulation and the code execution using the same inputs have compatible outputs. The approach presented in this paper shares similarities with what was presented in [19]. It relies on the fact that both the specification language and the code generated are executable. In our proposal, however, some results may also be obtained with non-executable specifications by relaxing the oracle strategy as presented on section 4.1.

3   Background

3.1   B-Method

The B-Method is a formal method that uses concepts of *first order logic, set theory* and *integer arithmetic* to specify *abstract state machines* that represent a software behavior. The consistency of these specifications can be guaranteed by proving that some automatically generated verification conditions are valid. The method also provides a refinement mechanism in which machines may pass through a series of refinements until they reach an algorithmic implementation, called B0, which can be automatically converted into code. Such refinements are also subject to *a posteriori* analysis through proofs.

A B machine usually has a set of *variables* that represent the software state and a set of operations to modify the state. Restrictions on possible values that variables can assume are formulated in the so-called machine *invariant*. The method also has a *precondition* mechanism for operations of a machine. To ensure that an operation behaves as expected, it is necessary to ensure its precondition is satisfied.

Figure 2 presents a simple example of B machine. The *Counter* machine specifies an increasing counter that can result in an overflow. The machine has two variables: *value* and *overflow* (line 4). Variable *value* stores the current value of the counter and variable *overflow* is a flag set when an overflow happens. The *inc* operation (lines 16–23) increases the value of the counter; it also detects overflow.

3.2   C4B and b2llvm

C4B, distributed and integrated with Atelier B 4.1, is a code generator tool that automatically produces C code from B implementations. The Atelier B IDE,

```
 1  MACHINE                         12  INITIALISATION
 2     Counter              ↲       13     value := 0 ||
 3  VARIABLES                       14     overflow := FALSE
 4     value, overflow              15  OPERATIONS
 5  INVARIANT                       16     inc =
 6     value ∈ INT ∧                17     BEGIN
 7     0 ≤ value ∧                  18        IF value ∈ 0..MAXINT-1
 8     value ≤ MAXINT ∧                        THEN
 9     overflow ∈ BOOL ∧            19           value := value+1
10     (overflow = TRUE            20        ELSE
                                    21           overflow := TRUE
          ⇒                         22        END
11           value = MAXINT)        23     END
                                    24  END
```

Fig. 2. Counter abstract machine

which include C4B, is tested and used by many projects in industry and academy. The input to C4B is an implementation written in the B0 language. Such implementation contains simple data types like integers (INT) and Booleans ($BOOL$), concrete variables, concrete constants, arrays, record types, importation (i.e., instantiation) of modules, B0 instructions (e.g., conditionals and loops), and operation calls.

b2llvm[4] is a compiler for B implementations that generates LLVM code. b2llvm has a small set of tests available in its project. This set was used as an initial validation of the tool. The input to b2llvm is a large subset of the B0 notation. The tool reads XML-formatted files representing the B implementation, and produces files in LLVM intermediate representation, also called LLVM IR. The XML input is generated by Atelier B.

Both C4B and b2llvm generate API files to provide declarations of the entities (types and functions) in C. This C API is needed to link C or C++ code to the generated (C or LLVM) code; such interface is necessary to compile tests. Particularly, the C API file generated by b2llvm contains pointer and structure type definitions to represent the state of the module, and declaration of the functions that correspond to the operations on that module. Each such function includes in its parameters a pointer to a structure representing the state of (an instance of) the module.

Figure 3 presents the steps of the B-Method and code generation process. The steps between the specification of the abstract machine and the refinement to implementation level are supported by formal verification. Neither the translation of the implementation to executable code is formally verified, nor the implementation of the code generation tools. This is where tests come into the picture: they are employed to extend the verification process to include the code generation tools as well.

---

[4] b2llvm project: https://www.b2llvm.org/b2llvm.

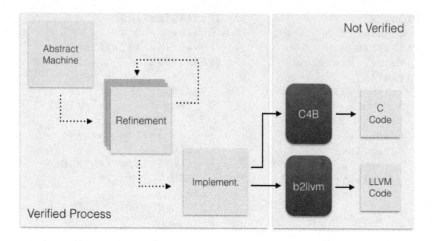

Fig. 3. The B-Method and the code generation process

4 Proposed Testing Strategy

In this section, we present in details the testing strategy used to verify the code generators in our case study.

Testing a code generation tool requires answering two questions:

1. Is the tool capable of generating code for the whole range of inputs it can receive? This requires a set of test inputs that can provide reasonable coverage for the tool.
2. Does the code generated by the code generation tool comply with the input model? To answer this question, it is necessary to check if the generated code implements the behaviour specified in the input model.

To answer these two questions, we propose a testing strategy that is a combination of Grammar-Based Testing and Model-Based Testing. Figure 1 gives an overview of this strategy.

The process starts with the generation of test models using grammar-based testing criteria. Using the specification of the B0 grammar, the tool generates a set of sentences. Each sentence is an input model. In general, if the grammar has cycles (recursively defined symbols), the set of all sentences is infinite, so the tool uses the coverage criteria to restrict the generated set to a finite, manageable, but still meaningful set. The tool used in our proposed testing strategy may use *Terminal Coverage (TC)* [2], *Production Coverage (PC)* [2] or *Context-Dependent Branch Coverage (CDBC)* [11] to guide the selection process of those sentences. Usually, a good test set should at least satisfy *Production Coverage*. This criterion produces a set of sentences that covers all the productions in the grammar. Therefore, this set is finite but with a good structural coverage of the grammar. *Context-Dependent Branch Coverage (CDBC)* goes one step further, requiring that the sentences on the test set not only cover all productions but each production for each non-terminal symbol on each of its uses (appearance of the symbol on the right-hand side of a production rule). This pairwise combination of production rules provides a much richer set of tests in most grammars.

Once the test models are generated, they are used as inputs for the code generation tools. The tool can either generate code for the test model or reject it and not generate code. When the second case happens, it is likely that the tool cannot support the rejected model. This can happen because the code generator cannot parse or generate code for some construct used or there is some semantic error in the test model. When a test model is rejected by a parser or code generation error it means that a bug or missing feature was encountered in the tool.

When the code generation tool is capable of generating code for a given test model, we have not any guarantee of its correctness. Indeed, the code generation tool may have generated faulty code for the test model. That is where model-based testing comes into place. We use the same input model used to exercise the code generator as input for an MBT tool, generating input data for the test of the implementation corresponding to this model, i.e., to test the output of the code generator. The generated test cases are then used to verify if this code implements the behaviour specified in the input model. Since the test cases are generated from the models used in the very beginning of the specification, they can be used to validate the conformance between what was specified in the beginning and the final implementation. Our proposed model-based testing approach uses *Input Space Partitioning* and *Logical Coverage* criteria such as: *Equivalent Classes, Boundary Value Analysis, Predicate Coverage, Clause Coverage, Combinatorial Clause Coverage* and *Active Clause Coverage* [15]. All these criteria are well established in the software testing community. The test cases generated aim to achieve the test requirements established by these criteria. So, the entire test generation process is guided to increase the coverage of these test requirements. For Input Space Partitioning, the generated test data will test all the combinations of partitions required by this type of coverage criteria. For Logical Coverage, the tests will exercise combinations of logical values for the predicates and clauses of the model, also taking into account the requirements of each criterion. The test cases thus generated can exercise different scenarios described in the input model, providing a good level of confidence about the correctness of the code generated if they pass on the generated test suite. If one of the test cases fails, it means that there are discrepancies between the model and the generated code caused by a fault in the translation process.

4.1   Used Toolset

To achieve the goals of the proposed testing strategy we used two tools that support the automatic generation of test models and test cases for the generated code. During the conducted case study, *LGen* and *BETA* were used as the *Grammar-Based Testing Tool* and the *Model-Based Testing Tool*, respectively, presented on Figure 1.

LGen. The Lua Language Generator (LGen[5]) [8,16] is a sentence generator based on syntax description using coverage criteria to restrict the set of generated sentences. This generator takes as input a grammar described in a notation based on Extended BNF (EBNF) and returns a set of sentences of the language corresponding to this grammar.

The process of generating sentences is implemented by a top-down left recursive descent algorithm which enumerate the sentences of specified language. With this algorithm, we guarantee that all sentences in the result test set is syntactically valid. If the grammar has cycles, the algorithm can restrict the number of their applications. Furthermore, the sentences generated by the algorithm are selected to increase the coverage of the coverage criterion used. The entire generating process is divided into two phases. The first is the translation of the grammar described in EBNF to a specification language described in Lua[6]. In the second, the generated Lua specification is used to generate a set of sentences.

LGen implements three coverage criteria: *Terminal Symbol Coverage, Production Coverage* [2] and *Context-Dependent Branch Coverage (CDBC)* [11]. These criteria are used to limit the number of generated sentences keeping a minimum quality and seeking a good set of tests. Derivation Coverage is attained, when possible, when no other coverage criterion is used, but although it is of theoretical interest, this criterion is impractical, because the number of derivations is often too big or even infinite.

BETA. BETA (B Based Testing Approach) is a MBT approach to generate unit tests from B-Method specifications. The approach is supported by a tool[7] that receives an abstract B machine as input and produces test case specifications and partial unit test scripts for each of its operations. The MBT approach proposed by BETA is used as a complement to the formal development with the B-Method.

The BETA tool is capable of defining *positive* and *negative* test cases for a software implementation. Positive test cases use input data that are valid according to the source specification and negative test cases use input data that are not predicted by the specification. BETA uses Equivalent Classes and Boundary Values Analysis techniques to partition the input space of an operation and combinatorial criteria such as *Each-choice* and *Pairwise* to combine the partitions into test cases. It also supports Logical Coverage criteria [2].

BETA also supports the implementation of some oracle strategies. These oracle strategies determine what kind of verifications are done by the test oracle. It currently supports four strategies inspired from [15]. They can be used separately (weaker verifications) or combined (stronger verifications). These strategies are: *Exception* (executes the test and verifies if any exception is raised), *Invariant checking* (executes the test and after its execution verifies if the invariant is preserved), *State variables checking* (executes the test and verifies if the values for

---

[5] The LGen project is hosted at http://lgen.wikidot.com.

[6] Lua language website: http://www.lua.org/.

[7] The BETA project is hosted at http://www.beta-tool.info.

the state variables are the ones expected) and *Return variables checking* (executes the test and verifies if the values returned by the operation are the ones expected).

The tool can generate test suites in different formats, such as HTML and XML test specifications and partial Java and C executable test scripts. For the case study presented in this paper, we used the C test scripts to test the output of the code generation tools.

5   The Case Study: Testing C4B and b2llvm

In this section, we describe how the testing strategy presented in section 4 was used to verify C4B and b2llvm. The objective here is not only to verify the code generators, but also to evaluate the effectiveness of the proposed testing strategy.

First, we used LGen to generate a set of test models with the intent of evaluating how the code generators handle different types of constructs used by the B0 notation. Since LGen generates tests based on the grammar of the input artefacts, we used the definition of the B0 grammar presented on the *B Language Reference manual*[8] as the basis to generate the test models. This grammar definition has 54 non-terminals, 75 terminals and 123 production rules.

The generated test models were edited to replace the lexical identifiers from the grammar by concrete values. The LGen is based on context-free grammar, for this reason it only generates syntactic valid test models. To increase the impact of the GBT based test set, we also add a small set of additional test cases with valid semantic and some combinations of instructions on it. After these modifications, the code generators were executed on each test model. Then, if the execution was successful, the generated code was run through a compiler to look for possible target language errors.

Proceeding with our testing strategy, we used BETA to generate a set of test cases to verify the functional equivalence between the code generated by C4B and b2llvm and their respective test models. For this part of the case study, we used a different set of test models, containing models that specified behaviours more meaningful and intricate than those of the artefacts generated by LGen, corresponding to scenarios someone would find in real B-Method projects. We decided to use this different set of test models so we could generate more interesting test cases for the code generators.

BETA uses the abstract machine that originated the code to generate test cases for it. Based on this abstract machine, it generates a set of test cases for each machine operation. Even though the chosen MBT tool is capable of generating positive and negative test cases, the negative ones are not considered in our verification process. The rationale for this decision is that we only want to verify if the code generated behaves as foreseen in the input model, whereas negative tests cases verify how the implementation behaves in situations that were not foreseen by the model. Since C4B and b2llvm directly translate the

---

[8] B language reference manual, version 1.8.6 from ClearSy. http://www.tools.clearsy.com/resources/Manrefb_en.pdf

information in the model into executable code we can not expect it to behave properly on unexpected scenarios.

Since both code generators generate APIs (Application Program Interface) in C, to allow the integration of the generated code with other programs, our tests are also being implemented in C, using test scripts generated by BETA. In some cases, the generated test scripts must be adapted. Indeed, as the test scripts are generated from an abstract model, that uses abstract data, and we are testing code resulting from the translation of a concrete model, which may well encode data differently than the abstract model does, it may be necessary to adapt the data structures used in the test cases.

As an example, figure 4 presents part of the generated test script corresponding to a single test case for the *inc* operation from the *Counter* machine. In the first part of the test, the state variables of Counter module are set in the state required by the test case (lines 9–10). After that, the operation under test is called (line 12). In the last part, there are assertions that verify if the results of the called method are the expected ones (lines 14–19).

As can be seen in the code, there is a difference in a variable name: the variable `overflow` of the abstract machine had its name changed to `error` in the implementation. This is a simple example that refinement from abstract to concrete data may require adaptation of the generated test drivers.

```
1   /**
2   * Test Case 1
3   * Formula: value = 0
4   */
5   void counter_inc_test_case_1(
        CuTest* tc)
6   {
7           counter$init$(&counter);
8
9           counter.error = false;
10          counter.value = 0;
11
12          counter$inc(&counter);
13
14          CuAssertTrue(tc, ,
15              counter.error == false);
16          CuAssertTrue(tc,
17              counter.value == 1);
18
19          check_invariant(tc, counter)
                ;
20  }
```

Fig. 4. Concrete test for *inc* operation from *Counter* machine

After these adaptations are made, the test must be linked with the C or LLVM code to be executed. The testing code and the generated code are compiled, resulting in an executable program. We must run this program to execute the tests. After the execution, the test results must be evaluated to verify that the code under test is in conformance with the abstract machine. It is expected that all tests must pass. If a test fails, it produces a message indicating that the code generator made a wrong translation to C or LLVM code.

5.1   Results

The results are organized considering both aspects of our testing strategy.

For the grammar-based aspect of the testing strategy, LGen generated 69 test models based on the B0 grammar definition, with production coverage. When we applied C4B to these models, it rejected 27 of them. These failures are due to the lack of support in the code generator for some syntactic constructions present in those models. One of them was rejected because C4B does not support expression record access for formal parameter instantiation and the remaining 26 were rejected because C4B does not support the renaming of models.

For the remaining 42, C4B was able to generate code, which was then compiled using the GNU C compiler (*gcc*). During this step, we identified problems in the code generated for three of the test models. The compiling errors on the code generated by C4B were: (1) an identifier declared as an array with a negative size, (2) a code block was not well defined, and (3) a parameter in a function call was missing. The first one was not an error inserted by C4B, but a semantic inconsistency of the syntactically correct input model which provoked an integer overflow. The other two were actual bugs. The chart (a) in Figure 5 presents the results of grammar-based testing for C4B.

For b2llvm, the code generator was able to produce code for 28 test models. For the remainder 41, problems were found and b2llvm was not able to generate code for them. There were 7 problems related to unsupported clauses, and 34 related to bugs in b2llvm[9]. Ultimately, all the 28 examples for which b2llvm could generate code were successfully compiled using the LLVM compiler (*llc*). The chart (b) in Figure 5 presents the results for b2llvm.

For the second aspect of our testing strategy, we used BETA to test semantic aspects of the code generated by b2llvm and C4B. In this case study, the tests were generated using Equivalent Classes (EC), Boundary Value Analysis (BV), Active Clause Coverage (ACC) and Combinatorial Clause Coverage (CoC) criteria. The same set of test models was used to test both code generators.

Table 1 presents information on the tests and the obtained results. The group of columns (a) presents information on the B test models we used: abstract machine name, number of lines and number of operations. The group of columns (b), (c) and (d) present the number of test cases generated by BETA and the

---

[9] The file format used by Atelier B to store parsed models suffered changes in the last version, which was used to perform this experiment. The b2llvm code generator was not fully updated to adapt to those changes in the input data format.

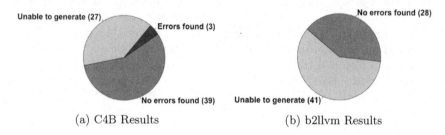

(a) C4B Results   (b) b2llvm Results

Fig. 5. Overview of the grammar-based tests generated with by LGen

number of tests that passed for b2llvm and C4B generated code using EC/BV, ACC, and CoC, respectively.

The capability to generate tests automatically using BETA allowed us to save a good amount of time and effort that would be needed to implement these tests manually, even with simple specifications and a small number of tests. The effort for this process can be summarized into: (1) running the test script generator; (2) adapting the test code with oracle information or other refinement related information, if needed; (3) running and evaluating the tests. The process of generating the test drivers with BETA, adapting the code and executing it was done in a few minutes for each B operation in the test model. The overall effort of generating and executing the test cases took approximately one day of work for each code generator.

Table 1. Overview of the model-based tests generated by BETA

(a) **B Modules**				(b) **EC/BV**			(c) **ACC**			(d) **CoC**		
N.	Machine	Lines	Ops	TCs	b2llvm	C4B	TCs	b2llvm	C4B	TCs	b2llvm	C4B
1	Counter	51	4	10	10	10	8	8	8	6	6	6
2	Swap	18	3	3	3	3	6	6	6	1	1	1
3	Calculator	48	6	10	10	10	26	26	26	6	6	6
4	Wd	27	3	5	5	5	5	5	5	4	4	4
5	Prime	10	1	4	4	4	5	5	5	3	3	3
6	Division	12	1	2	2	2	3	3	3	1	1	1
7	Team	36	2	3	3	3	7	7	7	4	4	4
8	BubbleSort	35	1	1	1	1	1	1	1	1	1	1
9	TicTacToe	67	3	13	13	13	12	12	12	8	8	8
10	Fifo	22	2	2	0*	2	4	0*	4	2	0*	2
11	Calendar	40	1	2	0*	2	25	0*	25	25	0*	25
12	ATM	28	3	3	0*	3	7	0*	7	2	0*	2
13	Timetracer	47	6	7	0*	4	11	0*	6	9	0*	4

The tests for the modules 1 to 9 had the same results for both code generation tools (see groups of columns (b), (c) and (d) of table 1). All tests generated by BETA passed, which means that no errors were found in the code generated by b2llvm and C4B for these modules. For machines number 10 to 13 (`Fifo`, `Calendar`, `ATM` and `Timetracer`), b2llvm was not able to generate code because it does not support some of the constructs used on these machines. Because of this, the tests were not performed for b2llvm. In this situation the tests created by BETA can be used to guide the implementation of these missing features in b2llvm.

In contrast, C4B was able to generate code for these machines. All tests for the modules 10 to 12 (`Fifo`, `Calendar` and `ATM`) passed. However, some tests for the machine number 13 (`Timetracer`) failed (three of AC/BV, five of ACC and five of CoC). After analyzing it, we found an error in the generated C code. The B implementation for `Timetracer` imports other B modules, so it is expected that the C code generated from it also calls other correspondent C modules. C4B was capable of generating code for all the modules of `Timetracer` but it did not import them where they were needed. Because of this, some tests failed. This error was reported to ClearSy, the company that develops Atelier B and C4B.

Using the testing strategy proposed in section 4, we found problems in both code generators. Using grammar-based testing through LGen we found that both code generators lack support for some constructs of the input language and, in some cases, generate non-compilable code. Besides, the MBT part of our strategy performed with BETA was able to find errors in the code generated by C4B related to importation of modules.

In the end, we believe this case study show that the proposed testing strategy is effective in finding errors in code generation tools, and is therefore beneficial to their validation. This strategy is a viable alternative to validate code generators since it required moderate effort, yet is able to uncover different classes of errors in such tools.

6   Conclusions and Future Work

In this paper, we presented a case study where testing techniques were used to verify two code generation tools for the B-Method. The strategy proposed for this verification is a combination of grammar-based testing and model-based testing. While grammar-based tests help to verify the translation capabilities of the code generators, the model-based testing aspect of the strategy supports the verification of functional equivalence between the input models and the generated code (correctness of the output of the code generators).

The case study was important not only to verify the code generation tools but also to evaluate the testing strategy that we proposed for this task. With moderate effort, we were able to find important problems and missing features on both code generation tools. The problems encountered during the case study were reported to the tool developers and will contribute to improve the reliability of C4B and b2llvm.

Even though our work here focused on tools for the B-Method, the proposed testing strategy could be used to test other code generation tools. LGen or a similar grammar-based testing tool can be used to generate test inputs for other types of artefacts, as long as the grammar for the corresponding language is available. A more restrictive requirement is the availability of a tool to perform the model-based testing part of the strategy. But, given the variety of existing MBT tools based on various kinds of input models, there might already exist a tool to support this task.

As future work, we will focus on evaluating and improving the quality of the generated test cases in both levels of testing, so that correctness can be asserted with greater confidence. Some lines of improvement are:

- *Use more sophisticated grammar-based testing criteria:* in this case study we used the Production Coverage criterion to improve the quality of the test set used in the first aspect of the testing strategy. Using it, we were able to reach a good coverage of the structure of the B0 grammar, ensuring a systematic coverage of the B0 language. However, this structural coverage of the grammar could be improved using a more sophisticated coverage criterion, such as the *Context-dependent branch coverage* [11]. Coverage of further unfolding of productions may also be considered for more rigorous tests.
- *Perform empirical studies:* to analyze the available criteria for both grammar-based testing and model-based testing. The objective of this studies would be to define a minimum set of criteria to increase the confidence of the users on their effectiveness.
- *Concretization of the test data:* currently, the test script generated by BETA must be adapted before it can be executed. The tool generates tests from an abstract model (B Machine) which usually uses abstract data structures (e.g. deferred sets) that cannot be used on the implementation level. Because of this, the values generated for the test cases may be too abstract. The support for concretization of the test data is already under development. When it is finished, the tool will be capable of generating test scripts that do not need any adaptations. It will increase the confidence in the generated tests since they will require less human input.

Acknowledgments. This work is partly supported by CAPES and CNPq grants 2057/14-0 (PDSE), 237049/2013-9, 573964/2008-4, (National Institute of Science and Technology for Software Engineering — INES, www.ines.org.br).

References

1. Abrial, J.-R.: The B-book: assigning programs to meanings. Cambridge University Press (1996)
2. Ammann, P., Offutt, J.: Introduction to Software Testing. Cambridge University Press, New York (2008)
3. ClearSy. Atelier B User Manual Version 4.0. Clearsy System Engineering (2009)

4. Déharbe, D., Medeiros, Jr., V.: Proposal: Translation of B Implementations to LLVM-IR. In: SBMF, Brasília - DF, SBMF (2013)
5. Goerigk, W., Dold, A., Gaul, T., Goos, G., Heberle, A., Von Henke, F.W., Hoffmann, U., Langmaack, H., Pfeifer, H., Ruess, H., et al.: Compiler correctness and implementation verification: The verifix approach (1996)
6. Gogolla, M., Vallecillo, A.: *Tract*able model transformation testing. In: France, R.B., Kuester, J.M., Bordbar, B., Paige, R.F. (eds.) ECMFA 2011. LNCS, vol. 6698, pp. 221–235. Springer, Heidelberg (2011)
7. Härtel, J., Härtel, L., Lämmel, R.: Test-Data generation for Xtext. In: Combemale, B., Pearce, D.J., Barais, O., Vinju, J.J. (eds.) SLE 2014. LNCS, vol. 8706, pp. 342–351. Springer, Heidelberg (2014)
8. Hentz, C.: Automatic Generation of Tests from Language Descriptions (Text in Portuguese). Master's thesis, UFRN, Natal, Brazil (2010)
9. Hoffman, D.M., Ly-Gagnon, D., Strooper, P., Wang, H.-Y.: Grammar-based test generation with yougen. Software: Practice and Experience **41**(4), 427–447 (2011)
10. Kossatchev, A.S., Posypkin, M.A.: Survey of compiler testing methods. Program. Comput. Softw. **31**(1), 10–19 (2005)
11. Lämmel, R.: Grammar testing. In: Hussmann, H. (ed.) FASE 2001. LNCS, vol. 2029, pp. 201–216. Springer, Heidelberg (2001)
12. Lämmel, R., Schulte, W.: Controllable combinatorial coverage in grammar-based testing. In: Uyar, M.U., Duale, A.Y., Fecko, M.A. (eds.) TestCom 2006. LNCS, vol. 3964, pp. 19–38. Springer, Heidelberg (2006)
13. Lattner, C., Adve, V.S.: LLVM: A compilation framework for lifelong program analysis & transformation. In: 2nd IEEE/ACM International Symposium on Code Generation and Optimization, pp. 75–88 (2004)
14. Leroy, X.: Formal verification of a realistic compiler. Commun. ACM **52**(7), 107–115 (2009)
15. Li, N., Offutt, J.: An empirical analysis of test oracle strategies for model-based testing. In: IEEE 7th International Conference on Software Testing, Verification and Validation (April 2014)
16. Moreira, A.M., Hentz, C., Ramalho, V.: Application of a Syntax-based Testing Method and Tool to Software Product Lines. In: 7th Brazilian Workshop on Systematic and Automated Software Testing, Brasília - DF (2013)
17. Necula, G.C.: Translation validation for an optimizing compiler. ACM Sigplan Notices **35**(5), 83–94 (2000)
18. Purdom, P.: A sentence generator for testing parsers. BIT Numerical Mathematics **12**(4), 366–375 (1972)
19. Stuermer, I., Conrad, M., Doerr, H., Pepper, P.: Systematic testing of model-based code generators. IEEE Transactions on Software Engineering **33**(9), 622–634 (2007)
20. Wimmer, M., Burgueño, L.: Testing M2T/T2M transformations. In: Moreira, A., Schätz, B., Gray, J., Vallecillo, A., Clarke, P. (eds.) MODELS 2013. LNCS, vol. 8107, pp. 203–219. Springer, Heidelberg (2013)
21. Zuck, L., Pnueli, A., Fang, Y., Goldberg, B.: VOC: A Methodology for the Translation Validation of Optimizing Compilers. Journal of Universal Computer Science **9**(3), 223–247 (2003)

Software Validation via Model Animation

Aaron M. Dutle$^{(\boxtimes)}$, César A. Muñoz, Anthony J. Narkawicz,
and Ricky W. Butler

NASA Langley Research Center, Hampton, Virginia 23681-2199, USA
aaron.m.dutle@nasa.gov

Abstract. This paper explores a new approach to validating software implementations that have been produced from formally-verified algorithms. Although visual inspection gives some confidence that the implementations faithfully reflect the formal models, it does not provide complete assurance that the software is correct. The proposed approach, which is based on animation of formal specifications, compares the outputs computed by the software implementations on a given suite of input values to the outputs computed by the formal models on the same inputs, and determines if they are equal up to a given tolerance. The approach is illustrated on a prototype air traffic management system that computes simple kinematic trajectories for aircraft. Proofs for the mathematical models of the system's algorithms are carried out in the Prototype Verification System (PVS). The animation tool PVSio is used to evaluate the formal models on a set of randomly generated test cases. Output values computed by PVSio are compared against output values computed by the actual software. This comparison improves the assurance that the translation from formal models to code is faithful and that, for example, floating point errors do not greatly affect correctness and safety properties.

1 Introduction

The formal verification of software written in widely used programming languages such as Java and C++ faces many hurdles. A typical approach for developing safety-critical software in these languages consists of specifying and verifying the critical components of the software as algorithms in a formal verification system, and then, translating either automatically or manually these formal models into code. In this approach, visual inspection and peer-review techniques are used to provide some assurance that the implemented code faithfully reflects the formal models. However, despite the best efforts, implementation errors can be accidentally introduced during the translation process.

The difficulty of the typical approach is increased by the large semantic gap that exists between modern programming languages and the functional specification languages often used in formal models. For example, imperative languages support control structures for iteration that must be cast as recursive functions in functional specification languages. This is complicated by the fact that iterations in modern languages may produce side effects on an arbitrary number of variables within their scope. In embedded systems, some of these complications

© Springer International Publishing Switzerland 2015
J.C. Blanchette and N. Kosmatov (Eds.): TAP 2015, LNCS 9154, pp. 92–108, 2015.
DOI: 10.1007/978-3-319-21215-9_6

are avoided by restricting the programming languages to certain constructs. However, for convenience and efficiency reasons, enforcing such restrictions is not always desirable or even possible. Another difficulty arises from the fact that modern programming languages utilize floating point arithmetic while formal verification is usually performed over the real numbers. Therefore, bridging the gap between implementations and their formally verified counterparts is a challenging problem in the validation and verification of critical software.

Significant value can be obtained by validating the numerical computations of a program against the actual theoretical values. Many subtle errors in the specification and implementation of an algorithm can be discovered and repaired by this process. For example, numerical errors can cause the software to make completely different decisions from what would be done if the computations were performed using exact values. The authors have found cases where two different implementations of a formally-verified conflict resolution algorithm [20], computed resolution maneuvers in opposite directions. This occurred even though the two implementations, one in Java and the other in C++, were syntactically almost identical. This undesirable behavior was due to the Java and C++ compilers producing a different order of evaluation of an expression, which resulted in different floating point results.

This paper explores a practical approach to the validation of software that implements formally-verified algorithms. The approach, which is called *model animation*, is based on animation[1] of formal specifications. The technique compares computations performed in the software implementations against those symbolically evaluated on the corresponding formal models. While model animation does not provide an absolute guarantee that the software is correct, it increases the confidence that the formal models are faithfully implemented in code. The proposed approach is illustrated on a library of kinematic software used for trajectory generation in conflict detection and resolution algorithms. The validated library, which implements formally-verified algorithms, is one of the core components of a prototype software for aircraft separation assurance. This prototype software is under development at NASA Langley and is being used for fast time simulations of advanced air traffic management (ATM) concepts.

2   Model Animation

In this paper, the concept of *software validation* refers to the process of checking that a software component meets its formal specification. The proposed software validation approach assumes the availability of formally-verified models of the software's critical algorithms in the specification language of an interactive theorem prover. It also assumes that the software implementations follow the

---

[1] The term animation used here refers to having a (usually static) specification actually perform calculation. In this sense, the formal model is brought to life, or *animated*. This is not to be confused with a tool such as PVSioWeb [16] which provides a graphical interface to, and interaction with, a PVS specification.

control and data structures of the formal models[2]. These two assumptions can be satisfied by either manual or automatic translation [13]. Furthermore, they do not have to be satisfied in any order. Indeed, an advantage of the proposed approach with respect to the correct-by-construction approach [17] is that formal models can be written a posteriori, which is usually done in the validation of legacy critical code. The model animation technique involves the following steps.

1. Automate the calculation of exact answers for specific inputs of the formal model. Where exact answers are not possible, e.g. formulas involving transcendental functions, provide semantic attachments that enable precise computations on the formal models.
2. Automatically generate input values and compare the symbolic evaluation of these values in the formal models to those computed by the software implementation, to determine if are equal up to a specified tolerance.

This approach is illustrated on core component of a prototype air traffic management (ATM) software package called Stratway, which is being developed at NASA Langley [10]. Stratway provides conflict detection and resolution algorithms using kinematic aircraft trajectories. These trajectories are generated in Stratway from a flight plan described by a sequence of 4D waypoints (aircraft position and time). The simplest model for flight based on this flight plan would be to assume that an aircraft follows a straight line trajectory with constant velocity between each successive pairs of waypoints. Of course, an aircraft cannot actually fly such a model consistently, since all but the most basic flight plans contain instantaneous changes in velocity and direction. On the other hand, high-fidelity modeling of how an aircraft would actually fly a given flight plan is both dependent on the dynamics of the aircraft, and the details of its control systems. The trajectories generated in Stratway strike a balance between these two extremes, producing trajectories with continuous velocities that obey the basic laws of motion. Instantaneous changes in direction are replaced with circular arcs, and instantaneous changes in ground or vertical speed are replaced with segments of constant acceleration [11]. The resulting kinematic flight plan is a sequence of points (called trajectory change points, or TCPs) where each segment between successive points is either 1) a constant velocity straight line segment, 2) a constant vertical acceleration segment, 3) a constant ground speed acceleration segment, or 4) a circular turn segment[2]. This kinematic flight plan is compact in its representation and also gives a realistic picture of an aircraft flying a given route.

The functions that compute the position and velocity of an aircraft throughout each type of segment, as well as functions for determining the amount of time needed to keep the velocity continuous throughout the flight plan, reside in a kinematics library used by Stratway. Much of the core functionality of Stratway,

---

[2] While this assumption is not strictly necessary for the approach to be carried out, this *syntactic similarity* is one reason for trusting the software implementation. The *behavioral similarity* justified by the outlined approach provides the other.

including trajectory generation and conflict detection and resolution algorithms, depends on the correctness of this library. Hence, strong assurance of the correctness of these basic kinematic functions is desired for a safety-critical application. On the other hand, Stratway is intended to be used as a convenient tool for simulation, and for testing new algorithms and concepts for air traffic management. Because of this, Stratway is available in both Java and C++ software libraries. The formal verification of the actual code is extremely challenging, which is why a practical approach to validate the software components of the library against their formal models was undertaken.

For the ATM software examined, the core algorithms used in the kinematic library were formally specified and verified in the Prototype Verification System (PVS) [21]. The formal verification of these algorithms involved several aspects. Foundational theorems are proved showing that the algorithms used for position and velocity obey basic Newtonian physics. For example, a function computing a velocity based on acceleration is proven to be equal to the integral of the acceleration. Putative theorems are also proven in the theorem prover to show the algorithms perform their desired task. For instance, for an algorithm designed to model an aircraft moving from its current altitude to a target altitude, one such theorem would say that the altitude at termination of the algorithm *is* the target altitude.

An assumption of the proposed approach is that the software implementations and the formal models share similar data and control structures. Ideally, variable and function names should be preserved. However, this is not always possible due to different naming conventions in the languages involved. The syntactic similarity allows for a simpler visual comparison of the different versions of the algorithms, which increases the confidence that they do the same computation. For the kinematic ATM software, the PVS formal models were manually translated into Java and C++ code. This paper focuses on the Java code, but the same approach can be used on the C++ code. Much of the kinematic ATM software analyzed in this project already existed, and the formalization was done to give a higher level of assurance of its correctness. For a few of the existing algorithms, the formal specification and putative theorems revealed subtle errors, which were subsequently corrected.

Algorithms written in functional specification languages, such as PVS, cannot always be evaluated due to the presence of non-computable operations over real numbers such as square root and trigonometric functions. This issue is addressed in the proposed approach by providing semantic attachments [9] that compute guaranteed approximations of real-valued functions. In the case of PVS, the animation of functional specifications, including semantic attachments, is supported by the animation tool PVSio [19]. PVSio provides semantic attachments for several real number functions that are guaranteed to be correct up to a given precision. These semantic attachments do not guarantee that all computations are correct up to that precision, as approximation errors accumulate, but they significantly improve the quality of numerical outputs over floating point computations.

One important aspect of the proposed approach is to determine an appropriate collection of test input values for each algorithm. The following process is used. First, for each parameter of an algorithm, an appropriate range for the parameter is determined. For example, an altitude parameter is restricted to be between 0 and 40,000 feet. Three models for testing are then used. In the first model, a sequence of inputs are randomly selected to lie within the specified ranges for the parameters, and the software and PVS output compared, checking to see if they are the same up to a defined tolerance. In the second model, the range of each parameter is split according to a mesh size. For example, the altitude parameter might be split into 1000 foot blocks. For an algorithm with N different inputs, this splits the input space into an N dimensional grid, and the software and PVS outputs are compared at each intersection point. The third method starts with the same grid as in method two, but instead of testing at the grid intersection points, a random point from inside each block that this grid defines is selected for comparison of the software and PVS outputs. For methods two and three, variation in the mesh size allows for a tradeoff between the level of assurance that the software and PVS algorithms agree and the amount of time and computer resources used.

3   Formalization and Implementation of ATM Kinematic Library

Among the several algorithms comprising Stratway's library, the algorithms that were validated using the proposed technique are those related to the generation of kinematic trajectories and, in particular, the algorithms that deal with turn dynamics, vertical acceleration, and ground speed acceleration. Furthermore, in order to complete the full specification, a host of additional helper algorithms and datatypes had to be specified. For example, a large collection of basic vector operations were implemented, including projections between 3D and 2D vectors, conversions to and from velocity vectors specified in Euclidean coordinates versus vectors in polar coordinates specified by track angle and ground speed, and many others.

In addition to specifying the algorithms that are used explicitly in the kinematics library, a wide variety of mathematical background must be built into the theorem prover in order to prove the foundational and putative theorems that provide assurance that the algorithms are specified correctly. For instance, in order to prove that a velocity function is the integral of a specified acceleration, the theory of integration must be accessible to the theorem prover. The NASA PVS Library[3] contains much of the required mathematical background (including integral calculus [6]), but the required mathematics is almost never fully ready to apply directly. For example, the vertical speed algorithms are essentially described by piecewise constant acceleration functions. In order to prove the corresponding foundational theorems, a theory of piecewise defined functions and their integration was written and employed.

---

[3] http://shemesh.larc.nasa.gov/fm/ftp/larc/PVS-library.

For brevity, the remainder of the section focuses on the case of turn dynamics.

3.1   Turn Dynamics in PVS

The kinematics library includes algorithms to compute the trajectory of an aircraft in a frictionless banked turn, which is turning to leave one leg and join another leg of a predetermined flight plan. The trajectory of such an aircraft traces out a circular arc. In PVS, algorithms are specified as strongly-typed functions. For instance, the following PVS function computes the position and velocity of a turning aircraft at a given time.

$$
\begin{aligned}
&\texttt{turnOmega}(\mathbf{s}_o, \mathbf{v}_o\colon \textsf{Vect3}, t\colon \textsf{real}, \omega\colon \textsf{real})\colon\; [\textsf{Vect3}, \textsf{Vect3}] \;\equiv\\
&\quad \texttt{IF}\;\; \omega = 0 \;\texttt{THEN}\;\; (\mathbf{s}_o + t\cdot\mathbf{v}_o, \mathbf{v}_o)\\
&\quad \texttt{ELSE}\;\; \texttt{LET}\\
&\qquad\quad v = \texttt{groundSpeed}(\mathbf{v}_o)/\omega,\\
&\qquad\quad \mathbf{s} = (\mathbf{s}_{ox} + v\cdot(\cos(\texttt{trk}(\mathbf{v}_o)) - \cos(t\omega + \texttt{trk}(\mathbf{v}_o))),\\
&\qquad\qquad\quad \mathbf{s}_{oy} - v\cdot(\sin(\texttt{trk}(\mathbf{v}_o)) - \sin(t\omega + \texttt{trk}(\mathbf{v}_o))),\\
&\qquad\qquad\quad \mathbf{s}_{oz} + t\,\mathbf{v}_{oz}),\\
&\qquad\quad \mathbf{v} = (\texttt{groundSpeed}(\mathbf{v}_o)\cdot\sin(t\omega + \texttt{trk}(\mathbf{v}_o)),\\
&\qquad\qquad\quad \texttt{groundSpeed}(\mathbf{v}_o)\cdot\cos(t\omega + \texttt{trk}(\mathbf{v}_o)),\\
&\qquad\qquad\quad \mathbf{v}_{oz})\;\texttt{IN}\\
&\qquad (\mathbf{s}, \mathbf{v})\\
&\quad \texttt{ENDIF}\;.
\end{aligned}
\tag{1}
$$

The parameters $\mathbf{s}_o$ and $\mathbf{v}_o$ are vectors in $\mathbb{R}^3$ that represent the initial position and velocity of the aircraft, respectively. The parameter t is the future time at which the state of the aircraft along its turn is computed. Finally, ω is the angular velocity. The output of this function is the position and velocity of the aircraft at the time t along its turn, which is relative to the current time. The function $\texttt{trk}$ used here computes the track angle of a vector as measured from true north.[4] For a banked turn, there is a simple relationship between the angular velocity ω and the radius R, given by the following equation.

$$
\omega = \texttt{dir}\cdot\texttt{groundSpeed}(\mathbf{v}_o)/R.
$$

The parameter $\texttt{dir}$ is either -1 or 1, depending on whether it is a right turn or a left turn, respectively.

The following theorem expresses the correctness of the function $\texttt{turnOmega}$. It states that for all times t, the distance between the position output of $\texttt{turnOmega}$ and the center of the turn is given by the turn radius.

---

[4] As typical in air navigation, angles are measured clockwise with respect to true north.

Theorem 1. *For all* $t \in \mathbb{R}$, $\mathbf{s}_o, \mathbf{v}_o \in \mathbb{R}^3$, $\omega \neq 0 \in \mathbb{R}$, *let* $v = \frac{groundSpeed(\mathbf{v}_o)}{\omega}$, $\mathbf{w} = \mathbf{s}_o + (v \cos(trk(\mathbf{v}_o)), -v \sin(trk(\mathbf{v}_o)), t\,\mathbf{v}_{oz})$, $(\mathbf{s}, \mathbf{v}) = turnOmega(\mathbf{s}_o, \mathbf{v}_o, t, \omega)$, *then*

$$\|\mathbf{s} - \mathbf{w}\| = |v|.$$

Theorem 1 implicitly states that $\mathbf{w}$ is the center of the turn. This theorem has been formally proved in PVS and its proof depends only on basic properties of sine and cosine. Figure 1 illustrates the geometric relations involved in Theorem 1.

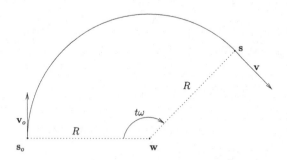

Fig. 1. Illustration of Theorem 1

3.2   Turn Dynamics in Java

The structural differences between PVS and Java play a large role in the way that the Java versions of algorithms are implemented. For example, some practices that are fairly common programming style in Java, such as exiting a program without returning a value, or returning a default failure value, are not possible in PVS. Another difference is that PVS functions must be provided all of their parameters, while a normal Java program may invoke or alter the values of any number of globally specified variables. For the kinematics library, all of the algorithms are written in Java as static methods to better reflect the functional specification style in PVS. Figure 2 illustrates the implementation of the function `turnOmega`, specified by Formula (1), in Java. While differences are apparent, the two versions are closely matched.

4   Model Animation of ATM Kinematic Library

The specification of an algorithm in a theorem prover such as PVS, along with an appropriate collection of theorems showing that the algorithm produces the desired output, allows for an extraordinarily high level of assurance that the algorithm is designed and implemented correctly. The translation of such an algorithm in a syntactically close way from the formal models to code carries

```
static Pair<Vect3,Velocity> turnOmega(Vect3 s0, Velocity v0, double t,
    double omega) {
    if (Util.almost_equals(omega,0))
        return new Pair<Vect3,Velocity>(s0.linear(v0,t),v0);
    double v = v0.gs()/omega;
    double theta = v0.trk();
    double xT = s0.x + v*(Math.cos(theta) - Math.cos(omega*t+theta));
    double yT = s0.y - v*(Math.sin(theta) - Math.sin(omega*t+theta));
    double zT = s0.z + v0.z*t;
    Vect3 ns = new Vect3(xT,yT,zT);
    Velocity nv = v0.mkTrk(v0.trk()+omega*t);
    return new Pair<Vect3,Velocity>(ns,nv);
}
```

Fig. 2. Java implementation of `turnOmega`

along much of this assurance of correctness. The final step in the proposed validation process is to evaluate the formal models on a selected collection of test inputs and to compare the outputs of this evaluation to the outputs computed by the code.

The reason why this model animation is important is two-fold. First, the algorithms that are examined invariably rely on simpler functions, which in turn rely on simpler functions, and so on, down to the basic functions defined in each respective language. While the syntactic similarity of the formal models and their implementations suggests that they perform the same computation, even slight differences in the lower-order functions could introduce significant differences in behavior. The comparison of the outputs of the two versions of the algorithm on a wide range of inputs can catch these invisible differences.

The second reason for the comparison of Java and PVS outputs is due to the inherent differences between how PVS and Java operate on numerical values. In PVS, like almost every other specification language, numerical operations are defined over real numbers. In contrast, Java, like almost every other programming language, uses floating point arithmetic. This means that for any algorithm which manipulates numerical values, calculations in Java may introduce estimations that make the output slightly different than what the calculation would produce if performed over the real numbers. For any one calculation, the difference between the expected real number output and the floating point estimate are generally small (on the order of 10^{-15}), but for an algorithm that performs hundreds of calculations, the effect of compounding small errors may lead to noticeable differences.

4.1 Test Generation

As mentioned in Section 2, three methods were chosen for selecting the input data for testing the output of the PVS specified algorithms versus the Java counterparts. All three methods assume that an appropriate range has been chosen for each input variable of the function under consideration. If d is the number of input variables, the allowable range of input values forms a d-dimensional hyper-rectangle in $\mathbb{R}^d$. For concision, any such rectangle will be referred to simply as a *box*.

The first method, which will be referred to as the *random* method, chooses a user specified number of points uniformly at random from the defined box. This method benefits from being simple to implement, and continuable in the sense that additional testing is unlikely to duplicate points, so further tests can be easily combined with previous results. The randomness aspect also helps mitigate the possibility that the outputs of a function match well for whole numbers or simple fractions, but not for long decimal expansions.

In the second method, referred to as the *grid* method, the user specifies a mesh size for each variable in the function being tested. For example, suppose the range for the variable t is $0 \leq t \leq 2$, and a mesh size of 0.5 is specified. Then the range for the variable t is split into the 4 subintervals $[0, 0.5], [0.5, 1], [1, 1.5]$, and $[1.5, 2]$. In general, if the range of variable t is $[a, b]$, and the mesh size is ϵ_t, then the number of subintervals created is roughly $(b - a)/\epsilon_t$. As should be expected, if the variable range is large, or the mesh size is small, the number of subintervals created can be very large. Each endpoint of a subinterval is used as a possible input for the given variable. For example, there are 5 inputs for the variable t above. These values are calculated for each variable, and every combination of the values is used as a test point. Essentially, the original range box is sliced in each dimension, and the intersection points of the slices are taken as test points for the function. The major benefit of this method versus the random method is guaranteed coverage of the input space. The main drawbacks are that the number of points created can be very large (depending on the number of variables, their ranges, and mesh sizes), and that the points tested may not represent "average" points, since they lack the randomness element of the first method.

The third method, called the *grid random* method, combines these two techniques. It first splits the range of each variable into subintervals using a user defined mesh size. Note that every possible choice of one such subinterval for each variable defines a sub box of the original range. This method selects one point uniformly at random from within each such box. This method benefits from the guaranteed coverage of the grid method, and the randomness of the random method, but is the most computationally expensive of the three.

The combination of the three methods above offer a number of advantages, in that they are simple to describe and implement while also allowing any plausible input value a non-zero probability of being selected. The grid and grid-random methods also provide for fairly uniform coverage of the input space. On the other hand, the methods above do not necessarily satisfy any code coverage criterion, such as MC/DC [12]. In general, *any* method that can generate test cases from either the software implementation or the formal specification can be used to produce the test inputs. Some of these possibilities are discussed in Section 5.

Once a method for determining function inputs has been selected, the following four steps must be performed in order to compare the outputs of a function under test.

1. Generate the set of test points according to the specified testing method.
2. Determine the output of the Java version of the function on each test point.
3. Determine the output of the PVS version of the function on each test point.
4. Compare the values of the two outputs, to determine if they agree up to some user-defined tolerance.

Because the Java versions of each function are purposely built for computation, and the actual inputs from end-users will be processed through Java, the first two steps are carried out using Java. To do this, a Java program was written specifically for each function and testing method. The output of the Java program is a collection of text files, each containing a list of formatted records in PVS syntax. Each record consists of a single test point, which lists the floating point input value of each variable in the function being tested, as well as the floating point output of the Java version of the function on evaluation at the test point.

4.2   Model Animation

To determine the output of a PVS function on a particular input, it is necessary to be able to evaluate the function on concrete input values. In PVS, this can be done through the ground evaluator [24] assuming that the functions are written in the executable fragment of PVS. Most functions in the ATM kinematic library are a priori computable, except that they rely on non-computable real-number functions such as square root and trigonometric functions. The PVS ground evaluator does not support evaluation of these kinds of functions.

To evaluate functions that are not supported by the ground evaluator, it is necessary to use semantic attachments [9]. A semantic attachment is a piece of code that links an uninterpreted PVS function to another function, possible another PVS function, for the sake of evaluation. For example, the square root function cannot be exactly evaluated, since it often returns an irrational number on a rational input. In a formal specification on the other hand, the precise square root function can be reasoned about, and properties proven about it theoretically. If a function in this formal specification is to be evaluated, some computable method to approximate the square root, the semantic attachment, is provided. Any time a square root is encountered in the execution of the specification, the semantic attachment is evaluted instead.

In general, semantic attachments are not safe as there is no guarantee that the semantic attachments soundly and completely realize the original functions. For instance, it is impossible to provide safe semantic attachments to irrational real-valued functions. Indeed, a semantic attachment has no guarantee to have any relation to the function it is attached to. Hence, in PVS, semantic attachments are allowed in the animation of specifications, but not in a formal proof.

Since writing semantic attachments is error prone, PVS includes the animation tool PVSio [19] that provides a predefined library of semantic attachments. The PVSio library of semantic attachments includes input/output operations, imperative features, and floating point arithmetic. For this project, PVSio has been extended with semantic attachments for exact arithmetic definitions of square root, sine, cosine, and arctangent. Concretely, if f is one of these mathematical functions, a semantic attachment `f_sa` is provided that satisfies the following property for all $x \in \mathbb{R}$

$$|\text{f\_sa}(x) - f(x)| \leq \epsilon, \tag{2}$$

where ϵ is a small positive number provided by the user. With these semantic attachments, all evaluations are then performed using exact arithmetic. However, it should be noted that Formula (2) does not guarantee that the computational error is always bounded by ϵ, as errors accumulate when combined in large numerical expressions. Overall, these semantic attachments provide a much better numerical precision than floating-point arithmetic and, since arithmetic is always exact for all the other operators, evaluation of numerical expressions is independent of the order of evaluation.

For this project, PVSio has also been extended with a library of semantic attachments that automate the process of checking test files in the format discussed in Section 4.1. This library provides functionality for reading text files, converting floating point inputs into exact rational number representations, symbolically evaluating these rational inputs in PVS, comparing the outputs to a given tolerance, and printing the results. This library, which is called PVSioChecker, is now part of the NASA PVS libraries.

4.3 Results

The five functions that were chosen for comparison between the PVS and Java versions were the following:

From the vertical speed algorithms, the functions tested were

- `vsAccelUntil`,
- `vsAccelUntilWithRampUp`,
- `vsLevelOut`.

From the ground speed algorithms, the function tested was

- `gsAccelUntil`,

From the turn algorithms, the function tested was

- `turnOmega`.

Each function was tested using all three test-point selection methods (random, grid, and grid random), where the upper and lower bounds for the majority of the parameters come from Stratway defaults. The only parameters lacking default values in Stratway are the horizontal position coordinates. For these, upper and lower bounds were chosen to be 1000 and -1000 nautical miles in each coordinate. Several of the bounds apply to multiple parameters. For instance, the bounds on ground speed apply to both the initial ground speed of the aircraft, and to the goal ground speed used in a `gsAccelUntil` maneuver. The parameters and corresponding bounds are listed in Table 1.

Table 1. Global bounds for input parameters

	s_{ox}, s_{oy}	altitude	ground speed	track angle
lower	-1000 nmi	500 ft	50 kn	0 deg
upper	1000 nmi	40,000 ft	700 kn	360 deg

	vertical speed	bank angle	acceleration[1]
lower	-5000 ft/min	-30 deg	0.1 m/s^2
upper	5000 ft/min	30 deg	2 m/s^2

[1]Bounds apply to ground speed and vertical speed acceleration.

The output of each function on a test point is a pair of vectors containing a calculated position and velocity for some point of the chosen maneuver. Given a test point, this pair of vectors is computed using both the PVS and the Java versions of the function, and if the PVS and Java outputs for any single coordinate differ by more than a tolerance value, which is set to 10^{-8}, the test point is marked as a *fail*. The precision used for the semantic attachments of real-valued functions is 10^{-15}. In general, the threshold for tolerance will depend on the particulars of the software under consideration. For the software considered here, the input data are positions and velocities of aircraft, which in the use-case are obtained through the Automatic Dependent Surveillance - Broadcast (ADS-B) system on each aircraft. At the highest level of fidelity that these systems may be certified at, the horizontal position is required to be accurate to with 3 meters, the vertical position accurate to within 45 meters, and the horizontal velocity accurate to within 0.3 meters/second[5] [1]. The minimum acceptable standards are far less precise. All calculations are performed in these units, and so a tolerance of 10^{-2} would likely be sufficient in this case. The tolerance used, 10^{-8} was selected because it reveals the edge of where the Java and PVS implementations differ. The precision for the semantic attachments was chosen through trial and error to be as small as possible without significantly increasing the computation time.

---

[5] There is no requirement for vertical velocity accuracy.

For each function and point selection method, Table 2 lists the number of records created, the number of fails, and the CPU time of testing.[6] Approximately 2 million test points were generated for each function, spread fairly evenly over the three testing methods. For the random method, the number of points to be tested is simple to explicitly specify. For the grid and grid random methods, the number of test points is governed by the step size chosen for each parameter. Each function has, as input, an initial 3D position and velocity, a time parameter, and some number of other parameters. Because each function has a parameter space of at least 8 dimensions, a decrease in step size by half in each parameter would result in at least 256 times as many records than before the decrease. Due to this, certain parameters of each function were given priority for allowing small step size. For instance, for the vertical speed algorithms, the altitude, vertical velocity, and vertical acceleration parameters were prioritized, since the horizontal position and velocity are simply projections in these algorithms. The step sizes were then calculated that would produce the desired number of test points.

In all, over 8 million test records were generated, and fewer than 0.01 % of the records failed with the specified tolerance of 10^{-8}. A few further notes about the results are in order. First, if the tolerance is increased to 10^{-6}, there are no failures at all. Second, the function testing whether two numbers are almost equal compares them in terms of *absolute* error. If compared in terms of *relative* error at the same tolerance, then there are again zero failures. Lastly, it is notable that almost all of the failures occurred in the function `turnOmega`. This is likely due to the function modeling a circular turn, while the other functions maintain straight-line trajectories. Because of this, the output of `turnOmega` is highly sensitive to any error in the calculation of several trigonometric functions. Nevertheless, a closer examination of the actual failures records for `turnOmega` was conducted. The examination revealed that nearly all failures occurred when the angular velocity parameter is below 0.2 deg/sec, and the time parameter is over 1000 seconds. This corresponds calculating a point over 16 minutes into a turn with a very slight bank angle. Such turns are rarely executed in reality, where the standard turn rate is approximately 3 deg/sec, taking just 2 minutes for a full 360 degree turn.

5   Related and Future Work

Model animation is a key feature of model-based development tools. For instance, MathWork's Simulink[7] is a widely-used simulation environment for the analysis of dynamical systems, which are specified using state charts. In the context of formal methods, tools like PVSio-web [16], which is also built on top of PVSio, and PetShop [22], which animate Petri nets, provide powerful features for prototyping and validating formal specifications. In [2], VDM models are animated

---

[6] All testing was performed on a 2014 Macbook Pro with a 2GHz Intel Core i7 processor and 8 GB of RAM.

[7] http://www.mathworks.com/products/simulink.

Table 2. Testing Results

vsAccelUntil				vsAccelUntilWithRampUp			
	Records	Fails	CPU time		Records	Fails	CPU time
Rand	1,000,000	0	11.32 hr	Rand	960,000	0	11.7 hr
Grid	622,080	0	4.11 hr	Grid	340,416	0	2.45 hr
G-R	332,659	0	2.88 hr	G-R	665,429	0	6.48 hr
totals	1,954,739	0	18.31 hr	totals	1,965,845	0	20.63 hr

vsLevelOut				gsAccelUntil			
	Records	Fails	CPU time		Records	Fails	CPU time
Rand	810,000	0	11.53 hr	Rand	330,000	0	12.29 hr
Grid	518,400	0	4.88 hr	Grid	315,000	0	11.8 hr
G-R	915,000	8	11.42 hr	G-R	340,000	0	11.7 hr
totals	2,243,400	8	27.83 hr	totals	985,000	0	35.79 hr

turnOmega				Global Totals			
	Records	Fails	CPU time		Records	Fails	CPU time
Rand	615,000	225	13.06 hr	Rand	3,715,000	225	59.9 hr
Grid	504,000	300	7.89 hr	Grid	2,299,896	300	31.13 hr
G-R	436,066	309	8.4 hr	G-R	2,689,154	317	40.88 hr
totals	1,555,066	834	29.35 hr	totals	8,704,050	842	131.91 hr

and used as oracles on generated test cases to uncover requirement errors. These works, however, do not aim at validating formal models against their software implementations as the approach proposed in this paper.

The approach presented in this paper is similar to the one supported by tools like QuickCheck [8] for Haskell and AutoTest [18] for Eiffel. These tools check software annotations on a set of randomly generated test cases. Similar tools exist for theorem provers [3] and other formal methods [26]. The presented approach also has similarities to the animation of EventB/B models using tools such as JeB [25] and ProB [14]. Indeed, JeB even provides support for a type of semantic attachment in the form of "hooks" for the user to supply Java code where a function in the specification is undefined. These tools, though, are generally intended for early testing of a specification, and for model checking. To the best knowledge of the authors, none of these tools attempt to bridge the gap between code and formal specifications due, for example, to numerical computations.

Concolic test [23] and other test generation techniques [7] combine concrete and symbolic execution of *code* to generate test cases that satisfy some coverage criteria. Generation of test cases is a step of the proposed approach. Hence, the software validation approach proposed in this paper can directly use these techniques. Indeed, an early reviewer of this paper suggested the following technique. Generate a test suite by determining a set of inputs that provide guaranteed path coverage on the formal specification, and another set of inputs that guarantee coverage on the software implementation. Using the full test suite would guarantee similar behavior of the software and its specification on every possible execution path for a concrete test value.

Future work involves employing the approach to validate more of the code utilized by the NASA air traffic management software under development, as well as further employing and developing tools to automate the code generation from specification. Another line of research is to develop a method for producing guaranteed output precision, or upper and lower bounds, for the symbolic evaluation of a function in PVS.

The NASA PVS library also contains a specification of floating point numbers and operations on them. Algorithms specified in this context can be translated to code in a more faithful way, and the behavior is likely to be much closer between the two. The hurdle to this pursuing this line of research is that proving properties of functions inside the context of floating point numbers is much more difficult.

6   Conclusion

Despite recent progress on the formal analysis of floating point programs [4,5,15], verification of software involving numerical computations is still a challenging problem. An alternative approach to software verification consists on the development of code from formally verified models of safety-critical algorithms. While this approach does not provide strong guarantees of software correctness, visual inspection of both the code and the formal models increases the confidence that the software behavior closely reflects its formal specification. This paper proposes a new approach that automates the validation of software implementations against their formal models. This approach, which is based on model animation, compares the output of algorithms implemented in a programming language to the results obtained from the symbolic evaluation of formal models enriched with semantic attachments. These semantic attachments enable symbolic evaluation of even irrational, real-valued functions, via precise numerical computations. The proposed approach is illustrated on an air traffic management system currently used at NASA for conducting research on advanced air traffic management concepts.

References

1. Federal Aviation Administration. Airworthiness approval of automatic dependent surveillance-broadcast (ADS-B) out systems. Advisory Circular AC 20–165A, FAA (November 2012)
2. Aichernig, B.K., Gerstinger, A., Aster, R.: Formal specification techniques as a catalyst in validation. In: Fifth IEEE International Symposim on High Assurance Systems Engineering, HASE 2000, pp. 203–206. IEEE (2000)
3. Berghofer, S., Nipkow, T.: Random testing in Isabelle/HOL. In: Cuellar, J., Liu, Z. (eds.) Software Engineering and Formal Methods, SEFM 2004, pp. 230–239. IEEE Computer Society (2004)
4. Boldo, S.: Deductive formal verification: how to make your floating-point programs behave. Thèse d'habilitation, Université Paris-Sud (October 2014)
5. Boldo, S., Marché, C.: Formal Verification of Numerical Programs: from C Annotated Programs to Mechanical Proofs. Mathematics in Computer Science 5, 377–393 (2011)
6. Butler, R.: Formalization of the integral calculus in the PVS theorem prover. Journal of Formalized Reasoning 2(1) (2009)
7. Cadar, C., Godefroid, P., Khurshid, S., Păsăreanu, C.S., Sen, K., Tillmann, N., Visser, W.: Symbolic execution for software testing in practice: preliminary assessment. In: Proceedings of the 33rd International Conference on Software Engineering, ICSE 2011, pp. 1066–1071. ACM, New York (2011)
8. Claessen, K., Hughes, J.: QuickCheck: a lightweight tool for random testing of Haskell programs. In: Proceedings of the Fifth ACM SIGPLAN International Conference on Functional Programming, ICFP 2000, pp. 268–279. ACM, New York (2000)
9. Crow, J., Owre, S., Rushby, J., Shankar, N., Stringer-Calvert, D.: Evaluating, testing, and animating PVS specifications. Technical report, Computer Science Laboratory, SRI International, Menlo Park, CA (March 2001)
10. Hagen, G., Butler, R., Maddalon, J.: Stratway: a modular approach to strategic conflict resolution. In: Preceedings of 11th AIAA Aviation Technology, Integration, and Operations (ATIO) Conference, Virgina Beach, VA (September 2011)
11. Hagen, G.E., Butler, R.W.: Towards a formal semantics of flight plans and trajectories. Technical Memorandum NASA/TM-2014-218862, NASA, Langley Research Center, Hampton VA 23681–2199, USA (December 2014)
12. Hayhurst, K.J., Veerhusen, D.S., Chilenski, J.J., Rierson, L.K.: A practical tutorial on modified condition/decision coverage. Technical Memorandum NASA/TM-2001-210876, NASA, Langley Research Center, Hampton VA 23681–2199, USA (May 2001)
13. Lensink, L., Smetsers, S., van Eekelen, M.: Generating verifiable java code from verified PVS specifications. In: Goodloe, A.E., Person, S. (eds.) NFM 2012. LNCS, vol. 7226, pp. 310–325. Springer, Heidelberg (2012)
14. Leuschel, M., Butler, M.: ProB: a model checker for B. In: Araki, K., Gnesi, S., Mandrioli, D. (eds.) FME 2003. LNCS, vol. 2805, pp. 855–874. Springer, Heidelberg (2003)
15. Marché, C.: Verification of the functional behavior of a floating-point program: an industrial case study. Science of Computer Programming 96(3), 279–296 (2014)
16. Masci, P., Oladimeji, P., Curzon, P., Thimbleby, H.: Tool demo: using PVSio-web to demonstrate software issues in medical user interfaces. In: 4th International Symposium on Foundations of Healthcare Information Engineering and Systems (FHIES2014) (2014)

17. Meyer, B.: Applying "Design by Contract". Computer **25**(10), 40–51 (1992)
18. Meyer, B., Fiva, A., Ciupa, I., Leitner, A., Wei, Y., Stapf, E.: Programs that test themselves. Computer **42**(9), 46–55 (2009)
19. Muñoz, C.: Rapid prototyping in PVS. Contractor Report NASA/CR-2003-212418, NASA, Langley Research Center, Hampton VA 23681–2199, USA (May 2003)
20. Narkawicz, A., Muñoz, C.: State-based implicit coordination and applications. Technical Publication NASA/TP-2011-217067, NASA, Langley Research Center, Hampton VA 23681–2199, USA (March 2011)
21. Owre, S., Rushby, J., Shankar, N.: PVS: a prototype verification. In: Kapur, D. (ed.) CADE 1992. LNCS, vol. 607, pp. 748–752. Springer, Heidelberg (1992)
22. Palanque, P., Ladry, J.-F., Navarre, D., Barboni, E.: High-Fidelity prototyping of interactive systems can be formal too. In: Jacko, J.A. (ed.) HCI International 2009, Part I. LNCS, vol. 5610, pp. 667–676. Springer, Heidelberg (2009)
23. Sen, K., Marinov, D., Agha, G.: CUTE: A concolic unit testing engine for C. In: Proceedings of the 10th European Software Engineering Conference Held Jointly with 13th ACM SIGSOFT International Symposium on Foundations of Software Engineering, ESEC/FSE-13, pp. 263–272. ACM, New York (2005)
24. Shankar, N.: Efficiently executing PVS. Technical report, Project report, ComputerScience Laboratory, SRI International, Menlo Park (1999)
25. Yang, F., Jacquot, J.-P., Souquières, J.: Jeb: safe simulation of event-b models in javascript. In: 2013 20th Asia-Pacific Software Engineering Conference (APSEC), vol. 1, pp. 571–576 (December 2013)
26. Yusuke, W., Shigeru, K.: Performance evaluation of a testing framework using quickcheck and hadoop. IPSJ Journal **53**(2), 7 (2012)

Sequential Generation of Structured Arrays and Its Deductive Verification

Richard Genestier[1], Alain Giorgetti[1,2]([✉]), and Guillaume Petiot[1,3]

[1] FEMTO-ST Institute, University of Franche-Comté, 25030 Besançon
CEDEX, France
[2] INRIA Nancy - Grand Est, CASSIS project, 54600 Villers-les-Nancy, France
[3] CEA, LIST, Software Reliability Laboratory PC 174, 91191 Gif-sur-Yvette, France
{richard.genestier,alain.giorgetti}@femto-st.fr, guillaume.petiot@cea.fr

Abstract. A structured array is an array satisfying given constraints, such as being sorted or having no duplicate values. Generation of all arrays with a given structure up to some given length has many applications, including bounded exhaustive testing. A sequential generator of structured arrays can be defined by two C functions: the first one computes an initial array, and the second one steps from one array to the next one according to some total order on the set of arrays. We formally specify with ACSL annotations that the generated arrays satisfy the prescribed structural constraints (soundness property) and that the generation is in increasing lexicographic order (progress property). We refine this specification into two programming and specification patterns: one for generation in lexicographic order and one for generation by filtering the output of another generator. We distribute a library of generators instantiating these patterns. After adding suitable loop invariants we automatically prove the soundness and progress properties with the Frama-C platform.

Keywords: Formal specification · Deductive verification · Combinatorial enumeration · Sequential generation · Imperative program

1 Introduction

Automated techniques for software testing are attractive because they produce many test cases in a more rational, reliable and affordable way than manual ones. We consider here unit testing for functions inputting a structured array. An array is said to be *structured* if it satisfies given constraints, such as being sorted or having no duplicate values. A challenge in input data generation for unit testing is to design and implement correct generators of complex data structures.

A recent trend in research in software verification aims at building verification environments that are themselves certified, in order to avoid erroneously validating safety properties of critical software. Randomized property-based testing has been formalized in Coq [15] to certify random generators. M. Carlier, C. Dubois and A. Gotlieb formally certify a constraint solver in Coq [6] as a piece of a

© Springer International Publishing Switzerland 2015
J.C. Blanchette and N. Kosmatov (Eds.): TAP 2015, LNCS 9154, pp. 109–128, 2015.
DOI: 10.1007/978-3-319-21215-9_7

certified testing environment. A certified constraint solver on a finite domain of arrays needs certified sequential generators of these structures to explore their domain. As a complement to random testing we address *Bounded Exhaustive Testing* (BET for short) with algorithms generating all the arrays with given length and structure. We formally specify the behavior of these exhaustive array generators. As an alternative to interactive proving, we annotate them with loop invariants and variants, so that their formal contracts can be proved automatically. The BET approach is relevant [19] because it offers the advantage of providing counterexamples of minimal size, and errors in the function to be tested can often be revealed using input arrays of small size.

For a predefined total order on all the arrays of the same length, a *sequential generator* of all arrays with a given structure is composed of two functions: the first function constructs the smallest array of a given length satisfying the structural constraint, and from any array, the second function constructs the next array in that order satisfying the constraint. We present a uniform approach to the rational implementation of sequential generators of structured arrays. They are implemented as C functions and formally specified in the ANSI C Specification Language (ACSL) [2]. We consider three behavioral properties for the generation functions. The *soundness* property asserts that both functions generate arrays satisfying the prescribed constraints. The *progress* property asserts that the second function generates arrays in increasing lexicographic order. It entails the termination of repeated calls to the second function. The *exhaustivity* property asserts that the generator does not omit any solution. According to the deductive approach promoted by Floyd [11], Hoare [13] and Dijkstra [9], we statically verify the soundness and progress properties. In addition, we execute the generator up to some array length to check dynamically the exhaustivity property, either by counting or by comparison with the output of another generator. For deductive verification, we use the WP plugin [8] of Frama-C, which implements the Weakest Precondition calculus for C programs annotated in ACSL, assisted by SMT solvers [21] to prove the verification conditions generated by WP. Frama-C is a framework for the analysis of C programs developed by CEA LIST and INRIA Saclay.

We also propose programming and specification patterns to facilitate the design of the generation functions and the verification of their properties. A first pattern formalizes the principle of generation in lexicographic order by modifying the end of the array. A second pattern describes generation by filtering the output of an existing generator. It is completed by a pattern outlining how to uniformly transform a first-order constraint into a Boolean function.

The contributions of this paper are (i) general programming and specification patterns to speed up the construction and verification of sequential generators, (ii) a verified library of C programs and ACSL specifications implementing sequential generation algorithms, and (iii) automated formal proofs of their soundness and progress properties.

After giving some definitions, Section 2 presents generation in lexicographic order through a running example and a general pattern. Section 3 illustrates generation by filtering with the same example and proposes patterns that make this method easy to apply to obtain and verify many sequential generators. Verification results for several generators constructed from these patterns are presented in Section 4. Section 5 presents some related work, and Section 6 concludes.

2   Generation in Lexicographic Order

In all that follows, array values are mathematical integers. Bounded exhaustive generation of arrays only makes sense when there are finitely many arrays of each length. To this end array values are assumed to be lower- and upper-bounded by two C integers, whose absolute value is usually small, so that the number of arrays to generate does not become too large. Moreover it can often be assumed that all the computations for new array values are performed within these bounds. Under these assumptions, array values can be safely represented by C integers with the type int, without any risk of arithmetic overflows.

Let $<$ denote the strict total order on integers, such that $i < i + 1$ for any integer i.

Definition 1. *The* lexicographic order *on integer arrays, denoted by $\prec$, is such that $b \prec c$ if and only if there is an index i ($0 \leq i \leq n - 1$) such that $b[i] < c[i]$ and $b[j] = c[j]$ for $0 \leq j \leq i - 1$, for all integer arrays b and c of length $n \geq 0$.*

The binary relation $\prec$ is a strict total order. All the programs presented in the paper generate structured arrays in increasing lexicographic order.

Section 2.1 defines sequential generation functions. Sections 2.2 and 2.4 respectively present the principle of generation in lexicographic order through the example of a family of structured arrays and through a formal pattern, while Section 2.3 presents a formalization of the progress property.

2.1   Sequential Generation Functions

Consider a family z of structured C arrays of length n whose values are of type int. A sequential generator of arrays in this family consists of two C functions, called the *(sequential) generation functions*. The first function

```
int first_z(int a[], int n, ...)
```

generates the first array a of length n in the family z. It returns 1 if there is at least one array of this length in this family. Otherwise, it returns 0. The second function

```
int next_z(int a[], int n, ...)
```

returns 1 and generates in the array a of length n the next element of the family z immediately following the one stored in the array a when the function is called, if this array is not the last one in the family. Otherwise, it returns 0. The function next_z is thereafter called the *successor function*. In the header of these two C functions, the dots represent other parameters which may be required for the generation of the structured array. We only consider the cases where none of these parameters is an additional structure.

A typical program successively generating in the unique variable a all the arrays of length n in the family z consists of a call `first_z(a,n,...)`; to the first function, a treatment of the first array, and then a treatment of all the subsequent arrays in the body of a loop `while (next_z(a,n,...) == 1)`.

2.2 Running Example

Catalogs such as the *fxtbook* [1] propose effective sequential generators of combinatorial structures stored in a structured array. We consider the combinatorial structure of restricted growth function as a running example.

Definition 2. *A* Restricted Growth Function *(RGF, for short) of size n is an endofunction a of $\{0,\ldots,n-1\}$ such that $a(0) = 0$ and $a(k) \leq a(k-1)+1$ for $1 \leq k \leq n-1$.*

An endofunction a of $\{0,\ldots,n-1\}$, and thus an RGF, can be represented by the C array $\boxed{a(0)\,|\,a(1)\,|\,\ldots\,|\,a(n-1)}$ of its n integer values. The *fxtbook* proposes an algorithm [1, page 235] to compute the RGF immediately following a given RGF a in ascending lexicographic order:

1. Find the maximum integer j such that $a(j) \leq a(j-1)$.
2. If this integer exists, increment the value $a(j)$ and fix $a(i) = 0$ for all $i > j$. The other values of a remain unchanged.
3. Otherwise, the generation is complete, a is the largest RGF and remains unchanged.

For example, the five RGFs of size 3 generated by this algorithm are 000, 001, 010, 011 and 012. The first RGF is the constant function equal to 0.

```
1  #include "global.h"
2  /*@ predicate is_non_neg(int *a, Z n) = ∀ Z i; 0 ≤ i < n ⇒ a[i] ≥ 0;
3   @ predicate is_le_pred(int *a, Z n) = ∀ Z i; 1 ≤ i < n ⇒ a[i] ≤ a[i-1]+1;
4   @ predicate is_rgf(int *a, Z n) = a[0] == 0 ∧ is_non_neg(a,n)
5   @   ∧ is_le_pred(a,n); */
6
7  /*@ requires n > 0 ∧ \valid(a+(0..n-1));
8   @ assigns a[0..n-1];
9   @ ensures is_rgf(a,n); */
10 void first_rgf(int a[], int n);
11
12 /*@ requires n > 0 ∧ \valid(a+(0..n-1));
13  @ requires is_rgf(a,n);
14  @ assigns a[1..n-1];
15  @ ensures is_rgf(a,n);
16  @ ensures \result == 1 ⇒ lt_lex{Pre,Post}(a,n); */
17 int next_rgf(int a[], int n);
```

Fig. 1. ACSL predicates and contracts of RGF generation functions (file **rgf.h**)

Figures 1 and 2 respectively show an ACSL specification and a C code for the sequential generation functions `first_rgf` and `next_rgf`. We explain through these examples the features of ACSL we use. To facilitate the reading of the specifications, some ACSL notations are replaced by mathematical symbols (e.g. keywords `\forall` and `integer` are respectively denoted by $\forall$ and $\mathbb{Z}$).

The file `rgf.h` given in Figure 1 and included in Figure 2 is composed of three predicates and two function contracts. The characteristic property of RGFs from Definition 2 is expressed between line 2 and line 5 of Figure 1 by the three ACSL predicates `is_rgf`, `is_non_neg` and `is_le_pred`. The constraint that the array values are in $\{0, \ldots, n-1\}$ is not specified because it is a consequence of the other constraints. In both function contracts an annotation `requires R;` specifies that the *precondition* R must be satisfied by the parameters of the function when it is called. On lines 7 and 12, we require that array `a` is of positive length `n` and is allocated in memory. It is also required (line 13) that the input array `a` of the successor function represents an RGF. An annotation of the form `assigns A;` before the header of a function declares in A the function parameters and global variables that it can modify. Thus, line 14 declares that all the values of array `a` can be changed except the first one `a[0]`.

An annotation `ensures E;` asserts that the *postcondition* E holds at the end of the function execution. The **soundness property** asserts that all the generated arrays satisfy the prescribed constraint, for the corresponding function to be an RGF. It is formally specified on lines 9 and 15 of Figure 1. The postcondition on line 16 is explained in Section 2.3.

The file `rgf.c` shown in Figure 2 is composed of one predicate and two function definitions specified in ACSL. The predicate `is_zero` defined on line 3 is introduced to express the loop invariant of the function `first_rgf` (line 8 of Figure 2). We now explain the C statements in the body of the function `next_rgf` in Figure 2. On line 20, a loop traverses the array from right to left to find a position from which the end of the array will be modified. This position is called the *revision index* of the array `a`. In this example, the revision index `rev` is reached when meeting the rightmost element (i.e. maximum index) less than or equal to its predecessor. If the search fails, then the final structure is reached (line 21). Otherwise, the contents of the array are changed from the revision index to the end, so that the new array also satisfies the constraint and is greater than the current array in lexicographic order. The way to effect this revision depends on the prescribed constraints of the array. For RGFs, the property `a[rev]` $\leq$ `a[rev-1]` of the revision index `rev` makes it possible to increment `a[rev]` (line 22) and fill the rest of the array with 0 (line 28) to obtain the next array satisfying the restricted growth constraint. Figure 2 also shows annotations concerning the loops of the functions. An annotation `loop invariant I;` immediately before a loop states that the formula I is an *(inductive) invariant* of this loop, i.e., a property that holds the first time the loop is entered and is preserved by each iteration of the loop body. For instance, the loop invariant on line 17 asserts that the revision index is the rightmost position from which the end of the array can be modified to obtain a greater array satisfying the constraint. Before the

```
1  #include "rgf.h"
2
3  /*@ predicate is_zero(int *a, Z b) = ∀ Z i; 0 ≤ i < b ⇒ a[i] == 0; */
4
5  void first_rgf(int a[], int n) {
6    int k;
7    /*@ loop invariant 0 ≤ k ≤ n;
8      @ loop invariant is_zero(a,k);
9      @ loop assigns k, a[0..n-1];
10     @ loop variant n-k; */
11   for (k = 0; k < n; k++) a[k] = 0;
12 }
13
14 int next_rgf(int a[], int n) {
15   int rev,k;
16   /*@ loop invariant 0 ≤ rev ≤ n-1;
17     @ loop invariant (∀ Z j; rev < j < n ⇒ a[j] > a[j-1]);
18     @ loop assigns rev;
19     @ loop variant rev; */
20   for (rev = n-1; rev ≥ 1; rev--) if (a[rev] ≤ a[rev-1]) break;
21   if (rev == 0) return 0;
22   a[rev]++;
23   /*@ loop invariant rev+1 ≤ k ≤ n;
24     @ loop invariant is_non_neg(a,k);
25     @ loop invariant is_le_pred(a,k);
26     @ loop assigns k, a[rev+1..n-1];
27     @ loop variant n-k; */
28   for (k = rev+1; k < n; k++) a[k] = 0;
29   return 1;
30 }
```

Fig. 2. Effective generation of RGFs in C/ACSL

second loop of the function next_rgf, three loop invariants successively assert that the loop variable k stays between rev+1 and n (line 23), that the k first values of the array are non-negative (line 24), and that the property is_le_pred is satisfied up to k (line 25). The annotation loop assigns line 26 asserts that the only values that the loop body can change are the elements of a between the indexes rev+1 and n-1. An annotation loop variant V; defines a *loop variant* V to ensure the termination of the loop. The entire expression must be non-negative at the beginning of each loop iteration and strictly decrease between two successive loop iterations. For example, as declared on line 27, the term n-k is a variant of the loop on line 28. The ACSL annotations in the body of the function first_rgf are similar and therefore not detailed.

Suppose that Figure 2 is the content of a file rgf.c. The static deductive verification of the function next_rgf with Frama-C and its plugin WP is realized by running the command frama-c -wp-fct next_rgf rgf.c. Frama-C indicates whether each proof obligation generated by WP is proved by the SMT solver Alt-Ergo and indicates the duration of each proof. Verification results are detailed in Section 4.

2.3 Progress Property

The progress property asserts that the successor function generates arrays in increasing lexicographic order. It is specified in ACSL by the postcondition

```
ensures  \result  == 1 ⇒ lt_lex{Pre,Post}(a,n);
```

on line 16 in Figure 1. The ACSL formula `lt_lex{L1,L2}(a,n)` formalizes that the array a at label **L1** is lexicographically less than at label **L2**. A label represents a position in the program. Every expression e in ACSL can be written `\at(e,L)`, meaning that e is evaluated at the label L. The predefined label `Pre` (resp. `Post`) in the postcondition refers to the state before (resp. after) execution of the function `next_rgf`.

The predicate `lt_lex` and two auxiliary predicates formalize Definition 1 in a header file `global.h` included in all the generators. These definitions are shown in Figure 3.

```
1 /*@ predicate is_eq{L1,L2}(int *a, Z i) =
2   @   ∀ Z j; 0 ≤ j < i ⇒ \at(a[j],L1) == \at(a[j],L2);
3   @ predicate lt_lex_at{L1,L2}(int *a, Z i) =
4   @   is_eq{L1,L2}(a,i) ∧ \at(a[i],L1) < \at(a[i],L2);
5   @ predicate lt_lex{L1,L2}(int *a, int n) =
6   @   ∃ int i; 0 ≤ i < n ∧ lt_lex_at{L1,L2}(a,i); */
```

Fig. 3. Progress predicates (file `global.h`)

2.4   Pattern of Generation in Lexicographic Order

The function `next_rgf` and the successor function of many other effective sequential generators of structured arrays follow a design principle here called *"suffix revision"*. Figure 4 presents this principle as a design pattern composed of C code and ACSL annotations, for the successor function `next_z` of a sequential generator in lexicographic order.

The family z of structured arrays is defined by a constraint formalized by the predicate `is_z` declared on line 4 of Figure 4. The successor function `next_z` revises the suffix of its input array a in two steps. First, it finds the rightmost array index satisfying some predicate called the *revision condition*. This index is called the *revision index* of the array a. Second, it modifies the contents of the array a from the revision index to the array end. The revision condition is formalized by the predicate `is_rev` (line 5) and the Boolean function `b_rev` (declared and specified on lines 8–13). The loop on line 32 explores the input array a from right to left to find the revision index `rev`. The loop invariant on line 29 states that the revision index is the rightmost index satisfying the revision condition. If the search fails (line 33), the input array is the last one and the function returns 0. Otherwise, the function `suffix` revises the array a from its revision index to its end, as specified by the `assigns` clause on line 17. Its postcondition on line 18 asserts that it increases the array value `a[rev]` at the revision index.

The successor function follows the suffix revision pattern if it satisfies the soundness and progress properties (respectively specified on line 24 and 25), but also the property that the successor function always computes the next array, i.e.

```
 1  #include "global.h"
 2
 3  /*@ axiomatic preds {
 4   @   predicate is_z(int *a, Z n) reads a[0..n-1];
 5   @   predicate is_rev(int *a, Z n, Z i) reads a[0..n-1];
 6   @ } */
 7
 8  /*@ requires n > 0 ∧ \valid(a+(0..n-1));
 9   @ requires 0 ≤ rev ≤ n-1;
10   @ assigns \nothing;
11   @ ensures \result == 0 ∨ \result == 1;
12   @ ensures \result ⟺ is_rev(a,n,rev); */
13  int b_rev(int a[], int n, int rev);
14
15  /*@ requires n > 0 ∧ \valid(a+(0..n-1));
16   @ requires 0 ≤ rev ≤ n-1;
17   @ assigns a[rev..n-1];
18   @ ensures a[rev] > \at(a[rev],Pre); */
19  void suffix(int a[], int n, int rev);
20
21  /*@ requires n > 0 ∧ \valid(a+(0..n-1));
22   @ requires is_z(a,n);
23   @ assigns a[0..n-1];
24   @ ensures soundness: is_z(a,n);
25   @ ensures \result == 1 ⟹ lt_lex{Pre,Post}(a,n); */
26  int next_z(int a[], int n) {
27    int rev;
28    /*@ loop invariant -1 ≤ rev ≤ n-1;
29     @ loop invariant (∀ Z j; rev < j < n ⟹ ! is_rev(a,n,j));
30     @ loop assigns rev;
31     @ loop variant rev; */
32    for (rev = n-1; rev ≥ 0; rev--) if (b_rev(a,n,rev)) break;
33    if (rev == -1) return 0;
34    suffix(a,n,rev);
35    return 1;
36  }
```

Fig. 4. Successor function pattern for suffix revision

that there exists no array in the family **z** between its input and output arrays, for the strict and total lexicographic order. An ingredient for its specification is the loop invariant on line 29. Its verification is further discussed in Section 4.1.

Suppose that Figure 4 is the content of a file suffix.c. The postcondition expressing the progress property and the loop invariant on line 29 are automatically proved by WP, with the command

frama-c -wp suffix.c -wp-prop=-soundness.

Note that the loop invariant on line 29 is not required to prove progress property. Indeed, the algorithm implemented by the function next_z corresponds to the definition of the lexicographic order: it leaves a prefix of the array **a** unchanged and increases its value at the revision index. The progress property is thus generically verified, because it is a consequence of the pattern. On the other hand, the soundness property cannot be verified at this level of generality, because it depends on the constraint on the array **a**.

By instantiating the predicates is_z and is_rev and the subfunctions b_rev and suffix in this pattern with appropriate code, we obtain a generator of a family **z** of structured arrays in lexicographic order, whose progress property can be verified automatically, assuming that the subfunctions satisfy their contracts.

In an instantiation of the pattern the subfunction contracts have to be completed so that the soundness property can also be verified automatically. For simple generators it is easier to replace the subfunction calls by a sequence of statements. For example, we can obtain the successor function `next_rgf` of Figure 2 by replacing the calls `b_rev(a,n,rev)` and `suffix(a,n,rev);` respectively by the statement

```
a[rev] ≤ a[rev-1];
```

and the sequence of statements

```
a[rev]++;
for (k = rev+1; k < n; k++) a[k] = 0;
```

3   Generation by Filtering

Generation *by filtering* consists of selecting in a family of structures those that satisfy a given constraint. Of course, the more structures are rejected, the less effective is the generator. However this simple generation approach quickly provides a first generator, whose implementation, specification and deductive verification come almost for free, as we will see throughout this section.

Section 3.1 illustrates the principle of generation by filtering with the example of RGFs. Section 3.2 formalizes this principle in a general pattern for all generators by filtering. The soundness property of the generation functions in this pattern is automatically proved. To instantiate this pattern, it is necessary to implement the constraint of substructures as a Boolean function. Section 3.3 provides a general pattern for this Boolean function and its specification. The soundness of the Boolean function with respect to the constraint is also automatically proved.

3.1   Example

The RGF family is a subfamily of the family of endofunctions of $\{0, ..., n-1\}$. Suppose we already have implemented, specified and automatically verified a generator of endofunctions of $\{0, ..., n-1\}$ consisting of two generation functions `first_endofct(a,n)` and `next_endofct(a,n)`. Figure 5 shows a sequential generator of RGFs filtering those endofunctions of $\{0, ..., n-1\}$ that are RGFs. The generation functions `first_rgf(a,n)` and `next_rgf(a,n)` call the C Boolean function `b_rgf`, which characterizes an RGF among the endofunctions of $\{0, ..., n-1\}$. The ACSL predicate `is_rgf` here is the conjunction of the predicates `is_le_pred` and `is_endofct`. The contracts of functions `first_rgf` and `next_rgf` are not shown, because they are very similar to those of Figure 1, except the postcondition expressing the soundness property for `next_rgf` which is now

```
ensures \result == 1 ⇒ is_rgf(a,n);
```

```
1  /*@ requires n > 0;                      25      @ tmp ≠ 0 ⇒ is_endofct(a,n);
2   @ requires \valid(a+(0..n-1));          26      @ loop assigns a[0..n-1],tmp; */
3   @ requires is_endofct(a,n);             27   while (tmp ≠ 0 ∧ b_rgf(a,n) == 0) {
4   @ assigns \nothing;                      28    tmp = next_endofct(a,n);
5   @ ensures \result == 0                   29   }
6   @   ∨ \result == 1;                      30   if (tmp == 0) { return 0; }
7   @ ensures \result == 1 ⇔ is_rgf(a,n);    31   return 1;
8   @*/                                      32  }
9  int b_rgf(int a[], int n) {               33
10   int i;                                  34  int next_rgf(int a[], int n) {
11   if (a[0] ≠ 0) return 0;                 35   int tmp = 0;
12   /*@ loop invariant 1 ≤ i ≤ n;           36   /*@ loop assigns a[0..n-1], tmp;
13    @ loop invariant is_le_pred(a,i);      37    @ loop invariant is_endofct(a,n);
14    @ loop assigns i;                      38    @ loop invariant
15    @ loop variant n-i; */                 39    @ le_lex{Pre,Here}(a,n); */
16   for (i = 1; i < n; i++)                 40   do {
17    if (a[i] > a[i-1]+1) return 0;         41    tmp = next_endofct(a,n);
18   return 1;                               42   } while (tmp ≠ 0 ∧ b_rgf(a,n) == 0);
19  }                                        43   if (tmp == 0) { return 0; }
20                                           44   return 1;
21  int first_rgf(int a[], int n) {          45  }
22   int tmp;
23   tmp = first_endofct(a,n);
24   /*@ loop invariant
```

Fig. 5. Generation of RGFs by filtering

```
1  /*@ predicate le_lex{L1,L2}(int *a, int n) = lt_lex{L1,L2}(a,n)
2   @   ∨ is_eq{L1,L2}(a,n); */
3
4  /*@ lemma trans_le_lt_lex{L1,L2,L3}: ∀ int *a; ∀ int n;
5   @   (le_lex{L1,L2}(a,n) ∧ lt_lex{L2,L3}(a,n)) ⇒ lt_lex{L1,L3}(a,n); */
```

Fig. 6. Predicate and lemma to specify and prove progress of a filtering successor function

The predicate and the lemma defined in Figure 6 are respectively introduced to specify on lines 38-39 a loop invariant for the filtering loop of the successor function and to automatically prove that invariant and thus the progress property for that function, assuming that the successor function of endofunctions ensures the progress property. The current array is indeed equal to the previous one at the beginning of the do .. while loop (lines 40-42). The pseudo-transitivity lemma trans_le_lt_lex helps the prover to derive the progress property – expressed with the strict order predicate lt_lex – from that loop invariant and the contract of the called function next_endofct.

3.2 General Pattern of Generation by Filtering

The generation of RGFs by filtering can be generalized to any family of arrays defined from more general arrays by additional constraints. Figure 7 provides a general pattern for the generation of arrays in a family z by filtering arrays in a family x that satisfy the additional constraint is_y implemented by the Boolean function b_y. The arrays in the family x are assumed to satisfy the constraint is_x. The contracts of the generation functions first_x, next_x, first_z and next_z are similar to the one of the functions first_rgf and next_rgf in

```
1  /*@ axiomatic preds {                    25   /*@ loop invariant tmp ≠ 0
2  @  predicate is_x(int *a, Z n)           26   @  ⇒ is_x(a,n);
3  @    reads a[0..n-1];                     27   @ loop assigns a[0..n-1], tmp; */
4  @  predicate is_y(int *a, Z n)           28   while (tmp ≠ 0 ∧ b_y(a,n) == 0) {
5  @    reads a[0..n-1];                     29   tmp = next_x(a,n);
6  @  predicate is_z(int *a, Z n) =         30   }
7  @    is_x(a,n) ∧ is_y(a,n);              31   if (tmp == 0) { return 0; }
8  @ } */                                    32   return 1;
9                                            33  }
10 int first_x(int a[], int n);             34
11 int next_x(int a[], int n);              35  int next_z(int a[], int n) {
12                                           36   int tmp;
13 /*@ requires n > 0;                      37   /*@ loop invariant is_x(a,n);
14 @ requires \valid(a+(0..n-1));          38   @ loop assigns a[0..n-1], tmp;
15 @ assigns \nothing;                      39   @ loop invariant
16 @ ensures \result == 0                   40   @  le_lex{Pre,Here}(a,n); */
17 @   ∨ \result == 1;                      41   do {
18 @ ensures \result == 1                   42   tmp = next_x(a,n);
19 @   ⇔ is_y(a,n); */                      43   } while (tmp ≠ 0 ∧ b_y(a,n) == 0);
20 int b_y(int a[], int n);                 44   if (tmp == 0) { return 0; }
21                                           45   return 1;
22 int first_z(int a[], int n) {            46  }
23   int tmp;
24   tmp = first_x(a,n);
```

Fig. 7. Pattern of generation by filtering

Section 3.1 and are therefore not reproduced in Figure 7. In this pattern, the ACSL predicates is_x, is_y and is_z are not defined. That's why they are declared in an ACSL axiomatic block, on lines 1-8 of Figure 7.

Assuming that the functions b_y, first_x and next_x satisfy their specifications, the soundness and progress properties of the functions first_z and next_z are automatically proved by Frama-C and WP assisted by Alt-Ergo.

The generator of RGFs by filtering (Figure 5) is obtained by instantiating the general pattern as follows: Replace each x, y and z respectively by endofct, rgf and rgf, and implement the property is_rgf as a Boolean function. Other examples of sequential generators using this pattern are given in Section 4. Thus, from a specified generator for a family of structured arrays, one can rapidly implement, specify and verify generators of their subfamilies.

3.3   General Pattern of Boolean Functions

We also propose patterns for the ACSL contract and the C code of a Boolean function corresponding to an array structural constraint expressed in first-order logic. If the constraint is a Boolean combination of atomic predicates, the correspondence is obvious: Boolean operators (such as conjunction or negation) either exist in C or can be readily expressed by a combination of C operators. Thus, the interesting cases are formulas with quantifiers. The case of a unique quantifier is too restrictive. The general case, where quantifiers are arbitrarily nested and combined with Boolean operators, would be too heavy to formalize, and the result would be painful to read. We have chosen to present the case of two nested quantifiers. This is enough to give an idea of what the general case would be, and this case is useful in itself.

```
1  /*@ axiomatic preds {
2    @   predicate is_x3(int *a, Z n, Z v1, Z v2) reads a[0..n-1];
3    @ }
4    @ predicate is_x2_gen(int *a, Z n, Z v1, Z v2) =
5    @   ∃ Z i2; 0 ≤ i2 < v2 ∧ is_x3(a,n,v1,i2);
6    @ predicate is_x2(int *a, Z n, Z v1) = is_x2_gen(a,n,v1,n);
7    @ predicate is_x1_gen(int *a, Z n, Z v1) = ∀ Z i1; 0 ≤ i1 < v1 ⇒ is_x2(a,n,i1);
8    @ predicate is_x1(int *a, Z n) = is_x1_gen(a,n,n); */
```

Fig. 8. Predicates for a constraint $\forall\exists$

```
1  /*@ requires n ≥ 0;                          25      if (b_x3(a,n,v1,i) == 1) return 1;
2    @ requires \valid(a+(0..n-1));             26      return 0;
3    @ assigns \nothing;                         27  }
4    @ ensures \result == 0 ∨                     28
5    @   \result == 1;                           29  /*@ requires n ≥ 0 ∧ \valid(a+(0..n-1));
6    @ ensures \result == 1 ⇔                     30    @ assigns \nothing;
7    @   is_x3(a,n,v1,v2); */                     31    @ ensures \result == 0 ∨
8  int b_x3(int a[],int n,int v1,int v2);        32    @   \result == 1;
9                                                33    @ ensures \result == 1 ⇔
10 /*@ requires n ≥ 0;                           34    @   is_x1(a,n); */
11   @ requires \valid(a+(0..n-1));             35  int b_x1(int a[],int n) {
12   @ assigns \nothing;                         36    int i;
13   @ ensures \result == 0 ∨                     37  /*@ loop invariant 0 ≤ i ≤ n;
14   @   \result == 1;                           38    @ loop invariant is_x1_gen(a,n,i);
15   @ ensures \result == 1 ⇔                     39    @ loop assigns i;
16   @   is_x2(a,n,v1); */                        40    @ loop variant n-i; */
17 int b_x2(int a[],int n,int v1) {              41    for (i = 0; i < n; i++)
18   int i;                                      42      if (b_x2(a,n,i) == 0) return 0;
19 /*@ loop invariant 0 ≤ i ≤ n;                 43    return 1;
20   @ loop invariant                            44  }
21   @   ! is_x2_gen(a,n,v1,i);
22   @ loop assigns i;
23   @ loop variant n-i; */
24   for (i = 0; i < n; i++)
```

Fig. 9. Pattern of Boolean functions for a constraint $\forall\exists$

Consider a constraint of the form $\forall i.\, 0 \leq i < n \Rightarrow (\exists j.\, 0 \leq j < n \wedge \varphi)$, where φ is a quantifier-free formula dependent on i and j expressing a constraint on an array of length n. In Figure 8 the constraint is decomposed into three ACSL predicates is_x1(a,n), is_x2(a,n,v1) and is_x3(a,n,v1,v2), respectively corresponding to the complete universal property, to the existential sub-formula and to the property φ it quantifies, for an array a of length n. The additional parameter v1 of the predicates is_x2 and is_x3 corresponds to the free variable i in the subformulas $(\exists j.\, 0 \leq j < n \wedge \varphi)$ and φ. Similarly, the additional parameter v2 of the predicate is_x3 corresponds to the free variable j in φ. This quantifier-free formula φ being arbitrary in this pattern, the corresponding predicate is_x3 is not defined, but only declared in an axiomatic block in lines 1-3 of Figure 8.

In Figure 9 the Boolean function b_x1 implements the ACSL predicate is_x1 in the sense that it returns 1 when its parameters satisfy the predicate, and 0 otherwise. The Boolean functions b_x2 and b_x3 respectively implement the predicates is_x2 and is_x3. For $k = 1,2$, the function b_xk implements a loop that sequentially evaluates the predicate is_x($k+1$) for all array elements. The loop invariants are specified using a generalization of the predicate is_xk, named is_xk_gen, defined in lines 4 and 7 of Figure 8.

Suppose that Figure 9 is the content of a file `allex.c`. Suppose that the Boolean function `b_x3` satisfies its specification. By the command `frama-c -wp allex.c -wp-skip-fct b_x3` we then automatically prove that the other functions satisfy their specification.

An immediate application of the previous pattern is the generation of surjections by filtering endofunctions. Indeed, a surjection f is an endofunction of $\{0, ..., n-1\}$ which satisfies the property $\forall i. 0 \le i < n \Rightarrow (\exists j. 0 \le j < n \land f(j) = i)$. A generator of surjections is easily obtained by merging the pattern of Boolean functions (Figures 9 and 8) with the one of generation by filtering (Figure 7), then by renaming `x1`, `x2`, `x`, `y` and `z` respectively as `im`, `eq_im`, `endofct`, `im` and `surj`, defining the predicate `is_x3` as

```
predicate is_x3(int *a, Z n, Z v1, Z v2) = a[v2] == v1;
```

and implementing the function `b_x3` with the unique statement

```
return(a[v2] == v1);
```

From the generator of endofunctions already used for RGFs in Section 3.1, the development and deductive verification of this surjection generator are effected in a few minutes. After this minimal work, we can make various simplifications to the surjection generator while preserving its deductive verification. For example, we can remove the parameter `n` of the predicate `is_x3`, which is not used in that example.

4   Verified Library

The patterns presented in the previous sections have been implemented and instantiated to produce a library of verified sequential generators of structured arrays.[1] In order to ensure that there are finitely many arrays of each length, all the generators of the library refine a generator of arrays whose codomain is finite. This generator named `fct` generates functions from $\{0, \ldots, n-1\}$ to $\{0, \ldots, k-1\}$ in increasing lexicographic order.

The literature in enumerative combinatorics [1,17] provides many effective algorithms to generate classical combinatorial structures, such as n tuples, permutations or combinations of k elements from n. Using the patterns in Section 3, we quickly obtain generators of these structures by filtering among functions. Then we implement, specify and verify more effective generators from the literature by instantiating the pattern of suffix revision (Section 2.4). Finally we use the generators obtained by filtering to validate them, as detailed in Section 4.1.

Metrics on the library are collected in Figure 10. The first column gives the name of the families of structures generated. These names are explained in the remainder of this section. The number of lines of code (resp. ACSL annotations) is recorded in the second (resp. third) column. The soundness and progress properties of these programs have been proved automatically with Frama-C Neon

---

[1] Archives `enum.*.tar.gz` of the library are available at http://members.femto-st.fr/richard-genestier/en and http://members.femto-st.fr/alain-giorgetti/en.

Array family	C	ACSL	goals	time (s)
suffix	9	12	25	1.929
filtering	14	33	51	5.524
allex	11	28	40	1.936
exall	12	27	40	1.921
all2	40	28	40	1.759
fct	13	25	42	5.622
subset	13	22	40	4.919
endofct	4	12	17	2.003
rgf ⊂ endofct	25	27	69	4.958
sorted1 ⊂ fct	19	27	67	4.743
sorted2 ⊂ fct	28	48	103	6.464
comb ⊂ fct	21	28	67	4.551
inj ⊂ fct	29	42	91	6.031
surj ⊂ fct	29	40	103	7.729
perm ⊂ fct	30	42	91	7.713
endoinj ⊂ inj	4	11	15	2.562
endosurj ⊂ surj	4	11	15	2.638
perm = endofct ∧ inj	17	21	60	7.211
perm = endofct ∧ surj	28	40	102	9.647
invol ⊂ perm	20	27	66	8.729
derang ⊂ perm	20	27	66	8.611
rgf	13	28	41	8.598
sorted	13	30	44	28.445
comb	18	33	46	Timeout
perm	23	29	50	8.903

Fig. 10. Verification results

20140301 and its WP plugin assisted by Why3 0.82 and the SMT solvers Alt-Ergo 0.95.2, CVC3 2.4.1 and CVC4 1.3. The fourth column shows the number of proof obligations (goals) generated by WP. The fifth column gives the time needed for the proof of these goals by the provers Alt-Ergo, CVC3 and CVC4 in seconds on a PC Intel Core i7-3520M 3.00GHz × 4 under Linux Ubuntu 14.04.

The first block of lines in Figure 10 concerns the patterns presented in Sections 2.4 and 3.2. The patterns allex, exall and all2 respectively correspond to a first-order constraint of the form $\forall\exists$, $\exists\forall$ and $\forall\forall$. Note that only the progress property is proved for the pattern suffix. The second block concerns the above-mentioned generator fct.

The third block in Figure 10 concerns specializations, defined as follows. When a family of arrays has other parameters than their length, one may fix the value of some of these parameters and thus obtain other generators. We say that we have *specialized* the family. For example, the specialization of the family of functions from $\{0, ..., n-1\}$ to $\{0, \ldots, k-1\}$ for $k = 2$ gives Boolean functions encoding the family subset of subsets of a set of n elements [1, page 203]. Its specialization to the case where $k = n$ yields the family endofct of endofunctions of $\{0, \ldots, n-1\}$.

The fourth block in Figure 10 concerns generation by filtering (Section 3). We denote by $z \subset x$ a generator of structures z by filtering among more general structures x. We denote by $z = x \wedge y$ a generator of structures z by filtering among more general structures x the ones having the additional property of structures y. For instance, rgf $\subset$ endofct denotes a generator of restricted growth functions filtered among endofunctions (presented in Section 3.1). From the generator fct we generate by filtering the following families:

- Sorted arrays of length n whose elements are in $\{0, \ldots, k-1\}$, by comparing each array value to the following one if it exists (sorted1),
- sorted arrays of length n whose elements are in $\{0, ..., k-1\}$, by comparing each array value to each other, i.e. using the pattern all2 (sorted2),
- combinations of p elements selected from n (comb $\subset$ fct),
- injections from $\{0, ..., n-1\}$ to $\{0, ..., k-1\}$ for $n \leq k$ (inj $\subset$ fct) and
- surjections from $\{0, ..., n-1\}$ to $\{0, ..., k-1\}$ for $n \geq k$ (generator surj $\subset$ fct).

The combination $\{e_0, \ldots, e_{p-1}\}$ with $0 \leq e_0 < \ldots < e_{p-1} \leq n-1$ is represented by the function c from $\{0, \ldots, p-1\}$ to $\{0, ..., n-1\}$ such that $c(i) = e_i$.

Combining specialization and filtering, we produce four generators of permutations on $\{0, ..., n-1\}$ (structure perm):

- perm $\subset$ surj (resp. perm $\subset$ inj) by specialization of surjections (resp. injections) from $\{0, ..., n-1\}$ to $\{0, ..., k-1\}$ (for $k = n$) and
- perm $=$ endofct $\wedge$ inj (resp. perm $=$ endofct $\wedge$ surj) by filtering of injections (resp. surjections) among endofunctions of $\{0, ..., n-1\}$.

The generator perm $=$ endofct $\wedge$ surj was detailed in Section 3.3. By filtering from permutations we also obtain involutions on $\{0, ..., n-1\}$ (invol $\subset$ perm) and derangements (fixed-point free permutations) on $\{0, ..., n-1\}$ (derang $\subset$ perm).

Family	nb. goals	time (s)
fct	43	6.858
subset	41	7.277
rgf	42	8.760
sorted	45	8.007
comb	48	29.094
perm	51	9.595

Fig. 11. Verification results for effective algorithms with an additional assertion

The fifth block in Figure 10 concerns effective generators in lexicographic order implemented by instantiating the pattern presented in Section 2. The generator rgf generates restricted growth functions with the algorithm from [1, page 235], as detailed in Section 2.2. The generator sorted produces sorted arrays from $\{0, ..., n-1\}$ to $\{0, ..., k-1\}$ in a more efficient manner than the generators sorted1 and sorted2. The generator comb produces combinations of p elements among n by the algorithm from [1, page 178]. The generator perm produces permutations on $\{0, ..., n-1\}$ by an adaptation of the algorithm from [1, page 243]. Column 4 shows that the proofs of these optimized generators are more complex, and thus take a longer duration, than for generators by filtering. Except for fct and subset, an extension of the timeout of the WP plugin to two minutes is required. In particular, the progress property of the generator comb is difficult to prove. However, an additional assertion

```
/*@ assert lt_lex_at{Pre,Here}(a,rev); */
```

at the end of the successor function substantially speeds up the longest proofs, as shown in Figure 11. Indeed, it specifies that the leftmost difference between the current array content (at label Here) and the former one (at label Pre) is at the revision index rev. This assertion helps the prover choosing the index rev to instantiate the existential quantifier in the predicate lt_lex.

4.1   Other Properties

We have also proved the postcondition

```
ensures \result == 0 ⇒ is_eq{Pre,Post}(a,n);
```

for the successor functions next_z of the generators by suffix revision. It expresses the property that the array a is not modified when the function returns 0, i.e. when no revision index is found, indicating that the lexicographically maximal array is reached. This property does not hold for a generation by filtering that instantiates the pattern presented in Section 3.2, when the maximal array in the subfamily z, say m_z, is not the maximal array in the family x, say m_x. In that case the function next_z considers all the arrays greater than m_z in the family x until reaching m_x and returns 0 while the array content has changed.

Exhaustivity. They are several ways to check the exhaustivity property asserting that all the arrays with a given structure are generated. (i) One can store all the generated arrays in a global array and then specify and prove that it contains all the arrays satisfying the constraint. Exhaustivity was formalized in this way for a generator of all the solutions to the n-queens problem [10]. The formal proof of exhaustivity with the Why3 verification tool [3] needs interactive steps. We discard this solution because we want to offer an approach where the verification is completely automated. (ii) Another solution is to specify that the successor function indeed always computes the next array, i.e. that there exists no array with the given structure between its input and output arrays, for the strict and total lexicographic order. This quantification over arrays makes the property more difficult to prove automatically than the soundness and progress properties. (iii) When the soundness and progress properties are already proved, the exhaustivity property can be validated up to some array length simply by counting the number of generated arrays and comparing it to the expected number either from a sequence of the

On-Line Encyclopedia of Integer Sequences (OEIS) [20] or from known counting formulas implemented as C functions. This work follows this third way. We have performed the validation for all the structures of the library, by increasing length up to the limit of the largest positive representable integer, beyond the number of structures one may expect to generate in a reasonable time.

We have also performed validations of a generator with another one. In the context of this work this validation is easy to implement, firstly because we can quickly obtain a reference generator by filtering and secondly because this generator and the effective one it is compared to produce arrays in the same lexicographic order whenever the latter follows the principle of suffix revision. In that case, the storage of generated arrays is not necessary: it is enough to generate arrays in parallel with each generator and then test their equality. For this validation, the generators by filtering rgf ⊂ fct, comb ⊂ fct, sorted ⊂ fct and perm ⊂ fct were used as reference implementations to validate the optimized generators rgf, comb, sorted and perm.

5   Related Work

Several techniques and tools help strengthening the trust in programs manipulating structured data. Randomized property-based testing (RPBT) consists in random generation of test data to validate given assertions about programs. RPBT has gained a lot of popularity since the appearance of QuickCheck for Haskell [7], followed by Quickcheck for Isabelle [4] and re-implementations for many programming languages, among which the C language with the tool quickcheck4c [23]. In RPBT a random data generator can be defined by filtering the output of another one, in a similar way as an exhaustive generator can be defined by filtering another exhaustive generator in BET.

A more generic approach is type targeted testing [18], wherein types are converted into queries to SMT solvers whose answers provide counterexamples. A more specific approach is contract-based testing, using contract languages. For Java programs the tools TestEra [14] and UDITA [12] automatically generate all non-isomorphic test cases within a given input size and evaluate soundness criteria, UDITA ensuring that some complex data structures are supported by the program. In case of violated soundness criteria, they produce concrete Java inputs as counterexamples, but the user has to write data generation methods and predicates. For C programs specified with ACSL, the tool StaDy [16] integrates the structural test generator PathCrawler [22] within the static analysis platform Frama-C. PathCrawler uses concrete execution and symbolic execution based on constraint solving and allows StaDy to guide the user in her proof work, showing inconsistencies between the code and the specification by the test coverage of all feasible paths of code and specification and producing counterexamples. StaDy helped us find errors in preliminary versions of some of our generators. Our work is even more specific: we provide a dedicated generator for each structure of interest. Although it requires more work, it is guaranteed to find the smallest counterexamples and is thus complementary to the other approachs.

Moreover we provide formally verified generators as building blocks for verified verification tools. To our knowledge, the deductive verification of exhaustive generators of constrained data structures has never been addressed yet.

6 Conclusion

The generation of arrays with a given structure in increasing length up to a given length can be very useful for automatically testing programs taking these arrays as inputs. Effective generation algorithms also provide interesting deductive verification problems. Therefore, we have undertaken to develop a library of structured array generators, formally specified and automatically verified. In order to reduce the cost of their specification and deductive verification, we propose general patterns for various families of generators, whose instantiation more easily yields correct programs. In particular, a pattern for the basic principle of filtering makes it possible to implement many generators from a small number of classical ones. The soundness and progress properties of these generators are automatically verified. We also provide a pattern for more effective generators, whose progress property is automatically verified. The soundness of the generators obtained by the instantiation of this pattern is more difficult to verify, but the Frama-C platform and its plugins provide significant help.

The use of deductive verification in combinatorics is not common. In this area, the most notable works are [5] and [10]. The first one specifies in ACSL and checks with Frama-C, a C function computing the conjugate of a partition of integers. The second work proves formally an enumeration of all the solutions to the n-queens problem. The formal proof is performed using the Why3 tool and the proof of exhaustivity is interactive.

Acknowledgments. The authors warmly thank J.-C. Filliâtre, J. Julliand, N. Kosmatov, C. Marché, T. Walsh and the anonymous referees for their suggestions and advice.

References

1. Arndt, J.: Matters Computational - Ideas, Algorithms, Source Code [The fxtbook] (2010). http://www.jjj.de
2. Baudin, P., Cuoq, P., Filliâtre, J.C., Marché, C., Monate, B., Moy, Y., Prevosto, V.: ACSL: ANSI/ISO C Specification Language. http://frama-c.com/acsl.html

3. Bobot, F., Filliâtre, J.C., Marché, C., Melquiond, G., Paskevich, A.: The Why3 platform 0.81 (March 2013). https://hal.inria.fr/hal-00822856
4. Bulwahn, L.: The new Quickcheck for Isabelle. In: Hawblitzel, C., Miller, D. (eds.) CPP 2012. LNCS, vol. 7679, pp. 92–108. Springer, Heidelberg (2012)
5. Butelle, F., Hivert, F., Mayero, M., Toumazet, F.: Formal proof of SCHUR conjugate function. In: Autexier, S., Calmet, J., Delahaye, D., Ion, P.D.F., Rideau, L., Rioboo, R., Sexton, A.P. (eds.) AISC 2010. LNCS, vol. 6167, pp. 158–171. Springer, Heidelberg (2010)
6. Carlier, M., Dubois, C., Gotlieb, A.: A certified constraint solver over finite domains. In: Giannakopoulou, D., Méry, D. (eds.) FM 2012. LNCS, vol. 7436, pp. 116–131. Springer, Heidelberg (2012)
7. Claessen, K., Hughes, J.: QuickCheck: a lightweight tool for random testing of Haskell programs. In: Proceedings of the Fifth ACM SIGPLAN International Conference on Functional Programming. SIGPLAN Not., vol. 35, pp. 268–279. ACM, New York (2000)
8. Correnson, L.: Qed. computing what remains to be proved. In: Badger, J.M., Rozier, K.Y. (eds.) NFM 2014. LNCS, vol. 8430, pp. 215–229. Springer, Heidelberg (2014)
9. Dijkstra, E.W.: A Discipline of Programming. In: Series in Automatic Computation, Prentice Hall, Englewood Cliffs (1976)
10. Filliâtre, J.-C.: Verifying two lines of C with Why3: an exercise in program verification. In: Joshi, R., Müller, P., Podelski, A. (eds.) VSTTE 2012. LNCS, vol. 7152, pp. 83–97. Springer, Heidelberg (2012). http://dx.doi.org/10.1007/978-3-642-27705-4
11. Floyd, R.W.: Assigning meanings to programs. In: Schwartz, J.T. (ed.) Mathematical Aspects of Computer Science. Proceedings of Symposia in Applied Mathematics, vol. 19, pp. 19–32. American Mathematical Society, Providence (1967)
12. Gligoric, M., Gvero, T., Jagannath, V., Khurshid, S., Kuncak, V., Marinov, D.: Test generation through programming in UDITA. In: Proceedings of the 32nd ACM/IEEE International Conference on Software Engineering, ICSE 2010, vol. 1, pp. 225–234. ACM, New York (2010)
13. Hoare, C.A.R.: An axiomatic basis for computer programming. Commun. ACM 12(10), 576–580 (1969)
14. Marinov, D., Khurshid, S.: TestEra: A novel framework for automated testing of Java programs. In: Proceedings of the 16th IEEE International Conference on Automated Software Engineering, pp. 22–31. IEEE Computer Society, Washington, DC (2001)
15. Paraskevopoulou, Z., Hriţcu, C.: A Coq framework for verified property based testing (2014). http://prosecco.gforge.inria.fr/personal/hritcu/publications/verified-testing-report.pdf
16. Petiot, G., Kosmatov, N., Giorgetti, A., Julliand, J.: How test generation helps software specification and deductive verification in Frama-C. In: Seidl, M., Tillmann, N. (eds.) TAP 2014. LNCS, vol. 8570, pp. 204–211. Springer, Heidelberg (2014)
17. Ruskey, F.: Combinatorial Generation Working Version (1j-CSC 425/520) (2003). http://www.1stworks.com/ref/RuskeyCombGen.pdf
18. Seidel, E.L., Vazou, N., Jhala, R.: Type targeted testing. In: Vitek, J. (ed.) ESOP 2015. LNCS, vol. 9032, pp. 812–836. Springer, Heidelberg (2015)

19. Sullivan, K.J., Yang, J., Coppit, D., Khurshid, S., Jackson, D.: Software assurance by bounded exhaustive testing. In: Proceedings of the ACM/SIGSOFT International Symposium on Software Testing and Analysis, ISSTA 2004, pp. 133–142. ACM (July 2004)
20. The OEIS Foundation Inc.: The On-Line Encyclopedia of Integer Sequences (2010). http://oeis.org
21. Weber, T.: SMT solvers: New oracles for the HOL theorem prover. International Journal on Software Tools for Technology Transfer **13**(5), 419–429 (2011)
22. Williams, N.: Abstract path testing with PathCrawler. In: Proceedings of the 5th Workshop on Automation of Software Test, AST 2010, pp. 35–42. ACM, New York (2010)
23. Zito, A.: quickcheck4c: A QuickCheck for C (2014). https://github.com/nivox/quickcheck4c

Checking UML and OCL Model Consistency: An Experience Report on a Middle-Sized Case Study

Martin Gogolla[✉], Lars Hamann, Frank Hilken, and Matthias Sedlmeier

Database Systems Group, University of Bremen, Bremen, Germany
{gogolla,lhamann,fhilken,ms}@informatik.uni-bremen.de

Abstract. This contribution reports on a middle-sized case study in which the consistency of a UML and OCL class model is checked. The class model restrictions are expressed by UML multiplicity constraints and explicit, non-trivial OCL invariants. Our approach automatically constructs a valid system state that shows that the model can be instantiated and thus proves consistency, i.e., shows that the invariants together with the multiplicity constraints are not contradictory.

1 Introduction

In the context of Model-Driven Engineering (MDE) assuring quality of software models by validation and verification approaches is of central concern. Thus testing and proving techniques and their combination is highly relevant, as several recent case studies from different domains and with different methodological aims demonstrate [1–3,9,11]. The work done here is carried out in the context of the design tool USE (UML-based Specification Environment) developed for UML (Unified Modeling Language) and OCL (Object Constraints Language). USE [5,7,8] is employed here for automatically checking the consistency (instantiability) of a UML class model enriched by OCL invariants. USE contains (what we call) a 'model validator' that constructs a system state on the basis of a configuration, which describes a search space for possible system states [10]. With this functionality and on the basis of a transformation into the relational logic of Kodkod [12], it is possible to check the UML and OCL model for consistency, for implications, for invariant independence and for possible completions of partially described system states, among other possible uses.

Here, we discuss a middle-sized case study with complex OCL constraints. We show that it is feasible to automatically check consistency for middle-sized UML and OCL models. Thus, by building a *test* case, i.e., an object model that instantiates the class model, we *prove* a property, namely model consistency or instantiability. The case study is a transformation model that describes the syntax (schemata) and the semantics (states) of the ER (Entity-Relationship) and the relational data model as well as the transformation between these two data models as the object model in Fig. 1 and the class model in Fig. 2 sketches. The notion 'semantics' refers here to those parts (classes and associations) of

© Springer International Publishing Switzerland 2015
J.C. Blanchette and N. Kosmatov (Eds.): TAP 2015, LNCS 9154, pp. 129–136, 2015.
DOI: 10.1007/978-3-319-21215-9_8

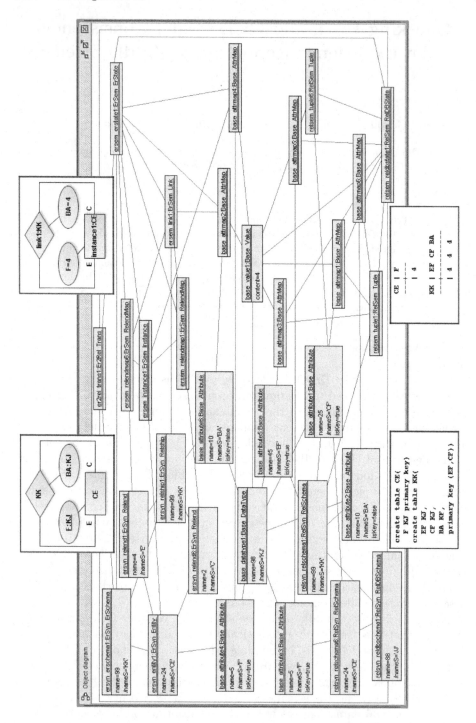

Fig. 1. Generated instantiation (object model) in UML and domain-specific notation

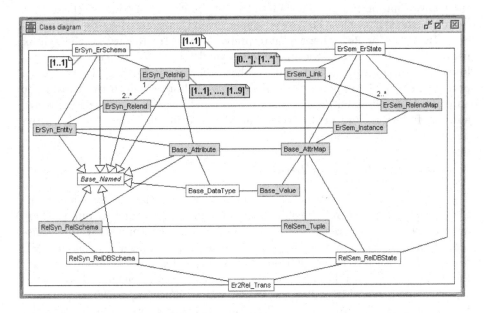

Fig. 2. Case study class model with model validator configurations indicated

Num Objects	Num Links	USE Response	Times [in milliseconds]		
			Translation	Translation	Solving
1..1	0..*	trivially unsat	358 ms	202 ms	0 ms
1..2	0..*	unsat	328 ms	811 ms	31 ms
1..3	0..*	unsat	359 ms	3292 ms	827 ms
1..4	0..*	sat	359 ms	11092 ms	8205 ms
1..5	0..*	sat	327 ms	31231 ms	45022 ms
1..6	0..*	sat	328 ms	73445 ms	8533 ms
1..7	0..*	sat	327 ms	158839 ms	231053 ms
1..8	0..*	sat	343 ms	301907 ms	149480 ms
1..9	0..*	sat	343 ms	557427 ms	459233 ms
1..1	1..*	trivially unsat	312 ms	203 ms	0 ms
1..2	1..*	unsat	328 ms	827 ms	16 ms
1..3	1..*	unsat	343 ms	3338 ms	78 ms
1..4	1..*	unsat	340 ms	10951 ms	219 ms
1..5	1..*	unsat	343 ms	30857 ms	3572 ms
1..6	1..*	sat	375 ms	74412 ms	134878 ms
1..7	1..*	sat	343 ms	157264 ms	17628 ms
1..8	1..*	sat	394 ms	301315 ms	120432 ms
1..9	1..*	sat	375 ms	551758 ms	607059 ms

Fig. 3. Applied 18 model validator configurations and USE results

the transformation model that handle the interpretation of 'syntax' classes; for example, the syntax class `Entity` is 'semantically' interpreted by the semantics class `Instance` or `RelSchema` is interpreted by `Tuple`. Regarding the syntax part, you see in Fig. 1 in the upper left a single (tiny) ER schema and in the lower left an equivalent relational database schema. Regarding the semantics part, you see in the upper right a single (tiny) ER state and in the lower right an equivalent relational database state. More details will be mentioned below, and the full UML and OCL model can be found in [4]. Later, Fig. 1 will be discussed further, as well.

2   Case Study Class Model

The case study is a transformation model. A transformation model is a descriptive model where the relationship between source and target is purely characterized by the (source,target) object model pairs determined by the transformation. A transformation model consists in our approach of a plain UML class model with restricting OCL invariants. Typically, there is an anchor class for the source model (class `ErSyn_ErSchema` in Fig. 2), an anchor class for the target model (class `RelSyn_RelDBSchema`), and a connecting class for the transformation (class `Er2Rel_Trans`). There are OCL invariants for restricting the source metamodel, for the target metamodel, and for the transformation. In this example, the transformation model consists of a single class and associations connecting the syntax and semantics parts.

We have studied parts of the case study before [6], however we have not yet handled the semantics parts from the right side of the class model with automatic techniques. In that earlier work, the class model for the syntax and the transformation parts included 10 classes, 11 associations, 22 invariants, and 6 OCL operations. Now, by including also the semantics part, we have 18 classes, 34 associations, 59 invariants, and 10 OCL operations. Thus the complexity of the case study has been more than doubled. In formal terms the OCL invariant coverage and their complexity grew from factor 247 to 775 (for details about the absolute numbers see [4], if needed; however, what is relevant here is the relationship between the numbers). The numbers indicate the coverage of the class model by the invariants and state the number of classes, attributes and associations touched by the constraints. The numbers are therefore one indication for the complexity of the invariants.

There are up to 6 nested quantifiers as, for example, in the invariant `Er2Rel_Trans::forTupleExistsOneInstanceXorLink` (see Fig.4 or [4] for more details, if needed). In the semantics part (not covered in [6]) the constraints also guarantee for the states the validity of key conditions (see for example `RelSem_Tuple::keyMapUnique` in Fig.4 or [4], if needed).

3   Model Validator Configuration

A model validator configuration determines the population of classes, associations, and attributes: (a) One specifies a mandatory upper and an optional lower

```
-- Entity-Relationship model syntax: Within one Entity, different
-- Attributes have different names

context self:ErSyn_Entity inv uniqueAttributeNamesWithinEntity:
  self.attribute->forAll(a1,a2 | a1.name=a2.name implies a1=a2)

-- Relational model semantics: Two different Tuples of one RelSchema
-- can be distinguished in every RelDBState where both Tuples occur by
-- a key Attribute of the RelSchema

context self:RelSem_Tuple inv keyMapUnique:
  RelSem_Tuple.allInstances->forAll(self2 |
    (self<>self2 and self.relSchema=self2.relSchema) implies
    self.relDBState->intersection(self2.relDBState)->forAll(s |
      self.relSchema.key()->exists(ka |
        self.applyAttr(s,ka)<>self2.applyAttr(s,ka))))

-- Transformation: For every Tuple in a RelDBState (1) there is either
-- exactly one Instance such that for every attrMap of the Tuple there
-- is exactly one attrMap in the Instance holding the same information
-- or (2) there is exactly one link such that for every attrMap of
-- Tuple the following holds: (A) if the attrMap belongs not to a key
-- Attribute, there is exactly one attrMap in the Link holding the
-- same information, and (B) if the attrMap belongs to a key
-- Attribute, there is exactly one RelendMap in the Link and exactly
-- one attrMap of the RelendMap such that the attrMap from the Tuple
-- and the attrMap from the Link hold the same information

context self:Er2Rel_Trans inv forTupleExistsOneInstanceXorLink:
  self.relDBState->forAll(relSt | self.erState->one(erSt |
    relSt.tuple->forAll(t | erSt.instance->one(i |
      t.attrMap->forAll(amRel | i.attrMap->one(amEr |
        amEr.attribute.name=amRel.attribute.name and
        amEr.value=amRel.value)))
    xor
    erSt.link->one(l | t.attrMap->forAll(amRel |
      ( amRel.attribute.isKey=false implies
        l.attrMap->one(amEr |
          amEr.attribute.name=amRel.attribute.name and
          amEr.value=amRel.value) )
      and
      ( amRel.attribute.isKey=true implies
        l.relendMap->one(rm |
          rm.instance.attrMap->select(amEr | amEr.attribute.isKey)->
          one(amEr |
            amRel.attribute.name =
              plus(times10(rm.relend.name),amEr.attribute.name)
          and amRel.value=amEr.value))))))))
```

Fig. 4. Typical OCL invariants (3 from 59) in the transformation model

bound for each class determining the maximal and minimal number of objects in the expected system state, (b) an optional lower and optional upper bound for each association determining the number of links, and (c) a finite value set for each attribute; attribute values may be determined by finite datatype value sets. The purpose of a configuration is to determine a finite search space for object models (system states) matching the class model and the constraints.

For proving consistency we have fixed some classes and associations in the applied configurations: All 'white' classes in Fig. 2 are fixed to have exactly one object (lower and upper bound '1'), and the associations between these classes are required to have exactly one link. The remaining 'grey' classes (and the associations with at least one participating 'grey' class) have been checked with a fixed lower bound and a varying upper bound: for the classes lower bound '1' and upper bounds equal to a single integer from '1, 2, ..., 9' have been used; for the associations the bounds '0..*' and '1..*' have been employed. One finds the results of running the model validator with these 18 configurations in Fig. 3.

Concerning the data types and attributes, the used configurations employ the range 0..99 for the data type `Integer` and the attributes `Base_Named::name:Integer` and `Base_Value::value:Integer`. Thus a name (for example, for an entity or for an attribute) is handled by the model validator as an `Integer` literal. In order to present a name more intuitively as a `String` literal, we encode the ten digits as letters: 0↦'A', 1↦'B', 2↦'C', 3↦'D', 4↦'E', 5↦'F', 6↦'G', 7↦'H', 8↦'J', 9↦'K'. This encoding is realized in terms of an operation and the derived attribute `Base_Named::nameS:String`. For example, the `Entity` object in the top left of Fig. 1 has `name=24` and `nameS='CE'`. The literal 4 occurring as the value of the `F` attribute in the top right of the figure has been chosen by the model validator from the mentioned range 0..99.

The solution found by the model validator when employing the 1..6/1..* configuration from Fig. 3 is pictured as an object model in Fig. 1. It is an automatically constructed test case proving model consistency on the basis of the stated configuration. The (tiny) test case covers an ER schema, an ER state, a relational database schema, and a relational database state.

4   Tool Response and Translation and Solving Times

The table in Fig. 3 gives an overview on performed experiments, i.e., 18 configurations with which the model validator has been executed (more configurations have been tested, but they are not documented here). The first and second column determine the configuration's setting for the object number bounds (in the 'grey' classes) and the link number bounds in the connected associations. The third column shows the three different responses made by the model validator: (a) 'trivially unsat' means that the configuration was recognized to be not instantiable by only analyzing the specified bounds; in this class model (see Fig. 2), for example, each ER relationship ('Relship') must be connected to at least 2 relationship end ('Relend') objects, and this cannot be satisfied by just allowing one 'Relend' object; (b) 'unsat' means that no instantiation can be found; and (c) 'sat' says that an instantiation has been found within the bounds and constructed as an object model. The three time specifications refer to the time needed (a) to translate the class model including the invariants into the relational logic of Kodkod, (b) to translate the relational formula and configuration into SAT (this step is performed by Kodkod), and (c) to solve the translated relational formula by the underlying SAT solver. For the experiments we have used the MiniSat solver.

The difference between the association bounds '0..*' and '1..*' concerns the instantiation. In the first case, not all associations must have links, whereas in the second case, links must be present for all associations: In the first case ER schemata without relationship attributes are allowed, whereas in the second case ER relationships must have attributes, i.e., the association between 'Relship' and 'Attribute' must be instantiated.

- In the '1..*' case, the restriction about the relationship attributes carries over to the relational data model and to the state part. In the '1..*' case, 'ErSem_Link' objects must have attribute values that are described by 'AttrMap' objects; therefore enough 'AttrMap' objects must be present (here, at least 6 'AttrMap' objects). The solution is only found after the object bounds have been set to '1..6' (see Fig. 1 showing six 'AttrMap' objects).
- In the '0..*' case, the solution is already found earlier when the object bounds are set to '1..4', because fewer 'AttrMap' objects are needed when there are no relationship attributes.

As a closing remark in the technical sections, let us consider the transformation model from a different perspective. Up to now, we have discussed the transformation model as transforming the ER model into the relational model, basically going in Fig. 2 from the upper part to the lower part. But formally, this direction is not expressed anywhere in the model in terms of the associations which can be navigated in both directions. One may look at the complete model also as a transformation from syntax to semantics, i.e., going in Fig. 2 from the left part to the right part.

5 Conclusion

We have shown that it is possible to automatically prove properties like consistency for UML and OCL models for non-trivial models in an automatic way. In the future, we want to carry over these results to other properties of UML and OCL models like invariant independence or implications from the stated constraints. The strength of the model validator has to be improved in order to be able to handle larger solution spaces, i.e., we want to allow more flexible configuration bounds. Better and more detailed feedback from the model validator in case of unsatisfiability should be given more attention. Larger case studies, like for example the UML metamodel, should be considered in order to show that the combination of tests and proofs can be applied for complex and real-world models.

References

1. Bishop, P.G., Bloomfield, R.E., Cyra, L.: Combining testing and proof to gain high assurance in software: a case study. In: 24th IEEE Int. Symp. Software Reliability (ISSRE), pp. 248–257. IEEE (2013)
2. Brucker, A.D., Feliachi, A., Nemouchi, Y., Wolff, B.: Test program generation for a microprocessor - a case study. In: Veanes, M., Viganò, L. (eds.) TAP 2013. LNCS, vol. 7942, pp. 76–95. Springer, Heidelberg (2013)
3. Dierkes, M.: Combining test and proof in MBAT - an aerospace case study. In: Pires, L.F., Hammoudi, S., Filipe, J., das Neves, R.C. (eds.) Proc. 2nd Int. Conf. Modelsward, pp. 636–644. SciTePress (2014)
4. Gogolla, M., Hamann, L., Hilken, F., Sedlmeier, M.: Additional Material for Checking UML and OCL Model Consistency (2015). http://www.db.informatik.uni-bremen.de/publications/intern/consis-casestudy-addon.pdf
5. Gogolla, M., Büttner, F., Richters, M.: USE: A UML-Based Specification Environment for Validating UML and OCL. Science of Computer Programming **69**, 27–34 (2007)
6. Gogolla, M., Hamann, L., Hilken, F.: Checking transformation model properties with a UML and OCL model validator. In: Amrani, M., et al. (eds.) Proc. 3rd Int. VOLT Workshop. CEUR Proceedings, vol. 1325, pp. 16–25 (2014)
7. Gogolla, M., Hamann, L., Hilken, F., Kuhlmann, M., France, R.B.: From application models to filmstrip models: an approach to automatic validation of model dynamics. In: Fill, H., Karagiannis, D., Reimer, U. (eds.) Proc. Modellierung (MODELLIERUNG 2014), GI, LNI 225, pp. 273–288 (2014)
8. Hamann, L., Hofrichter, O., Gogolla, M.: Towards integrated structure and behavior modeling with OCL. In: France, R.B., Kazmeier, J., Breu, R., Atkinson, C. (eds.) MODELS 2012. LNCS, vol. 7590, pp. 235–251. Springer, Heidelberg (2012)
9. Kosmatov, N., Lemerre, M., Alec, C.: A case study on verification of a cloud hypervisor by proof and structural testing. In: Seidl, M., Tillmann, N. (eds.) TAP 2014. LNCS, vol. 8570, pp. 158–164. Springer, Heidelberg (2014)
10. Kuhlmann, M., Gogolla, M.: From UML and OCL to relational logic and back. In: France, R.B., Kazmeier, J., Breu, R., Atkinson, C. (eds.) MODELS 2012. LNCS, vol. 7590, pp. 415–431. Springer, Heidelberg (2012)
11. Ledru, Y., du Bousquet, L., Dadeau, F., Allouti, F.: A Case Study in Matching Test and Proof Coverage. ENTCS **190**(2), 73–84 (2007)
12. Torlak, E., Jackson, D.: Kodkod: a relational model finder. In: Grumberg, O., Huth, M. (eds.) TACAS 2007. LNCS, vol. 4424, pp. 632–647. Springer, Heidelberg (2007)

A Constraint Optimisation Model for Analysis of Telecommunication Protocol Logs

Olga Grinchtein[1]([⊠]), Mats Carlsson[2], and Justin Pearson[3]

[1] Ericsson AB, Stockholm, Sweden
olga.grinchtein@ericsson.com
[2] SICS, Stockholm, Sweden
Mats.Carlsson@sics.se
[3] Uppsala University, Uppsala, Sweden
justin.pearson@it.uu.se

Abstract. Testing a telecommunication protocol often requires protocol log analysis. A protocol log is a sequence of messages with timestamps. Protocol log analysis involves checking that the content of messages and timestamps are correct with respect to the protocol specification. We model a protocol specification using constraint programming (MiniZinc), and we present an approach where a constraint solver is used to perform protocol log analysis. Our case study is the Public Warning System service, which is a part of the Long Term Evolution (LTE) 4G standard. We were able to analyse logs containing more than 3000 messages with more than 4000 errors.

Keywords: Telecommunication protocol · Testing · Constraint programming

1 Introduction

In this paper we investigate the use of constraint programming to implement a part of a test harness for equipment involved in the Long Term Evolution (LTE) 4G standard [1,2], in particular the broadcast of public warning messages [3]. The protocol specification includes a number of messages with complex timing requirements between them. The contribution of the paper is a new approach to analyse the correctness of protocol logs. The main novelty is that we use constraint programming [4] to directly model the protocol and use a constraint solver as a test harness in order to find incorrect behavior in logs. Some results of this paper appeared in the workshop paper [5] presented as work in progress.

In this work, we model a part of the protocol directly in the MiniZinc [6] language (see Section 2). This approach requires a script that reads a protocol log that is a plain text, creates arrays of MiniZinc parameters, and assigns values to the parameters according to the information provided in the log. We also have variables that represent correct timestamps of some messages. There are parameters such as delays of messages for which we know only boundary values,

J.C. Blanchette and N. Kosmatov (Eds.): TAP 2015, LNCS 9154, pp. 137–154, 2015.
DOI: 10.1007/978-3-319-21215-9_9

which adds complexity to the model. The complexity of the model also depends on the number of messages, and we use a technique to partition timestamps of messages into classes. Protocol log analysis in this case is an optimisation problem. We use a constraint solver to find the optimal solution minimising the number of unsatisfied constraints.

The rest of this paper is structured as follows: in Section 2 we give a very brief overview of constraint programming and MiniZinc; in Section 3 we explain main steps of the approach by an example; in Section 4 we give the necessary telecommunication background to understand the case study; in Section 5 we give in some detail the constraint model that is required to test the protocol logs for correctness; in Section 6 we describe optimisation technique to reduce complexity of the model; and in Section 7 we present experimental results.

2   MiniZinc and Constraint Programming

Constraint Programming [4] (CP) is a framework for modelling and solving combinatorial problems including verification and optimisation tasks. A constraint problem is specified as a set of *decision variables* that have to be assigned values so that the given constraints on these variables are satisfied, and optionally so that a given objective function is minimised or maximised. Constraint solving is based on the constructive search for such an assignment. Constraint propagation plays an important role: a constraint is not only a declarative modelling device, but has an associated propagator, which is an algorithm to prune the search space by removing values that cannot participate in a solution to that constraint. The removal can trigger other propagators, and this process continues until a fixpoint is reached, at which time the next assignment choice must be made.

MiniZinc [6] is a constraint modelling language, which has gained popularity recently due to its high expressivity and large number of available solvers that support it. It also contains many useful modelling abstractions such as quantifiers, sets, arrays, and a rich set of global constraints. MiniZinc is compiled into FlatZinc, a constraint solving language which specifies a set of built-in constraints that a constraint solver must support. The compilation process is based on flattening by introducing auxiliary variables, substituting them for nested subexpressions, and selecting the appropriate FlatZinc constraints. Common sub-expression elimination plays an important role as well. All the constraints presented in this paper are shown in a form that is very close to their MiniZinc version. We use fzn-gecode, the Gecode FlatZinc back-end.

An application of constraint programming to testing in industry is reported in [7] and [8]. In [9] constraint solving is used to derive test cases that distinguish between a piece of code and a mutation of that piece of code. More recently there has been a lot of work on using recent advances in constraint programming applied to white box testing of Java or C [10,11]. In [12] constraint programming is used to generate protocol logs to test telecommunication test harness.

3   Overview of the Approach by an Example

We analyse protocol logs that consists of a sequence of messages with timestamps. An abstract sequence of protocol messages is shown in Figure 1. This is not a real log, but we use it to illustrate the approach. The radio base station transmits three messages M1, M2 and M3 to the mobile phone. Message M1 does not contain any parameters. Message M2 contains the parameter y and message M3 contains the parameters z_1 and z_2. The first message M1 the mobile phone reads with some delay, and we introduce decision variable *delay*, which is between 0 and 100 milliseconds.

$10:00:00.000$ M1$\{\}$ $10:00:01.600$ M3$\{z_1 = 1, z_2 = \text{aaba}\}$
$10:00:00.080$ M2$\{y = 80\}$ $10:00:01.920$ M3$\{z_1 = 2, z_2 = \text{abab}\}$
$10:00:00.400$ M3$\{z_1 = 1, z_2 = \text{aaba}\}$ $10:00:02.900$ M1$\{\}$
$10:00:00.720$ M3$\{z_1 = 2, z_2 = \text{abab}\}$ $10:00:03.120$ M3$\{z_1 = 1, z_2 = \text{aaba}\}$
$10:00:01.040$ M3$\{z_1 = 4, z_2 = \text{aaaa}\}$ $10:00:03.440$ M3$\{z_1 = 2, z_2 = \text{abab}\}$
$10:00:01.450$ M1$\{\}$ $10:00:04.350$ M1$\{\}$
$10:00:01.580$ M2$\{y = 320\}$

Fig. 1. Sequence of messages in a log

We introduce three arrays of parameters M1Time, M2Time and M3Time that represent timestamps in milliseconds since the beginning of the log of corresponding messages in the log. In this example they will have the values

$$\text{M1Time} = [0, 1450, 2900, 4350]$$
$$\text{M2Time} = [80, 1580]$$
$$\text{M3Time} = [400, 720, 1040, 1600, 1920, 3120, 3440]$$

In the example the parameter y can take two values and parameters z_1 and z_2 can take four values. We introduce three arrays of parameters M2y, M3z1 and M3z2 which represent content of the messages in the log. In this example they will have the values

$$\text{M2y} = [1, 2]$$
$$\text{M3z1} = [1, 2, 4, 1, 2, 1, 2]$$
$$\text{M3z2} = [1, 2, 4, 1, 2, 1, 2]$$

In the example there are two cases in the transmission of messages M3 by the radio base station. After each message M1 the radio base station transmits several messages M3. After a M1 message, which is transmitted within 1500 milliseconds, the M3 messages follow with z_1 equal to $1, 2, 3$ and 4. After messages M1, which are transmitted after 1500 milliseconds, the messages M3 follow with z_1 equal to 1 and 2. Between the two messages M1 should be the M3 messages with all possible values of the parameter z_1. This can be captured with the constraint

$(\forall 1 \leq i \leq 3)$
$\quad ((\texttt{M1Time}_i < 1500 - delay \wedge$
$\quad (\forall 1 \leq j \leq 4)(\exists 1 \leq k \leq 7)\texttt{M1Time}_i < \texttt{M3Time}_k < \texttt{M1Time}_{i+1} \wedge \texttt{M3z1}_k = j)$
$\quad \vee$
$\quad (\texttt{M1Time}_i \geq 1500 - delay \wedge$
$\quad (\forall 1 \leq j \leq 2)(\exists 1 \leq k \leq 7)\texttt{M1Time}_i < \texttt{M3Time}_k < \texttt{M1Time}_{i+1} \wedge \texttt{M3z1}_k = j))$

where two disjuncts in the constraint represent two cases of transmission of messages M3. If disjuntcs are not satisfiable, then we have errors in the log. We introduce the Boolean decision variable $M3contentinc_i$ equal to 1 indicates an error in the log and rewrite the constraint as

$(\forall 1 \leq i \leq 3)$
$\quad ((\texttt{M1Time}_i < 1500 - delay \wedge$
$\quad (\forall 1 \leq j \leq 4)(\exists 1 \leq k \leq 7)\texttt{M1Time}_i < \texttt{M3Time}_k < \texttt{M1Time}_{i+1} \wedge \texttt{M3z1}_k = j)$
$\quad \vee$
$\quad (\texttt{M1Time}_i \geq 1500 - delay \wedge$
$\quad (\forall 1 \leq j \leq 2)(\exists 1 \leq k \leq 7)\texttt{M1Time}_i < \texttt{M3Time}_k < \texttt{M1Time}_{i+1} \wedge \texttt{M3z1}_k = j))$
$\quad \leftrightarrow M3contentinc_i = 0$

After defining constraints we can use constraint solver to find solution by minimising sum of Boolean decision variables in the array *M3contentinc*. In the example from Figure 1, regardless of the value of *delay*, we have $M3contentinc_1 = 1$, since there is no message M3 with the parameter $z_1 = 3$ between first and second messages M1. However, if $delay = 20$, then $\texttt{M1Time}_2 = 1450 < 1500 - delay$ and $M3contentinc_2 = 1$, since there are no messages M3 with z_1 equal to 3 and 4 between second and third messages M1. Thus, the minimum number of errors is one, while *delay* is between 50 and 100. To analyse real protocol logs, we also need to define constraints on timestamps and content of messages, but they are more complex. We present such a constraint model in Section 5.

4   Public Warning System for LTE

In our case study we use a constraint solver to test a part of Public Warning System (PWS). The Public Warning System is a technology that broadcasts Warning Notifications to multiple users in case of disasters or other emergencies.

4.1   E-UTRAN Architecture

LTE (Long Term Evolution) [1] is the global standard for the fourth generation of mobile networks (4G). Radio Access of LTE is called evolved UMTS Terrestrial Radio Access Network (E-UTRAN)[2]. A E-UTRAN consists of eNodeBs (eNBs), which is just another name for radio base stations. Our setup consists of an eNB, a simulated Mobility Management Entity (MME) that forwards PWS messages to the eNB, and some simulated User Equipment (UE). The functions of these entities are described in more detail below.

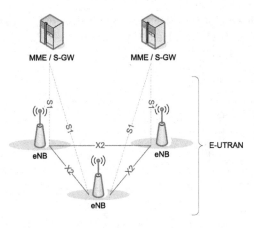

Fig. 2. E-UTRAN architecture [2]

An eNB connects to User Equipment via the air interface. The eNBs may be interconnected with each other by means of the X2 interface. The eNBs are also connected by means of the S1 interface to the EPC (Evolved Packet Core), more specifically to the MME (Mobility Management Entity) by means of the S1-MME interface, and to the Serving Gateway (S-GW) by means of the S1-U interface [13]. The MME performs mobility management; security control; distribution of paging messages; ciphering and integrity protection of signaling; and provides support for PWS message transmission. S-GW is responsible for packet routing and forwarding. The functions of eNBs include radio resource management; IP header compression and encryption, selection of MME at UE attachment; routing of user plane data towards S-GW; scheduling and transmission of paging messages and broadcast information; and measurement and reporting configuration for mobility and scheduling [1]. An eNB is responsible for the scheduling and transmission of PWS messages received from MME.

4.2   The Earthquake and Tsunami Warning System

The earthquake and Tsunami warning system (ETWS) is a part of PWS that delivers Primary and Secondary Warning Notifications to the UEs within an area where Warning Notifications are broadcast [3]. We show in Figure 3 the network structure of PWS architecture.

Fig. 3. PWS architecture [14]

The Cell broadcast Entity (CBE) can be located at the content provider and sends messages to the Cell Broadcast Center. The Cell Broadcast Center (CBC) is part of EPC and connected to the MME.

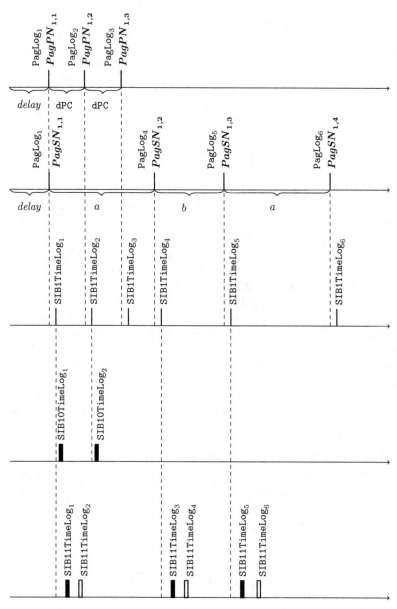

Fig. 4. An example of acquiring primary and secondary notification messages by UE

Table 1. Parameters and *decision variables* in the models

delay	Time difference between time when eNB starts to transmit primary notification and/or secondary notification and the time when UE reads first paging message.
nPrim	Number of primary notifications.
delayPN	An array of timestamps of primary notifications. The size of the array is nPrim.
nSec	Number of secondary notifications.
delaySN	An array of timestamps of secondary notifications. The size of the array is nSec.
dPC	The length of a paging cycle.
ndPC	The number of paging cycles, which is configured in eNB.
PagPN	An array of timestamps of paging messages of primary notification. The size of the array is ndPC · nPrim
nBR	An array of NumberofBroadcastRequested + 1 of secondary notifications. The size of the array is nSec.
nBRmax	Maximum number in array nBR.
PagSN	An array of timestamps of paging messages of secondary notifications. The size of the array is nBRmax · nSec.
PagLog	An array of timestamps of paging messages from the log. The size of the array is nPagLog.
rPer	An array of lengths of repetition periods. The size of the array is nSec.
SIB1TimeLog	An array of timestamps of SIB1 messages from the log. The size of the array is nSIB1Log.
SIB1TypeLog	An array of values from 0 to 3 that indicate whether SIB1 messages contain schedulingInfoList for SIB10 and/or SIB11 messages. The size of the array is nSIB1Log.
SIB10TimeLog	An array of timestamps of System Information messages with SIB10 from the log. The size of the array is nSIB10Log
SIB11TimeLog	An array of timestamps of System Information messages with SIB11 from the log. The size of the array is nSIB11Log.
siPerSIB10	Periodicity of SIB10.
siPerSIB11	Periodicity of SIB11.
nSeg	An array of number of segments in secondary notifications.

The CBE sends emergency information to the CBC. The CBC identifies which MMEs need to be contacted and sends a Write-Replace Warning Request message containing the warning message to be broadcast to the MMEs. The MME sends a Write-Replace Warning Confirm message that indicates to the CBC that the MME has started to distribute the warning message to eNBs. The MME forwards Write-Replace Warning Request to eNBs in the delivery area. The eNB determines the cells in which the message is to be broadcast based on information received from MME [14]. If a Warning Type IE (information element) is included in a Write-Replace Warning Request message, then the eNB broadcasts a Primary Notification. If Warning Message Contents IE is included in a Write-Replace Warning Request message, then the eNB schedules a broadcast of the warning message according to the value of Repetition Period IE (rPer) and Number of Broadcasts Requested IE (NumberofBroadcastRequested) [15]. To inform a UE about the presence of an ETWS primary notification and/or ETWS secondary notification, a paging message is used. A UE attempts to read paging messages at least once every defaultPagingCycle (dPC). If a UE receives a Paging message including an ETWS-indication, then it starts receiving ETWS primary notification or ETWS secondary notification according to schedulingInfoList contained in SystemInformationBlockType1 (SIB1). ETWS primary notification is contained in SystemInformationBlockType10 (SIB10) and ETWS secondary notification is contained in SystemInformationBlockType11 (SIB11). The messages SIB10 and SIB11 are transmitted in System Information (SI) messages with different periodicity. If a secondary notification contains a large message, then it is divided into several segments, which are transmitted in System Information messages.

In Table 1 we present a description of some parameters that are constants and *decision variables* used in models. Parameters, which represent the content of SIB10 and SIB11 messages, are omitted. In Figure 4 we show an example of a correct reception of paging messages, SIB1, SIB10 and SIB11 messages of the first warning message by UE, where $a = (\lfloor rPer_1/dPC \rfloor + 1) \cdot dPC$, $\lfloor rPer_1/dPC \rfloor$ is the number of whole paging cycles during a repetition period, $b = \lfloor rPer_1/dPC \rfloor \cdot dPC$, $ndPC = 3$, $nBR_1 = 4$ and $nSeg_1 = 2$. Horizontal lines in Figure 4 represent timelines. The first timeline is used to represent timestamps of paging messages of primary notification, and the second timeline is used to represent timestamps of paging messages of secondary notification. Vertical lines in first and second timelines represent timestamps of paging messages; vertical lines in the third timeline represent timestamps of SIB1 messages; rectangles in the fourth timeline represent timestamps of SIB10 messages; and rectangles in the fifth timeline represent timestamps of SIB11 messages. Unfilled and filled rectangles in the fifth timeline indicate two different message segments.

4.3   Replacement of Warning Messages

If a warning message is being broadcast in a certain area and the eNB receives a Write-Replace Warning Request message with an identity which is different from

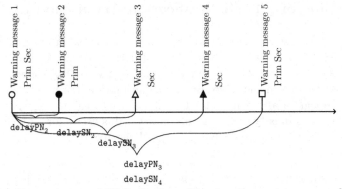

(a) Transmission of Write-Replace Warning Request messages by MME to eNB. Different shapes on the top of the vertical lines represent different warning messages.

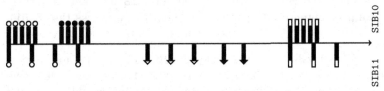

(b) Transmission of primary and secondary notifications for each warning message by eNB to UE. A shape on top (bottom) of a rectangle shows to which warning message SIB10 (SIB11) message corresponds.

Fig. 5. Replacement of Write-Replace Warning Request messages

the warning messages being broadcast, the eNB schedules the received warning message for broadcast for that area. Figure 5 illustrates the replacement of warning messages. Figure 5(a) shows timestamps of five Write-Replace Warning request messages (Warning message 1-5) which contain the content of primary notifications (Prim) and/or secondary notifications (Sec). For example Warning message 1 contains the content of primary and secondary notifications and Warning message 2 contains the content of primary notification. The horizontal line is the timeline and vertical lines represent timestamps of warning messages. Warning message 2 is received by eNB $delayPN_2$ milliseconds after Warning message 1 was received. Warning message 5 is received $delayPN_3 = delaySN_4$ milliseconds after Warning message 1 is received. In Figure 5(b) vertical rectangles represent timestamps of SIB10 and SIB11 messages which eNB transmit to UE. It can happen that SIB10 (SIB11) messages from a previous warning message continues to transmit after the new warning message is received, if the new message does not contain a content of primary (secondary) notification. For example, when Warning message 2 is received, eNB continues transmit SIB11 messages from Warning message 1 and start to transmit new SIB10 messages.

5   Modelling of ETWS Notification Acquisition by UE

Our goal is to analyse a UE protocol log that contains paging messages, SIB1, SIB10, and SIB11 messages. We defined a Model that consists of constraints on timestamps and the content of these messages. We divided the Model into three submodels, each of them checks for different information in a protocol log. Some constraints appear in all submodels. The division into submodels was made in order to reduce complexity of the overall model and is useful for a quick check of partial information in case when Model takes a long time to solve. The submodels are

- PagingModel that checks that the log contains all required paging messages, and that the number and timestamps of paging messages are correct
- SIB1Model that checks that the log contains all required SIB1 messages, and that the schedulingInfoList is correct
- PrimSecModel checks that the log contains SIB10 messages with correct timestamps, content and identity numbers. It also checks that SIB11 messages have correct timestamps, content, segments and identity numbers.

The recommended values for dPC, siPerSIB10, siPerSIB11 and rPer satisfy constraints dPC > siPerSIB10, rPer > siPerSIB11 and rPer > dPC, which we assume in all our models. Other values are possible, but would require different testing strategies. We also assume that the first message in the log is a paging message and we assign value 0 to $PagLog_1$. We assign to the array SIB10TimeLog of timestamps of SIB10 messages, and to the array SIB11TimeLog of timestamps of SIB11 messages values, which are time differences between timestamps of the messages in the log and the timestamp of the first paging message in the log. The main ingredient of the model is *delay*, which is an integer decision variable in the model that can be between 0 and dPC. It represents the delay of first paging message. We use binary search as a search strategy for *delay*. We use arrays of Boolean decision variables which are equal to 1 if the corresponding constraints are unsatisfiable. Then we search for a solution that minimises *objective* that is the sum of the Boolean variables.

5.1   Delays of Warning Messages as Decision Variables

The arrays delayPN and delaySN represent timestamps of warning messages sent to eNB by a MME. Since these timestamps are constant and some variable delay can occur, we introduce arrays of decision variables *delayPN50* and *delaySN50* which represent extra delay of warning messages. We assume that delays are less than 50 milliseconds.

Simply introducing a decision variable between 0 and 50 as an extra delay will increase complexity of the problem drastically. When there is extra delay some paging messages, SIB1, SIB10 and SIB11 could belong to the previous warning message. Thus, we can set values to extra delay $delayPN50_i$ by calculating distances between timestamps of SIB1, SIB10 and SIB11 messages and timestamp

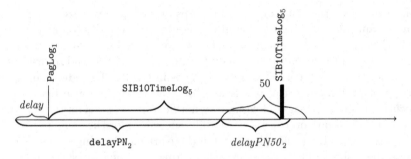

Fig. 6. Illustration of $\texttt{setdelayPN50}(2, \texttt{nSIB10Log}, \texttt{SIB10TimeLog})$

of ith warning message and choose distance with less than 50 milliseconds as a value for $delayPN50_i$. We constrain $delayPN50$ by expression:

$$
\begin{aligned}
&(\forall 1 \leq i \leq \texttt{nPrim}) \\
&\quad (delayPN50_i = 0 \\
&\quad \vee \\
&\quad (\texttt{dPC} - ((\texttt{delayPN}_i - delay) \quad \text{mod} \quad \texttt{dPC}) < 50 \wedge \\
&\qquad delayPN50_i = \texttt{dPC} - ((\texttt{delayPN}_i - delay) \quad \text{mod} \quad \texttt{dPC}) + 1) \\
&\quad \vee \\
&\quad \texttt{setdelayPN50}(i, \texttt{nSIB1Log}, \texttt{SIB1TimeLog}) \\
&\quad \vee \\
&\quad \texttt{setdelayPN50}(i, \texttt{nSIB10Log}, \texttt{SIB10TimeLog}) \\
&\quad \vee \\
&\quad \texttt{setdelayPN50}(i, \texttt{nSIB11Log}, \texttt{SIB11TimeLog}))
\end{aligned}
\tag{1}
$$

where

$$
\begin{aligned}
&\texttt{setdelayPN50}(i, k, \texttt{TimeLog}) = \\
&(\exists 1 \leq j \leq k) \\
&\quad (0 \leq \texttt{TimeLog}_j - \texttt{delayPN}_i + delay < 50 \wedge \\
&\qquad delayPN50_i = \texttt{TimeLog}_j - \texttt{delayPN}_i + delay + 1)
\end{aligned}
\tag{2}
$$

Figure 6 shows illustration of $\texttt{setdelayPN50}(2, \texttt{nSIB10Log}, \texttt{SIB10TimeLog})$, where $delayPN50_2 = \texttt{SIB10TimeLog}_5 - \texttt{delayPN}_2 + delay + 1$.

The array $delaySN50$ is defined in a similar way. Then we replace in the model $\texttt{delayPN}_i$ by $\texttt{delayPN}_i + delayPN50_i$ and $\texttt{delaySN}_i$ by $\texttt{delaySN}_i + delaySN50_i$. We have a constraint to guarantee that if $\texttt{delayPN}_i = \texttt{delaySN}_j$ then $delayPN50_i = delaySN50_j$, $1 \leq i \leq \texttt{nPrim}$ and $1 \leq j \leq \texttt{nSec}$.

5.2 Modeling of Timestamps of Paging Messages

The first timeline in Figure 4 shows timestamps of paging messages, which are part of transmission of primary notification and the second timeline shows timestamps of paging messages, which correspond to secondary notification. Since paging messages of primary and secondary notifications look identical in the logs, we introduce one array `PagLog` of timestamps of paging messages from the log, which contain timestamps of paging messages of primary and secondary notifications in the order as they appear in the log. However paging messages of primary and secondary notifications have different periodicity and we need to distinguish them in order to check correctness of messages in the log. Periodicity of paging messages of primary notifications is `dPC`, but the time difference between two consecutive paging messages of secondary notification depends on the repetition period of notification and can take two different values for the same notification as shown in Figure 4. On the other hand, if there are more paging messages in the log than there should be or there are other errors in paging messages in the log, `SIB10` and `SIB11` messages can still be correct, but we cannot use timestamps of paging messages from the log. Therefore we introduce the array of correct timestamps of paging messages of primary notification *PagPN* and the array of correct timestamps of secondary notification *PagSN*. We post constraints on these arrays which calculate periodicity of paging messages. These constraints appear in all models.

5.3 Description of the `PagingModel`

We check that all required paging messages of primary and secondary notifications are present in the log. We check that every paging message in the log is a paging message of primary notification or paging message of a secondary notification.

5.4 Description of the `SIB1Model`

We have several constraints to check the timing and content of `SIB1` messages. The constraint (3) is an example of constraint, that checks the correctness of messages. In (3) we check that if the `SIB1` message is between the first paging message of primary notification and the last paging message of primary notification, then it contains scheduling information for `SIB10`. The array `SIB1TimeLog` contains timestamps of `SIB1` messages in the log. `SIB1TypeLog` is array of values from 0 to 3 that indicates whether `SIB1` contains `schedulingInfoList` for `SIB10` and/or `SIB11`. Then we post a constraint

$$
\begin{aligned}
(\forall 1 \leq k \leq \text{nSIB1Log}) \\
\quad ((((\exists 1 \leq i \leq \text{nPrim} - 1) \\
\quad (\text{SIB1TimeLog}_k \geq \text{delayPN}_i + delayPN50_i - delay \wedge \\
\quad ((PagPN_{i,\text{ndPC}} = -1 \wedge \text{SIB1TimeLog}_k < \\
\quad \text{delayPN}_{i+1} + delayPN50_{i+1} - delay) \vee \\
\quad (PagPN_{i,\text{ndPC}} \neq -1 \wedge \text{SIB1TimeLog}_k \leq PagPN_{i,\text{ndPC}}))) \\
\quad \vee \\
\quad (\text{SIB1TimeLog}_k \geq \text{delayPN}_{\text{nPrim}} + delayPN50_{\text{nPrim}} - delay \wedge \\
\quad \text{SIB1TimeLog}_k \leq PagPN_{\text{nPrim},\text{ndPC}})) \\
\quad \leftrightarrow (\text{SIB1TypeLog}_k = 1 \vee \text{SIB1TypeLog}_k = 3)) \\
\quad \leftrightarrow SIB1PrimTypeinc_k = 0 \quad\quad\quad\quad\quad\quad\quad\quad (3)
\end{aligned}
$$

where the Boolean variable $SIB1PrimTypeinc_k$ equal to 1 indicates an error in log. Since we can assign different values to $PagPN$ and $PagSN$ due to unknown value for $delay$, we use constraints and arrays of Boolean decision variables from `PagingModel` in `SIB1Model`. Minimisation of sum of Boolean decision variables from `PagingModel` helps reduce variations in the values of the timestamps in $PagPN$ and $PagSN$.

5.5   Description of the `PrimSecModel`

The model `PrimSecModel` checks correctness of timing and content of `SIB10` and `SIB11` messages in the log. For example, we check that notifications have correct identity numbers. We also check the correctness of sequences of `SIB11` segments, and that there are messages every paging cycle and repetition period. As in `SIB1Model` we use constraints and arrays of Boolean decision variables from `PagingModel` also in `PrimSecModel`.

6   Partitioning of Timestamps of Messages

If the log is large and contains for example 1000 `SIB10` messages, then we can have many constraints of the form

$$(\forall 1 \leq i \leq \texttt{nPrim})(\exists 1 \leq k \leq 1000).\phi(i, k) \tag{4}$$

$$(\forall 1 \leq k \leq 1000)(\exists 1 \leq i \leq \texttt{nPrim}).\phi'(i, k) \tag{5}$$

and

$$(\forall 1 \leq i \leq \texttt{nPrim})(\forall 1 \leq j \leq \texttt{ndPC})(\exists 1 \leq k \leq 1000).\phi''(i, j, k) \tag{6}$$

where k is index of `SIB10` message in the log, `nSIB10Log` $= 1000$ and ϕ, ϕ' and ϕ'' are some constraints. Even with small values for `nPrim` and `ndPC`, MiniZinc cannot process such constraints. However, we can partition messages into classes, where a message belongs to class i if its timestamp is between $\texttt{delayPN}_i - \texttt{dPC}$ and $\texttt{delayPN}_{i+1} + \texttt{dPC}$, where $1 \leq i \leq \texttt{nPrim} - 1$ or greater than $\texttt{delayPN}_i - \texttt{dPC}$ if $i = \texttt{nPrim}$. It can happen that the message belongs to several classes, but it helps to significantly reduce the size of constraint, it does not change the set of solutions, and makes the approach practical. For example, for `SIB10` messages we can have arrays of integers f^{min} and f^{max} such that

$$f_i^{min} = \min_{1 \leq k \leq \texttt{nSIB10Log}} \{k | \texttt{delayPN}_i - \texttt{dPC} \leq \texttt{SIB10TimeLog}_k \leq \texttt{delayPN}_{i+1} + \texttt{dPC}\},$$

where $1 \leq i \leq \texttt{nPrim} - 1$ and

$$f_{\texttt{nPrim}}^{min} = \min_{1 \leq k \leq \texttt{nSIB10Log}} \{k | \texttt{SIB10TimeLog}_k \geq \texttt{delayPN}_{\texttt{nPrim}} - \texttt{dPC}\}$$

$$f_i^{max} = \max_{1 \leq k \leq \texttt{nSIB10Log}} \{k | \texttt{delayPN}_i - \texttt{dPC} \leq \texttt{SIB10TimeLog}_k \leq \texttt{delayPN}_{i+1} + \texttt{dPC}\},$$

where $1 \leq i \leq \texttt{nPrim} - 1$ and $f_{\texttt{nPrim}}^{max} = \texttt{nSIB10Log}$.

Since `delayPN`, `SIB10TimeLog` and `dPC` are constants, we can easily calculate f^{min} and f^{max} and rewrite (4) as

$$(\forall 1 \leq i \leq \texttt{nPrim})(\exists f_i^{min} \leq k \leq f_i^{max}).\phi(i,k) \tag{7}$$

Similary, we can define arrays of integers g^{min} and g^{max} and more complex arrays of integers $\gamma_{i,j}^{min}$ and $\gamma_{i,j}^{max}$ and rewrite (5) as

$$(\forall 1 \leq k \leq 1000)(\exists g_k^{min} \leq i \leq g_k^{max}).\phi'(i,k) \tag{8}$$

and (6) as

$$(\forall 1 \leq i \leq \texttt{nPrim})(\forall 1 \leq j \leq \texttt{ndPC})(\exists \gamma_{i,j}^{min} \leq k \leq \gamma_{i,j}^{max}).\phi''(i,j,k) \tag{9}$$

Similar calculations have been done for paging messages, `SIB1` and `SIB11` messages.

7 Experiments

We used our constraint model to find errors in real logs, and generated logs of different size with injected errors. The experiments were done on the computer equipped with 8GB RAM and an Intel Core i5-3210M processor (2.50GHz).

7.1 Analysis of Real Logs

We analysed nine real logs, which were documented and were in an internal archive of Ericsson. Each log was captured in a UE simulator after sending two Write-Replace Warning Request messages from a MME simulator to an eNB. The logs have different structures, and represent all possible combinations of primary and secondary notifications in case of two warning messages. For example, the first warning message contains primary and secondary notifications, and the second warning message contains primary notifications; or another example, the first warning message contains secondary notifications, and the second warning message contains secondary notifications. Nine combinations are possible in case of two warning messages. The size of logs is between 138KB and 578KB. The number of paging messages is between 8 and 26, the number of `SIB1` messages is between 8 and 26, the number of `SIB10` messages is between 0 and 75, and the number of `SIB11` messages is between 0 and 24.

The running time for the `Model` was a few seconds for each log, and the found *objective* was between 0 and 70. The optimisation as presented in Section 6 was not needed. Eight logs have the property that the Boolean decision variables, which have value 1 in optimal solution, have the same value in all other solutions. Thus, the found errors are present in all solutions for different values of *delay*. This was checked by adding to the model a constraint with negated conjunction of values of non-zero Boolean decision variables of optimal solution, then MiniZinc reported that the model is unsatisfiable. One log does not have such property, but it has the property that there is only one solution with the value of *objective* being optimal, and the difference between other solutions and optimal solution is at least 6 errors.

Table 2. Analysis of correct generated logs

		log1	log2	log3	log4	log5
	nPrim	30	25	20	15	10
	nSec	30	25	20	15	10
PagingModel	nPagLog	625	510	419	307	218
	time	0:03:59	0:02:39	0:00:22	0:00:11	0:00:07
	time,gecode	0:00:04	0:00:02	0:00:02	0:00:01	0:00:01
	objective	0	0	0	0	0
SIB1Model	nSIB1Log	625	510	419	307	218
	time	0:04:21	0:02:56	0:00:42	0:00:21	0:00:11
	time,gecode	0:00:04	0:00:03	0:00:02	0:00:01	0:00:01
	objective	0	0	0	0	0
PrimSecModel	nSIB10Log	3062	2628	2091	1435	1057
	nSIB11Log	2753	2209	1500	1052	867
	time	0:16:47	0:12:46	0:03:49	0:02:13	0:01:27
	time,gecode	0:00:05	0:00:03	0:00:02	0:00:02	0:00:01
	objective	0	0	0	0	0
Model	time	0:20:59	0:14:31	0:04:46	0:02:45	0:01:43
	time,gecode	0:00:05	0:00:04	0:00:03	0:00:02	0:00:02
	objective	0	0	0	0	0

7.2 Analysis of Generated Logs

We generated logs, with and without errors, in order to understand how the model scales. The generation of protocol logs was described in [12] where SICStus Prolog [16] was used as constraint solver. We extended the approach and used Gecode[17] and C++ for log generation. Note that this was not a pure constraint model, but it included some imperative pre and post processing steps.

Table 2 shows results of the analysis of generated correct logs, where the found *objective* is 0. The optimization presented in Section 6 was used. The total time includes translation of models to FlatZinc using `mzn-gecode` and execution time of Gecode on the compiled FlatZinc using `fzn-gecode`. We can see that a very large log with 625 paging messages, 625 SIB1 messages, 625 SIB10 messages, 3062 SIB10 messages, and 2753 SIB11 messages requires 21 minutes to compile to FlatZinc. While `fzn-gecode` found the solution in a few seconds. A log that is three times smaller containing 10 primary and 10 secondary notifications requires 2 minutes to compile to FlatZinc and only 2 seconds to find solution.

In Table 3 we present the results of the analysis of generated logs where errors were introduced. All logs in Table 3 are incorrect versions of Log6. The Log7 to Log15 were generated by changing the timestamp of messages (t), removing messages (r), adding extra messages (a) and changing the content of messages (c). In Log7 and Log8 some paging messages are not correct. In Log9 and Log10 some SIB1 messages are not correct. In Log11 and Log12 some SIB10 messages

Table 3. Analysis of generated logs with injected errors

		log6	log7	log8	log9	log10	log11	log12	log13	log14	log15
	nPrim					20					
	nSec					20					
	errors in messages		r,a paging	t paging	r,c SIB1	t,c SIB1	r SIB10	t,c SIB10	r,t,c SIB11	r,a,t,c all	r,a,t,c all
PagingModel	nPagLog	374	174	374	374	374	374	374	374	374	398
	time	0:00:23	0:00:27	0:01:23						0:00:58	0:23:15
	time,gecode	0:00:02	0:00:08	0:01:02						0:00:39	0:22:56
	objective	0	413	155						192	789
SIB1Model	nSIB1Log	374	374	374	75	374	374	374	374	383	473
	time	0:00:39	0:00:41	0:01:30	0:01:07	0:04:23				0:01:22	0:32:16
	time,gecode	0:00:02	0:00:06	0:00:50	0:00:38	0:03:44				0:00:45	0:31:33
	objective	0	413	155	684	395				304	1386
PrimSecModel	nSIB10Log	1875	1916	1994	1871	1858	406	1922	1888	1683	2034
	nSIB11Log	1430	1429	1429	1429	1429	1430	1429	1143	1295	1242
	time	0:03:38	0:03:45	0:04:49			0:03:28	0:07:54	0:04:11	0:06:24	1:25:55
	time,gecode	0:00:03	0:00:08	0:00:58			0:01:00	0:04:11	0:00:59	0:02:57	1:22:21
	objective	0	413	155			220	3611	2061	4267	6789
Model	time	0:05:27	0:04:48	0:06:04	0:04:42	0:08:38	0:04:22	0:08:34	0:05:14	0:07:12	1:40:13
	time,gecode	0:00:03	0:00:09	0:01:04	0:00:45	0:03:40	0:01:00	0:03:46	0:01:01	0:02:46	1:35:18
	objective	0	413	155	684	395	220	3611	2061	4379	7396

are not correct, and in Log13 some SIB11 messages are not correct. In Log14 and Log15 there are errors in all types of messages. It took 7 minutes to find solution for Model of Log14, which consists of 3735 messages and 4379 errors. This is still a good result, since in a real environment it would require more than 30 minutes to collect a log of the same order of magnitude as Log14.

However, as the analysis of Log15 shows, when there are significantly incorrect timestamps of messages the solving time can increase significantly. It appears that incorrect timestamps of messages are harder for the solver to handle, since they are appear in constraints more often.

8   Learning Delay

Constraint programming can be used to analyse small logs if some parameter is unknown. This is often the case with logs in an archive. There was a log in the archive, with two warning notifications, that was not well documented. There was no information about the delay of second warning message. The warning messages consisted of primary and secondary notifications, that is $delayPN_2 = delaySN_2$. We estimated that $delayPN_2$ must be less than 80 seconds. The log was 1,5 MB and there were 23 paging messages, 183 SIB10 messages and 40 SIB11 messages in the log. We used `delayPN`$_2$ as decision variable in `PagingModel`. It took one second for constraint solver to find a solution with the *objective* being 0. That is it found a value of `delayPN`$_2$ such that all paging messages in log are correct. We used the generated value of `delayPN`$_2$ in `Model` and got a solution after 9 seconds with the *objective* strictly greater than 0. We also used `delayPN`$_2$ as a decision variable in `Model` and got a solution after 6 minutes with the same objective value.

9   Conclusion

There are a number of advantages of using MiniZinc and constraint programming: it was easy to translate the required parts of the telecommunication specification [3] directly into MiniZinc; these MiniZinc specifications are automatically translated into a constraint program that can be used to test protocol logs for correctness directly; the MiniZinc specification is a declarative specification of the protocol behaviour rather than the procedural implementation that is usually used for implementation of the checker; and finally adding more functionality to the MiniZinc implementation is done by simply adding more constraints.

Constraint solvers can easily handle complex requirements on timestamps. We used the MiniZinc model to analyse real logs and also larger generated logs with a lot of errors, which shows its usability in practice. The constraint solver was able to handle big domains of parameters, and we do not need to reduce or scale the domains. Protocol log analysis with constraint programming can be a part of test automation and can be useful for functional testing as well as in regression testing. Further, we believe that the protocol itself has independent interest as a useful case study for other formal modelling approaches. As a future work we plan to apply the approach to other case studies and protocols.

Acknowledgments. The authors would like to thank Noric Couderc for fruitful discussions on protocol log generation with Gecode. The first author is supported by VINNMER Program 2011-03229 funded by Swedish Governmental Agency for Innovation Systems. The third author is supported by grant 2012-4908 of the Swedish Research Council(VR).

References

1. Chadchan, S., Akki, C.: 3GPP LTE/SAE: An overview. International Journal of Computer and Electrical Engineering **2**(5), 806–814 (2010)
2. 3GPP: Evolved universal terrestrial radio access (e-utra) and evolved universal terrestrial radio access network (e-utran); overall description; stage 2. TS 36.300, 3rd Generation Partnership Project (3GPP)
3. 3GPP: Public warning system (PWS) requirements. TS 22.268, 3rd Generation Partnership Project (3GPP)
4. Rossi, F., van Beek, P., Walsh, T., eds.: Handbook of Constraint Programming. Elsevier (2006)

5. Carlsson, M., Grinchtein, O., Pearson, J.: Protocol log analysis with constraint programming (work in progress). In: Proceedings of the 12th International Workshop on Satisfiability Modulo Theories, SMT, pp. 17–26 (2014)
6. Nethercote, N., Stuckey, P.J., Becket, R., Brand, S., Duck, G.J., Tack, G.R.: MiniZinc: towards a standard CP modelling language. In: Bessière, C. (ed.) CP 2007. LNCS, vol. 4741, pp. 529–543. Springer, Heidelberg (2007)
7. Mossige, M., Gotlieb, A., Meling, H.: Testing robotized paint system using constraint programming: an industrial case study. In: Merayo, M.G., de Oca, E.M. (eds.) ICTSS 2014. LNCS, vol. 8763, pp. 145–160. Springer, Heidelberg (2014)
8. Mossige, M., Gotlieb, A., Meling, H.: Using CP in automatic test generation for ABB robotics' paint control system. In: O'Sullivan, B. (ed.) CP 2014. LNCS, vol. 8656, pp. 25–41. Springer, Heidelberg (2014)
9. DeMilli, R., Offutt, A.J.: Constraint-based automatic test data generation. IEEE Transactions on Software Engineering 17(9), 900–910 (1991)
10. Williams, N., Marre, B., Mouy, P., Roger, M.: PathCrawler: automatic generation of path tests by combining static and dynamic analysis. In: Dal Cin, M., Kaâniche, M., Pataricza, A. (eds.) EDCC 2005. LNCS, vol. 3463, pp. 281–292. Springer, Heidelberg (2005)
11. Carlier, M., Dubois, C., Gotlieb, A.: FocalTest: a constraint programming approach for property-based testing. In: Cordeiro, J., Virvou, M., Shishkov, B. (eds.) ICSOFT 2010. CCIS, vol. 170, pp. 140–155. Springer, Heidelberg (2013)
12. Balck, K., Grinchtein, O., Pearson, J.: Model-based protocol log generation for testing a telecommunication test harness using clp. In: DATE (2014)
13. 3GPP: General packet radio service (GPRS) enhancements for evolved universal terrestrial radio access network (E-UTRAN) access. TS 23.401, 3rd Generation Partnership Project (3GPP)
14. 3GPP: Technical realization of cell broadcast service (CBS). TS 23.041, 3rd Generation Partnership Project (3GPP)
15. 3GPP: Evolved universal terrestrial radio access (E-UTRA); S1 application protocol (S1AP). TS 36.413, 3rd Generation Partnership Project (3GPP)
16. Carlsson, M., Ottosson, G., Carlson, B.: An open-ended finite domain constraint solver. In: Hartel, P.H., Kuchen, H. (eds.) PLILP 1997. LNCS, vol. 1292, pp. 191–206. Springer, Heidelberg (1997)
17. Gecode Team: Gecode: A generic constraint development environment (2006). http://www.gecode.org

Experimental Evaluation of a Novel Equivalence Class Partition Testing Strategy

Felix Hübner [(✉)], Wen-ling Huang, and Jan Peleska

Department of Mathematics and Computer Science, University of Bremen,
Bremen, Germany
{felixh,huang,jp}@informatik.uni-bremen.de
http://informatik.uni-bremen.de/agbs

Abstract. In this paper, a novel complete model-based equivalence class testing strategy is experimentally evaluated. This black-box strategy applies to deterministic systems with infinite input domains and finite internal state and output domains. It is complete with respect to a given fault model. This means that conforming behaviours will never be rejected, and all nonconforming behaviours inside a given fault domain will be uncovered. We investigate the question how this strategy performs for systems under test whose behaviours lie *outside* the fault domain. Furthermore, a strategy extension is presented, that is based on randomised data selection from input equivalence classes. While this extension is still complete with respect to the given fault domain, it also promises a higher test strength when applied against members outside this domain. This is confirmed by an experimental evaluation that compares mutation coverage achieved by the original and the extended strategy with the coverage obtained by random testing.

Keywords: Model-based testing · Equivalence class partition testing · Adaptive random testing · SysML · State Transition Systems

1 Introduction

Background. In [13], two of the authors have presented a novel complete input equivalence class partition (IECP) testing strategy. Typically used in a model-based testing (MBT) scenario, the strategy is applicable to all concrete test models whose behavioural semantics can be described by a deterministic variant of Kripke Structures, with input variables from potentially infinite domains, but with finite-range internal state variables and finite output domains. The test suite construction is performed in relation to a given fault model $\mathcal{F} = (\mathcal{S}, \sim, \mathcal{D})$ with reference model $\mathcal{S}$, conformance relation $\sim$, and fault domain $\mathcal{D}$. $\mathcal{S}$ specifies the expected behaviour of the SUT. In general, the conformance relation is a not necessarily symmetric relation specifying the conditions for the behaviour of a system under test (SUT) to be still acceptable in comparison with $\mathcal{S}$. In the context discussed here, we use I/O-equivalence $\sim$ as conformance relation which means that the SUT and reference model $\mathcal{S}$ produce the same observable

© Springer International Publishing Switzerland 2015
J.C. Blanchette and N. Kosmatov (Eds.): TAP 2015, LNCS 9154, pp. 155–172, 2015.
DOI: 10.1007/978-3-319-21215-9_10

sequences of states, when restricted to inputs and outputs. The fault domain $\mathcal{D}$ consists of a (usually infinite) set of models $\mathcal{S}'$ from this domain, that may conform to the reference model $(\mathcal{S}' \sim \mathcal{S})$ or not.

A test suite is then *complete with respect to* $\mathcal{F}$, if and only if all tests of the suite will pass for every $\mathcal{S}' \in \mathcal{D}$ conforming to $\mathcal{S}$, and at least one test will fail when executed against a non-conforming member of $\mathcal{D}$. The *test hypothesis* states that the true behaviour of the SUT is equivalent to one of the models in the fault domain, as far as visible at the black-box interface. Summarising, the complete IECP testing strategy uncovers every erroneous behaviour of the SUT, provided that its true behaviour can be captured by a member $\mathcal{S}'$ of the fault domain, and SUTs that are I/O-equivalent to $\mathcal{S}$ will never fail a test of the suite.

The investigation of completeness properties has a long tradition as a research topic; references to the associated literature are given in Section 5.

Test model (SysML)   Semantic representation

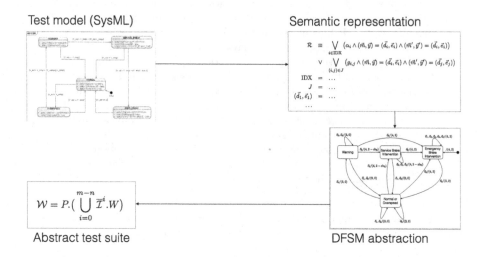

Fig. 1. Tool-supported workflow

Workflow and Tool Support. In Fig. 1 the workflow associated with our test approach is shown. Test models are represented in a concrete modelling formalism; for the models presented in this paper SysML [18] has been used. As explained in Section 2, the test model is translated into a state transition system whose behavioural semantics is expressed by means of initial condition and transition relation in propositional form. From the transition relation, equivalence classes are calculated. These give rise to an abstraction as a deterministic finite state machine (DFSM). Applying well-known complete testing strategies for DFSM, an abstract test suite is derived. Each test case of this suite is represented as a sequence of input equivalence classes. Selecting concrete input data from each of these classes by means of an SMT solver, a complete test suite for the original test model is generated. The whole process is automated and has been integrated in the model-based test automation tool RT-Tester [20].

Objectives and Main Contribution. Apart from their theoretical value, complete testing strategies are of considerable importance for verification and validation (V&V) of safety critical systems. There test suites have to be justified with respect to their test case selection and the resulting test strength, in order to obtain certification credit. The completeness property, however, depends on the assumption that the true SUT behaviour is reflected by a member of the fault domain $\mathcal{D}$ (test hypothesis). Widening $\mathcal{D}$ typically affects the size of the test suite in an exponential way. Therefore just using very large fault domains is not an approach that will be feasible in practise. This leads to the question of how complete test suites perform *outside* the fault domain, and this investigation is the main objective of this paper. To this end, three test strategies are evaluated with respect to their strength: (A) conventional random testing – this serves as a lower bound of test strength, to be surpassed by any more sophisticated strategy. (B) The original complete IECP strategy from [13], and (C) an extension of the latter which is based on randomised selection of inputs from each input equivalence class (IEC). These three strategies are described in more detail in Section 2.

An experimental evaluation (see Section 4) is performed which is based on two test models that are introduced in Section 3: a speed monitor from the European Train Control System and an airbag controller for vehicles. Applying the three strategies against a collection of mutants, the experimental evaluation confirms significant test strength improvements of strategy (B) over (A), and the highest test strength is achieved by (C).

Apart from this main contribution, the evaluation results indicate how the fault domain should be configured: in contrast to fault domains for DFSMs (these only depend on the assumed maximal size of the SUT's DFSM state space), our fault domains depend on an additional parameter affecting the size of the IECs. The evaluation indicates that the best choice for $\mathcal{D}$ is an IEC granularity that still reflects the different control conditions imposed by the reference model and the boundary value conditions. However, instead of further refining the IECP (this would result in a dramatic increase of the test suites), it is better to increase the number of input values randomly selected from each IEC in each state.

2 Model-Based Random Testing and Equivalence Class Partition Testing

2.1 Random Testing

In *model-based random testing*, test cases are created by generating random values as SUT inputs. To this end, the input interface signatures of the SUT are extracted from the model, so that the random values are created in the appropriate data ranges. Apart from this, the input data creation is not guided further by the model. Additionally, the model is used as a test oracle, so that the observed SUT behaviour can be compared to the expected behaviour specified by the model.

When performing black-box tests of SUTs with internal states, the SUT behaviour depends on the *sequence* of inputs provided since the last SUT reset.

As a consequence, test cases are specified by sequences of random inputs. Models serving as test oracles need to simulate the internal state changes to be performed by the SUT on each input, in order to predict the SUT reactions in a correct way. While random testing is quite easy to mechanise, its test strength is usually rather weak, because the test case selection does not take into account the required SUT behaviour. On the other hand, random testing is an obvious candidate for assessing the test strength of more refined model-based testing strategies: any successful refined strategy should have a test strength that is significantly higher than the random testing approach.

2.2   Equivalence Class Partition Testing

Semantic Domain. The novel equivalence class partition testing strategy presented in [13] is applicable to deterministic, livelock-free systems with conceptually infinite input domains and finite internal state and output domains. "Conceptually infinite" means that the domains are too large to be explicitly enumerated for test purposes. This includes physical models with real-valued inputs, but can also apply to finite but very large data types such as 64 bit integers or doubles as used in typical programming languages or modelling formalisms. As pointed out in [5,6,13], this class of systems is quite significant in the embedded systems domain: typical candidates are controllers processing analogue inputs and deriving discrete control decisions from these inputs, such as thrust reversal controllers in aircrafts, or the speed monitors and airbag controllers described in this paper.

The strategy has been proven to be complete on the semantic domain of *Reactive Input Output State Transition Systems (RIOSTS)* $\mathcal{S} = (S, s_0, R, V, D)$. These systems have state spaces S, initial state $s_0 \in S$, and transition relations $R \subseteq S \times S$. Their state spaces consist of valuation functions $s : V \to D$, where V is a set of variable symbols and D is the union of all variable domains. The variable symbols can be partitioned into $V = I \cup M \cup O$, where I comprises input variables, M (internal) model variables, and O output variables. RIOSTS distinguish between *quiescent* states $s \in S_Q$ and *transient* states $s' \in S_T$, such that $S_Q \cup S_T$ partitions the state space S. Transitions from quiescent states only change input valuations, while internal model variables and output variables remain unchanged. The resulting post-states may be quiescent or transient. Transitions from transient states always have uniquely determined quiescent post-states (so we only allow deterministic RIOSTS here), and the associated transitions leave the inputs unchanged. This concept represents a natural abstraction of timed formalisms, where delay transitions allow for time to pass and inputs to be changed, while discrete transitions produce output and change internal state, but are executed in zero time [3, p. 687].

By associating atomic propositions AP with free variables in V, any RIOSTS can be extended to a Kripke Structure [9] $K(\mathcal{S}) = (S, s_0, R, V, D, L, AP)$. The labelling function $L : S \to 2^{AP}$ maps $s \in S$ to the set of all atomic propositions $p \in AP$ that evaluate to **true**, when replacing every free variable v of p by its valuation $s(v)$ in state s.

Notation. In the exposition below, variable symbols are enumerated with the naming conventions $I = \{x_1, \ldots, x_k\}$, $M = \{m_1, \ldots, m_p\}$, $O = \{y_1, \ldots, y_q\}$. We use notation $\boldsymbol{x} = (x_1, \ldots, x_k)$ for input variable vectors, and their valuation in state s is written as $s(\boldsymbol{x}) = (s(x_1), \ldots, s(x_k))$. $D_I = D_{x_1} \times \cdots \times D_{x_k}$ denotes the Cartesian product of the input variable domains. Tuples $\boldsymbol{m}, \boldsymbol{y}$ and D_M and D_O are defined over model variables and outputs in an analogous way. By $s \oplus \{\boldsymbol{x} \mapsto \boldsymbol{c}\}$, $\boldsymbol{c} \in D_I$ we denote the state s' which coincides with s on all variables from $M \cup O$, but maps the input vector to valuation $s'(\boldsymbol{x}) = \boldsymbol{c}$. For $(s_1, s_2) \in R$ we also use the shorter expression $R(s_1, s_2)$. Restricting a state s to variable symbols from a set $U \subseteq V$ is denoted by $s|_U$. This function has domain U and coincides with s on this domain.

Application to Concrete Modelling Formalisms. The test strategy described below is elaborated on the semantic domain of RIOSTS. Every concrete modelling formalism whose behavioural semantics can be represented by RIOSTS is automatically equipped with such a test strategy: the concrete model M is translated into its corresponding RIOSTS $\mathcal{S}$. Then the test strategy is applied to $\mathcal{S}$, and this results in a set of test cases, each case represented by a finite sequence of inputs to the SUT. When executing the test cases, the transition relation of $\mathcal{S}$ is used to determine whether the SUT's reactions to these input sequences are adequate. In this article, concrete models are expressed by SysML state machines, and these can be associated with RIOSTS semantics which is consistent with the semi-formal specification of state machine behaviour in the UML/SysML standards [17, 18].

Equivalence Classes. We use the term *trace* to denote finite sequences of states, input vectors, or output vectors. Applying a trace $\iota = \boldsymbol{c}_1 \ldots \boldsymbol{c}_n$ of input vectors $\boldsymbol{c}_i \in D_I$ to an RIOSTS $\mathcal{S} = (S, s_0, R, V, D)$ residing in some quiescent state $s \in S$ stimulates a sequence of state transitions, each pair of consecutive states connected by the transition relation R, and with associated output changes as triggered by these inputs. Restricting this sequence to quiescent states, this results in a trace of states $\tau = s_1.s_2 \ldots s_n$ such that $s_i(\boldsymbol{x}) = \boldsymbol{c}_i, i = 1, \ldots, n$, and $s_i(\boldsymbol{y})$ is the last STS output resulting from application of $\boldsymbol{c}_1 \ldots \boldsymbol{c}_i$ to state s.[1] This trace τ is denoted by s/ι. The restriction of s/ι to output variables is denoted by the trace $(s/\iota)|_O$. Since transient states have unique quiescent post-states, $(s/\iota)|_O$ is a uniquely determined output trace. Two quiescent states s, s' are *I/O-equivalent*, written $s \sim s'$, if every non-empty input trace ι, when applied to s and s', results in the same outputs, that is, $(s/\iota)|_O = (s'/\iota)|_O$. Two STS $\mathcal{S}, \mathcal{S}'$ with the same input domain are I/O-equivalent, if their initial states are I/O-equivalent. Note that $s \sim s'$ asserts equivalent I/O-behaviour *in the future*, while it still admits that states s and s' show different output valuations, i.e. $s|_O \neq s'|_O$.

---

[1] Observe that the restriction to quiescent states does not result in a loss of information. Every transient state has the internal and output variable valuations coinciding with its quiescent pre-state, and its input valuation is identical to that of its quiescent post-state.

Since I/O-equivalence $\sim$ is an equivalence relation on quiescent states, we can factorise S_Q with respect to $\sim$. The *initial input equivalence class partitioning (IECP)* $\mathcal{I} \subseteq \mathbb{P}(D_I)$ associated with $S_Q/_\sim$ is the coarsest partitioning of D_I such that for all $\mathbf{q} \in S_Q/_\sim$, $X \in \mathcal{I}$, there exists a uniquely determined I/O-equivalence class $\delta(\mathbf{q}, X) \in S_Q/_\sim$, such that

$$\forall s \in \mathbf{q}, c \in X : s/c \in \delta(\mathbf{q}, X) \tag{1}$$

and there exists a well-defined output $\omega(\mathbf{q}, X) \in D_O$, such that

$$\forall s \in \mathbf{q}, c \in X : (s/c)|_O = \omega(\mathbf{q}, X) \tag{2}$$

It is shown in [13] that $S_Q/_\sim$ is finite if the RIOSTS $\mathcal{S}$ has finite internal state domains and finite output domains, while the input domains may be infinite. Moreover, the coarsest partitioning $\mathcal{I}$ exists, and it is finite and uniquely determined under these prerequisites. For these RIOSTS, properties (1) and (2) induce an abstraction to DFSMs with state space $S_Q/_\sim$, input alphabet $\mathcal{I}$, and output alphabet D_O: (1) specifies a well-defined total transition function $\delta : S_Q/_\sim \times \mathcal{I} \to S_Q/_\sim$, and (2) a well-defined output function $\omega : S_Q/_\sim \times \mathcal{I} \to D_O$. When partitioning $\mathcal{I}$ further to a refined IECP $\overline{\mathcal{I}}$, the characteristic properties (1),(2) are preserved.

A finite sequence $X_1 \ldots X_k, X_i \in \mathcal{I}$ is called an *abstract test case*: concrete test input vectors c_i can be selected from each X_i, and, when applied to the initial state s_0, this selection induces a trace $s_1 \ldots s_k$ of quiescent states, such that

$$\exists \mathbf{q}_1, \ldots, \mathbf{q}_k \in S_Q/_\sim : \forall i \in \{1, \ldots, k\} : s_i \in \mathbf{q}_i \wedge \mathbf{q}_i = \delta(\mathbf{q}_{i-1}, X_i)$$

The IECP properties imply that the *expected results* associated with this test case are then specified by the output trace $\omega(\mathbf{q}_{i-1}, X_i), i = 1, \ldots, k$.

In [13] an algorithm for calculating $S_Q/_\sim$ and $\mathcal{I}$ is given. This algorithm produces propositions over variables from V, specifying the members of $S_Q/_\sim$ and $\mathcal{I}$, respectively. Making use of an SMT solver, the algorithm allows for identifying the reachable I/O-equivalence classes $\mathbf{q} \in S_Q/_\sim$. As a consequence, every proposition characterising an abstract test case $X_1 \ldots X_k$ is actually feasible: this means that we can find concrete traces in $\mathcal{S}$ such that, after deleting the transient states, the resulting quiescent state sequence $s_0.s_1 \ldots s_k$ fulfils $s_i \in \mathbf{q}_i$ for $i = 0, \ldots, k$ and $s(\boldsymbol{x}) \in X_i$ for $i = 1, \ldots, k$.

In the case studies described in Section 4, input equivalence classes are unions of convex subset of $\mathbb{R}^n$. It should be noted, however, that the notion of I/O-equivalence and IECPs introduced here is far more general, since arbitrary propositional specifications of I/O-equivalence classes can be handled by the underlying theory. The input equivalence classes identified in [13, Example 1], for example, contain members z specified by conditions $z \bmod m = n$.

Fault Models. For the semantic domain of RIOSTS, the fault models $\mathcal{F} = (\mathcal{S}, \sim, \mathcal{D}(\mathcal{S}, m, \overline{\mathcal{I}}))$ are specified as follows. The reference models $\mathcal{S}$ are semantic RIOSTS representations of models elaborated in concrete formalisms, such that the expected behaviour of the SUT is specified by S up to I/O-equivalence. We use I/O-equivalence as conformance relation.

Positive integer m fulfils $m \geq n$, where n is the number of I/O-equivalence classes of S. IECP $\overline{\mathcal{I}}$ is a refinement of the initial coarsest IECP $\mathcal{I}$ associated with S. Then the members S' of the fault domain $\mathcal{D}(S, m, \overline{\mathcal{I}})$ are RIOSTS specified as follows.

1. The states of S' are defined over the same I/O variable space $I \cup O$ as defined for the model S.
2. Initial state s'_0 of S' coincides with initial state s_0 of S on $I \cup O$.
3. S' generates only finitely many different output values.
4. S' has a well-defined reset operation allowing to re-start the system from its initial state.
5. The number of I/O-equivalence classes of S' is less or equal m.
6. If $\mathcal{I}, \mathcal{I}'$ are the initial coarsest IECP of S, S', respectively, fulfilling the characteristic properties (1), (2), then $\overline{\mathcal{I}}$ fulfils the following *adequacy condition*:

$$\cdot \quad \forall X \in \mathcal{I}, X' \in \mathcal{I}' : (X \cap X' \neq \varnothing \Rightarrow \exists \overline{X} \in \overline{\mathcal{I}} : \overline{X} \subseteq X \cap X') \qquad (3)$$

The intuition behind the adequacy condition 6 is as follows. Every possible behaviour of a fault domain member S' can be exercised by visiting a state in some I/O-equivalence class $\mathbf{q}'$ and applying an input of some IECP member $X' \in \mathcal{I}'$ to this state. Using the refined IECP $\overline{\mathcal{I}}$ in the test suite as described below, ensures that an input from $\overline{X} \subseteq X' \in \mathcal{I}'$ will be selected when S' resides in $\mathbf{q}'$, so the behaviour associated with $(\mathbf{q}', X')$ will be stimulated in at least one of the test cases. If, when in a state of $\mathbf{q}'$, S' conforms to the behaviour of S for all inputs from $X \setminus X'$, but fails for inputs from $X \cap X'$, inputs selected from $\overline{X} \subseteq X \cap X'$ will uncover this error.

Conversely, suppose now that the reference model S behaves differently, when IECs $X_1, X_2 \in \mathcal{I}$ are applied in some state $\mathbf{q}$. Suppose further that S' fails to make this case distinction in a corresponding state $\mathbf{q}'$. Then there exists $X' \in \mathcal{I}'$ such that S' shows the same behaviour for all $c \in X'$, but $X_1 \cap X' \neq \varnothing$ and $X_2 \cap X' \neq \varnothing$, so two different behaviours should be visible according to the reference model. Now the adequacy condition guarantees that there exist two IEC $\overline{X}_1, \overline{X}_2 \in \overline{\mathcal{I}}$, such that $\overline{X}_1 \subseteq X_1 \cap X'$ and $\overline{X}_2 \subseteq X_2 \cap X'$. As a consequence, if inputs from every input class of $\overline{\mathcal{I}}$ are exercised, the behavioural differences for inputs from $X_1 \cap X'$ and $X_2 \cap X'$ will be revealed. Summarising, the adequacy condition ensures that the IECP $\overline{\mathcal{I}}$ from where input data to the SUT is selected is fine-grained enough to stimulate every possibly deviating behaviour of S and S'. These facts are exploited in the complete test strategy described next.

Complete Finite Test Suite. The complete DFSM abstraction $\mathcal{M}$ of S with states $S_Q/_\sim$, input alphabet $\overline{\mathcal{I}}$, transition function and output function as characterised in (1), (2), allows for application of finite complete DFSM testing strategies, such as the *W-Method* introduced in [8,25]. The general form of a W-Method test suite is

$$W = P.\left(\bigcup_{i=0}^{m-n} \overline{\mathcal{I}}^i.W \right) \tag{4}$$

where P is the state transition cover, $\overline{\mathcal{I}}^i$ denotes the input trace segments of length i, and W is the characterisation set. Every test of W consists of a (possibly empty) input trace from P, concatenated with an arbitrary input trace of length zero up to $m - n$, and terminated by an input trace from the characterisation set. P is the union of a *state cover* C and a *transition cover* $C.\overline{\mathcal{I}}$: C contains the empty trace ε, and for any state $\mathbf{q}$ of $\mathcal{M}$, there exists an input trace in C which, when applied to the initial state, ends at $\mathbf{q}$. The transition cover is defined by $C.\overline{\mathcal{I}} = \{\iota.X \mid \iota \in C, X \in \overline{\mathcal{I}}\}$. Summarising, the input sequences of a state transition cover ensure that (1) every state of the reference DFSM $\mathcal{M}$ associated with the reference model $\mathcal{S}$ is visited, and (2) every transition from every state is exercised. A characterisation set is a set of input traces distinguishing each pair of states in a minimal DFSM. Using minimisation algorithms such as the one specified in [12], characterisation sets can be constructed as a by-product of the minimisation process.

The test suite generated according to (4) is called an *abstract test suite*, because its elements are abstract test cases as defined above: the inputs to be used in each test case are not yet represented by concrete input vectors $\mathbf{c}$, but by input equivalence classes $\overline{X} \in \overline{\mathcal{I}}$. For creating an executable test suite, inputs $\mathbf{c} \in \overline{X}$ have to be selected for every $\overline{X} \in \overline{\mathcal{I}}$.

The W-Method is complete for the fault model of all DFSM over the same input and output alphabet and with at most m states. It is shown in [13] that the associated test suites with concrete inputs $\mathbf{c} \in \overline{X}$ are also complete for $\mathcal{F} = (\mathcal{S}, \sim, \mathcal{D}(\mathcal{S}, m, \overline{\mathcal{I}}))$. This completeness result is independent on the choice of concrete input data selected from each input equivalence class $X \in \overline{\mathcal{I}}$.

The fault domain $\mathcal{D}(\mathcal{S}, m, \overline{\mathcal{I}})$ introduced above can be extended by increasing m or by refining $\overline{\mathcal{I}}$. Increasing m increases the maximal length of input sequences in test cases in a linear way. This affects the size of the test suite exponentially, but allows for fault domain members with higher *recurrence diameters* r [4]: this is the length of the longest loop-free path in a Kripke structure. Erroneous SUT behaviour that only occurs at the end of such a longest loop free path may only be detected if the test cases use input sequences that are long enough to traverse the SUT state up to the length of the recurrence diameter.

Refining $\overline{\mathcal{I}}$ increases the size of the IECP, and this size increases the number of test cases in a polynomial way. It has to be noted, however, that uniformly refining all members of $\overline{\mathcal{I}}$ – for example, by using a sub-paving strategy as it is well known from interval analysis [14] – increases the size of the IECP exponentially with each new refinement step. The resulting fault domain contains members $\mathcal{S}'$ possessing narrower *trapdoors*: these are refined input guard conditions $g \wedge \delta$ applicable in certain $\mathcal{S}'$-states, where $\mathcal{S}'$ should behave uniformly for all inputs satisfying g. The true behaviour of $\mathcal{S}'$, however, conforms to the expected behaviour modelled by $\mathcal{S}$ only for inputs fulfilling $g \wedge \neg\delta$, while erroneous behaviour is revealed for inputs satisfying $g \wedge \delta$.

2.3   Randomisation of Equivalence Partition Tests

As we have seen above, enlarging the fault domain $\mathcal{D}(\mathcal{S}, m, \overline{\mathcal{I}})$ via m or $\overline{\mathcal{I}}$ seriously affects the size of the resulting complete test suite $\mathcal{W}$. We therefore investigate an alternative approach in this paper that aims at increasing the test strength of $\mathcal{W}$ for SUTs $\mathcal{S}''$ whose true behaviour is reflected by RIOSTS *outside* $\mathcal{D}(\mathcal{S}, m, \overline{\mathcal{I}})$. For obvious reasons it is assumed that these SUTs still fulfil the RIOSTS compatibility requirements 1 – 4 of the fault domain definition. This means that $\mathcal{S}''$ may have more than m I/O-equivalence classes and may need an IECP that is more fine-grained than $\overline{\mathcal{I}}$, but it is still assumed that $\mathcal{S}''$ is an RIOSTS using the same I/O variables and possessing the same visible initial state and fulfilling a reset condition.

To this end, we observe that the completeness property of the test suites introduced above does not depend on the concrete values selected from each input equivalence class $\overline{X} \in \overline{\mathcal{I}}$. For members $\mathcal{S}' \in \mathcal{D}(\mathcal{S}, m, \overline{\mathcal{I}})$ it would suffice to fix one input vector $c_{\overline{X}}$ for every $\overline{X} \in \overline{\mathcal{I}}$. Alternatively, we could also choose different members at random, each time an input from some class $\overline{X}$ is required according to the abstract test suite definition. While this alternative would not affect the suite's completeness property when applied against members of $\mathcal{D}(\mathcal{S}, m, \overline{\mathcal{I}})$, it favourably affects the test strength against RIOSTS outside $\mathcal{D}(\mathcal{S}, m, \overline{\mathcal{I}})$: the chances for uncovering trapdoors are obviously increased. This approach results in an *adaptive random testing strategy*, where the selection of input data is no longer performed uniformly over the complete input domain, but selectively for each input equivalence class $\overline{X} \in \overline{\mathcal{I}}$. Moreover, the random values from such an $\overline{X}$ are only applied when an $\overline{X}$-input is required according to the abstract test suite constructed from Equation (4).

Technically the randomisation is implemented by running an SMT solver repeatedly to find concrete values of every input equivalence class $\overline{X} \in \overline{\mathcal{I}}$. The abstract test suite constructed from Equation (4) is a sequence on input equivalence classes. According to our equivalence class construction [13], an input equivalence class $\overline{X} \in \overline{\mathcal{I}}$ is defined by a proposition[2] $g_{\overline{X}}$, containing solely variables in I. Using an SMT solver to solve $g_{\overline{X}}$ results in a concrete input vector $c \in \overline{X}$. Rerunning the solver for the same $\overline{X}$ and prohibiting existing solutions $c_1, \ldots, c_{n-1}$ with a refined constraint $g_{\overline{X}} \wedge \bigwedge_{i=1}^{n-1} \neg c_i$ will result in a new solution c_n, i.e. a new concrete input $c_n \in \overline{X}$ of the input equivalence class. The negation of existing solution yields an exponential growth of the runtime of the SMT solver in the worst case. Therefore two other heuristics were implemented:
(a) the internal heuristics of the SAT solver have been randomized to get a "random" solution of $g_{\overline{X}}$. (b) Interval analysis can be used to find a subpaving, that is an inner approximation of $g_{\overline{X}}$. From this subpaving random elements can be selected using a random number generator. As another runtime optimization the

---

[2] The proposition is guaranteed to have a solution, since it describes an input equivalence class, which has at least one member and thus at least one assignment that fulfills the proposition.

input selection can be parallelized. Once the input equivalence class partitioning $\overline{\mathcal{I}}$ is available, candidates from every input equivalence class $\overline{X}$ can be calculated separately and in parallel, to find as many different concrete values as needed.

It has to be noted, however, that the complete test suite generated according to (4) will not guarantee that every pair $(\mathbf{q}, \overline{X})$ with $\mathbf{q} \in S/_\sim$ and $\overline{X} \in \overline{\mathcal{I}}$ will be exercised the same number of times. Therefore we add test cases to ensure a minimal number a each $(\mathbf{q}, \overline{X})$ is exercised, each time with a new random selection $c \in \overline{X}$. For these additional test cases we just repeat suitable cases from $\mathcal{W}$. If p estimates the probability to detect a trapdoor when selecting a random value in $(\mathbf{q}, \overline{X})$, then the probability to uncover this during the randomised test suite is $1 - (1 - p)^a$.

3   Reference Models

We use two test models as the basis for the experimental evaluation of the IECP strategy discussed in this paper, one from the railway domain, the other from the automotive domain. Their functional properties are described in this section.

Ceiling Speed Monitor. The main on-board controller of trains that are part of the *European Train Control System (ETCS)* executes a variety of automated train protection functions. One of these functional modules is the *Ceiling Speed Monitor (CSM)*, whose core behaviour is specified by the SysML state machine shown in Fig. 2. This state machine has been modelled from the ETCS standard [24]. The CSM inputs the current estimated train speed V_{est} and the current admissible maximal speed V_{MRSP} and reacts to overspeeding situations. The reactions are visible on the driver machine interface (DMI) (outputs DMICmd, DMIdisplaySBI), and the CSM may interact with the service and emergency brakes (output TICmd).

As soon as the train starts overspeeding ($V_{est} > V_{MRSP}$), the CSM performs a transition from NORMAL to OVERSPEEDING, and an overspeed indication is displayed on the DMI. If the actual speed exceeds the V_{MRSP}-dependent threshold $V_{MRSP} + \mathsf{dV_{warning}}(V_{MRSP})$, the DMI indication changes to WARNING. If the higher threshold $V_{MRSP} + \mathsf{dV_{sbi}}(V_{MRSP})$ is violated, the CSM automatically triggers the service brakes. When in one of the control modes OVERSPEED, WARNING, or SERVICE_BRAKE, DMI indications and braking interventions are automatically reset as soon as the speed is back in the admissible range $V_{est} \le V_{MRSP}$. If, however, the train continues overspeeding until the highest threshold $V_{MRSP} + \mathsf{dV_{ebi}}(V_{MRSP})$ is violated, the CSM triggers the emergency brakes. From the associated state EMER_BRAKE, the transition to NORMAL is only performed when the train has come to a standstill.

While internal state and output domains of the CSM are finite, the inputs V_{est}, V_{MRSP} represent speed values ranging from zero to the maximal train speed. This domain is too large to enumerate all possible value combinations during test campaigns. Therefore an IECP strategy has to be applied. A more detailed description of the CSM model can be found in [5,6].

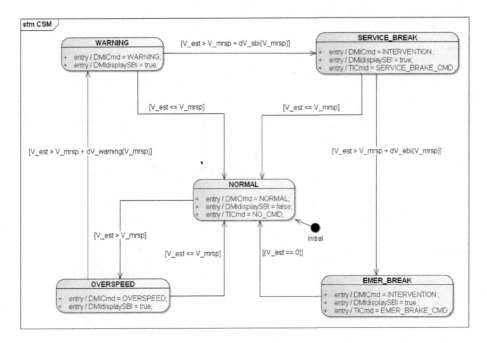

Fig. 2. State machine of the Ceiling Speed Monitor

Airbag Controller. The second test model describes an airbag controller. This system has two analog inputs s1 and s2 that are acceleration sensors used by the controller to detect a crash situation and decide whether the airbag shall be fired or not (output fire). While the airbag may ensure passenger safety in crash situations, its accidental activation is harmful in situations, when no crash is present but indicated by erroneous sensor data. Therefore certain safety mechanisms have to be applied to guarantee (up to a certain degree of confidence) that the airbag is only fired, if a real crash situation is present. Additionally, defect sensors should be recognised and notified (output defect). The state machine in Fig. 3 models the functionality ensuring the safe operation of the airbag controller.

The system reads the sensor values s1 and s2 cyclically on every rising and falling edge (input t). Both sensor values are checked for plausibility. The sensor values are considered plausible, if the value of sensor one (s1) does not exceed or drop below the value of sensor two (s2) by more than 5 percent, i.e. $s1 \in [0.95 \cdot s2, 1.05 \cdot s2]$. If the sensor values are plausible and an acceleration greater than 3 is measured in 3 consecutive cycles, the airbag is fired. This is done by setting output variable fire to 1. If instead the sensor values are implausible, internal variable error_ctr is incremented. This variable holds the number of implausible measurements, and if it reaches a value equal to 3, the output variable defect is set to 1, causing a shutdown of the complete airbag system and activating the service lamp to indicate a sensor defect of the airbag. After at least 3 consecutive cycles with plausible sensor values, the internal variable error_ctr is reset.

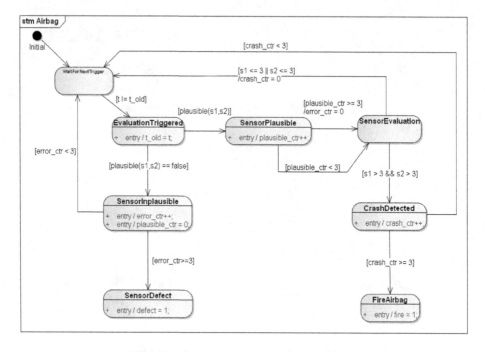

Fig. 3. State machine of the airbag controller

4   Experimental Results

Experimental Setup. The three test strategies (A) conventional random test-ing strategy, (B) original IECP testing strategy, and (C) randomised IECP test-ing strategy described in Section 2 have been integrated in an experimental extension of the RT-Tester tool which performs automated model-based testing from SysML models [20]. The algorithm described in [13] has been implemented there, in order to identify I/O-equivalence classes and the associated coarsest initial IECP in propositional form. Using the SMT solver integrated in RT-Tester, random candidates from each IEC can be calculated.

For the experimental evaluation correct Java implementations were generated from each model. The java implementation was performed by hand in a straight forward way, resulting in 148 and 70 lines of code for the ceiling speed monitor and the airbag controller respectively. Next, mutants were automatically gener-ated from each implementation with the tool µJava [16]. All applicable operators were executed to generate single-fault mutants. For our concrete implementa-tions these operators were as follows: arithmetic operator replacement (AOR) and insertion(AOI), relational operator replacement (ROR), conditional opera-tor replacement (COR) and insertion (COI), logical operator insertion (LOI) and statement deletion (SDL).[3] Note that the mutation tool is unaware of any conformance relation. Therefore the generated mutants have been manually investigated, and after discarding I/O-equivalent mutants, this resulted in a collection of 351 erroneous implementations for the ceiling speed monitor, and 199 for the airbag controller.

Afterwards the test suites specified below were executed against these SUTs in order to measure the mutation score of the test suite. The mutation score is the ratio of mutants, that were "killed" by a test suite[4], to the total number of non-I/O-equivalent mutants. The mutation score is used as an indicator of each test suite's strength.

Table 1. Specification of fault domains

$\mathcal{D}$	Description
$\mathcal{D}_1$	$\mathcal{I}$ is the initial coarsest IECP derived from the reference model. It is assumed that the SUT has the same number of I/O-equivalence classes as the reference model, i.e. $m = n$.
$\mathcal{D}_2$	$\mathcal{I}$ is a refinement of the initial coarsest IECP that reflects all case distinctions visible in guard conditions of the model. $m = n$.
$\mathcal{D}_3$	$\mathcal{I}$ is a refinement of the initial coarsest IECP that reflects all case distinctions and all boundary value conditions. $m = n$.

The strategies (B) and (C) were applied to different fault domains as described in Table 1. For the randomised IECP strategy (C), an additional parameter $min \geq 1$ was introduced, specifying the minimal number of times a random selection should be performed for each combination $(\mathbf{q}, X)$ of I/O-equivalence class and input equivalence class of the reference model. For $min > 1$, test cases from the original IECP testing strategy according to Equation (4) were repeated with different random value selections, so that at least min selections were performed for each $(\mathbf{q}, X)$.

When generating test suites according to strategies (B) and (C), the choice of fault domain, and – for strategy (C) – min value determines the number of test cases (i.e. input sequences) and their length. When applying random testing, test suites of the same shape were used: for each test case of a suite generated with strategy (B) or (C), a corresponding random test case of the same length was applied.

Experimental Results

Ceiling speed monitor. In Table 2 the experimental results for the Ceiling Speed Monitor are shown. Though in test suite $(B, \mathcal{D}_1)$ the original IECP strategy (B)

---

[3] The insertion operators of the μJava tool are only applicable to unary operators $(+,-,++,--,!,\tilde{\ })$. Since our implementations did not contain any of these operators, the complementary deletion operators are missing from the list above.

[4] A mutant is killed, if at least one test case of the test suite did not pass.

performs significantly better than random testing (A), when only the coarsest IECP from fault domain $\mathcal{D}_1$ is used, the mutation score of 62% is far too low for achieving certification credit for such a safety-critical application. The low score is caused by the fact that the test suite (B,$\mathcal{D}_1$) uses an IECP that not even considers all case distinctions visible in guard conditions of the original model. Therefore faulty implementations outside $\mathcal{D}_1$ that violate these case distinctions will not be detected by this suite. In contrast to that, when distinguishing all guard conditions and adding IECs representing boundary test conditions – this is done in suite (B,$\mathcal{D}_3$) – the mutation score of 93% is acceptable. The strength of the randomised strategy (C) is clearly revealed in suite (C,$\mathcal{D}_3$,1): with the same number of 610 test cases as in suite (B,$\mathcal{D}_3$), a mutation score of 100% is achieved.

Table 2. Results for the Ceiling Speed Monitor

		IECP-Tests (B) / (C)		(A) (Random Testing)		
Suite B,C	No. TC	Mutation Score	Line Cov.	No. TC	Mutation Score	Line Cov.
(B,$\mathcal{D}_1$)	21	62 %	86 %	21	34 %	75 %
(C,$\mathcal{D}_1$,1)	21	76 %	97 %	21	34 %	75 %
(C,$\mathcal{D}_1$,10)	183	82 %	97 %	183	54 %	87 %
(C,$\mathcal{D}_1$,25)	453	82 %	97 %	453	72 %	97 %
(B,$\mathcal{D}_2$)	186	87 %	100 %	186	63 %	92 %
(C,$\mathcal{D}_2$,1)	186	88 %	100 %	186	63 %	92 %
(C,$\mathcal{D}_2$,10)	882	94 %	100 %	882	84 %	97 %
(B,$\mathcal{D}_3$)	610	93 %	100 %	610	80 %	97 %
(C,$\mathcal{D}_3$,1)	610	100 %	100 %	610	80 %	97 %
(C,$\mathcal{D}_3$,10)	3002	100 %	100 %	3002	92 %	97 %

Column No. TC records the number of test cases applied. (B,$\mathcal{D}_i$) denotes application of strategy (B) with fault domain $\mathcal{D}_i, i = 1, 2, 3$, (C,$\mathcal{D}_i$,q) denotes application of strategy (C) with fault domain $\mathcal{D}_i, i = 1, 2, 3$ and min = q. Columns 'Line Cov.' record the line coverage achieved with the execution of the respective test suite.

In contrast to the results for the airbag controller shown below, random testing (A) achieves a surprisingly high mutation score of 92%, when the highest number of 3002 test cases is used. The performance of random testing is obviously correlated to the number of test cases. An increase in the number of test cases clearly increases the probability of finding a mutation. This is due to the fact that the ceiling speed monitor has a very low recurrence diameter of 2: from every control mode, every other mode can be reached by at most 2 RIOSTS transitions, when setting V_{est} and V_{MRSP} accordingly. Furthermore, the guard conditions are quite wide, so that the probability of finding random inputs letting any of the guards evaluate to `true` is high.

Airbag Controller. As table 3 confirms, our approach has a test strength that is significantly higher than the test strength of naive random testing. A mutation score of 89 % can be reached already in test suite (B,$\mathcal{D}_1$). Combined with randomisation, the mutation score can be lifted up to 97 % (test suite (C,$\mathcal{D}_1$,10)). Combined further with boundary value testing, (C,$\mathcal{D}_3$,1) is able to uncover every single fault mutation.

Table 3. Results for the Airbag Controller

		IECP-Tests (B) / (C)		(A) Random Testing		
Suite	No. TC	Mutation Score	Line Cov.	No. TC	Mutation Score	Line Cov.
(B,$\mathcal{D}_1$)	368	89 %	97 %	368	66 %	94 %
(C,$\mathcal{D}_1$,1)	368	96 %	100 %	368	66 %	94 %
(C,$\mathcal{D}_1$,10)	3816	97 %	100 %	3816	68 %	97 %
(B,$\mathcal{D}_3$)	3248	99 %	100 %	3248	68 %	94 %
(C,$\mathcal{D}_3$,1)	3248	100 %	100 %	3248	68 %	94 %

Notation in analogy to Table 2.

Note that the mutation score for naive random testing remains roughly constant, because the airbag controller has a higher recurrence diameter than the ceiling speed monitor, so that long traces are needed to reach a system state that is suitable to uncover a fault. Additionally the input equivalence classes are quite narrow. This explains, that an increase in the number of test cases has no or very limited effect on the mutation score of random testing, since the remaining 32 percent of mutations are only revealed by long specialised traces that have very low probabilities to be chosen at random.

Threats to Validity. We presented two reference models in the comparative test strength evaluation for the strategies (A), (B), and (C). The selection of test models may have an impact on the observed results. To reduce this threat, we used two models with opposing characteristics. The ceiling speed monitor has a very small recurrence diameter, a small number of internal states, and relatively wide input equivalence classes. The airbag controller on the other hand has many internal states, a high recurrence diameter and narrow input equivalence classes. It has been shown that the IECP testing strategies (B) and (C) are applicable to both systems and resulted in good test strength with an acceptable number of test cases. To counter threats to validity that might be caused by the mutant generator, other mutation generation tools have been applied as well. The PITest[5] tool uses a subset of the mutation operators the μJava tool uses. The Major mutation framework [15] uses the same mutation operators plus constant value replacement. Due to space restrictions only the results for the μJava tool were presented. Still, the results of both other tools were very similar to the results presented in the tables above.

---

[5] See http://pitest.org/. Additionally, this tool was very helpful to measure the line coverage that has been shown in the tables above.

Our experimental setup uses specific implementations in Java to generate mutants from. The implementation style may have an influence on the generated mutants which in turn has an impact on the observed mutant score. The use of code mutations was motivated from the fact, that real faults are very likely to be introduced on the code level. As our approach is to be applied to arbitrary blackbox systems, potentially implemented in other programming languages and/or combinations of hardware and software, the real faults might look different from our experimental faults. To counter this threat, we also experimented with mutations of the SysML model, applying mutant operators on the state machines. Double fault mutations were included as well, in contrast to the code mutations, where only single fault mutations were observed. These experiments also provided results for our strategies (B,C) that were comparable to the results presented here. There may remain some threats to validity resulting from the fact that some characteristic faults, e.g. memory leaks as a typical fault type in languages like C/C++, or faults resulting from HW/SW integration have not been considered yet in the mutations applied.

5   Related Work

The framework for constructing complete test suites in general, and for introducing equivalence class testing methods preserving completeness in particular, has been laid out in [11]. Notable examples for complete test methods have been given for various formalisms (FSM,Timed Automata, process algebras) in [8,10,19,22,23,25], further references on the state of the art of automated model-based testing are given in [1,21]. Adaptive random testing [7] focuses on techniques to evenly spread the test cases over the complete input domain. Most research concentrates on testing non-reactive software modules, where test cases are specified by single input vectors instead of the input sequences considered in our reactive systems setting. An example of the application of adaptive random testing and search-based testing to realtime embedded systems is given in [2].

6   Conclusion

In this paper, a complete equivalence class testing strategy has been experimentally evaluated with respect to its test strength, when applied to SUTs whose behaviour is outside the fault domain for which the completeness assertion applies. The experiments show that this strategy has significantly greater strength in comparison to conventional random testing. Moreover, a randomisation of the equivalence class testing strategy has been proposed that increases the test strength even further by selecting different values from each input equivalence class, whenever a member of this class is required as input according to the original strategy. The resulting test suite was additionally extended in order to ensure a minimal number of random selections from each input class applied in each I/O-equivalence class of the reference model.

At the same time it is clear that this "randomisation in the $\overline{\mathcal{I}}$-dimension" does not increase the test strength, if $\mathcal{S}''$ has a larger recurrence diameter than $\mathcal{S}$, and if erroneous behaviour of $\mathcal{S}''$ is only revealed at the end of a longest loop-free path. Therefore we suggest to add a "randomisation in the m-dimension" by attaching a random input sequence of a given fixed length at the end of each test case for in-depth exploration of the SUT behaviour. Observe that in most embedded system tests, the costs for resetting the SUT are higher than those for increasing the test suite length. Therefore increasing the length of test cases is generally acceptable, while increasing the number of test cases is usually a costly decision. The effect of increasing the test case length is currently investigated by the authors. Note that this requires more complex mutations increasing the recurrence diameter and inserting erroneous behaviours at the end of maximal loop-free paths only.

References

1. Anand, S., Burke, E.K., Chen, T.Y., Clark, J.A., Cohen, M.B., Grieskamp, W., Harman, M., Harrold, M.J., McMinn, P.: An orchestrated survey of methodologies for automated software test case generation. Journal of Systems and Software **86**(8), 1978–2001 (2013)
2. Arcuri, A., Iqbal, M.Z., Briand, L.: Black-Box system testing of real-time embedded systems using random and search-based testing. In: Petrenko, A., Simão, A., Maldonado, J.C. (eds.) ICTSS 2010. LNCS, vol. 6435, pp. 95–110. Springer, Heidelberg (2010)
3. Baier, C., Katoen, J.: Principles of model checking. MIT Press (2008)
4. Biere, A., Heljanko, K., Junttila, T., Latvala, T., Schuppan, V.: Linear encodings of bounded LTL model checking. Logical Methods in Computer Science **2**(5) (November 2006), arXiv: 0611029, arXiv: cs/0611029
5. Braunstein, C., Haxthausen, A.E., Huang, W., Hübner, F., Peleska, J., Schulze, U., Vu Hong, L.: Complete model-based equivalence class testing for the ETCS ceiling speed monitor. In: Merz, S., Pang, J. (eds.) ICFEM 2014. LNCS, vol. 8829, pp. 380–395. Springer, Heidelberg (2014)
6. Braunstein, C., Huang, W.l., Peleska, J., Schulze, U., Hübner, F., Haxthausen, A.E., Hong, L.V.: A SysML test model and test suite for the ETCS ceiling speed monitor. Tech. rep., Embedded Systems Testing Benchmarks Site (April 30, 2014). http://www.mbt-benchmarks.org
7. Chen, T.Y., Kuo, F.C., Merkel, R.G., Tse, T.H.: Adaptive random testing: the art of test case diversity. Journal of Systems and Software **83**(1), 60–66 (2010)
8. Chow, T.S.: Testing software design modeled by finite-state machines. IEEE Transactions on Software Engineering SE **4**(3), 178–186 (1978)
9. Clarke, E.M., Grumberg, O., Peled, D.A.: Model Checking. The MIT Press, Cambridge (1999)
10. Fujiwara, S., von Bochmann, G., Khendek, F., Amalou, M., Ghedamsi, A.: Test selection based on finite state models. IEEE Transactions on Software Engineering **17**(6), 591–603 (1991)
11. Gaudel, M.-C.: Testing can be formal, too. In: Mosses, P.D., Nielsen, M. (eds.) CAAP 1995, FASE 1995, and TAPSOFT 1995. LNCS, vol. 915, pp. 82–96. Springer, Heidelberg (1995)

12. Gill, A.: Introduction to the theory of finite-state machines. McGraw-Hill, New York (1962)

13. Huang, W.l., Peleska, J.: Complete model-based equivalence class testing. International Journal on Software Tools for Technology Transfer, 1–19 (2014). http://dx.doi.org/10.1007/s10009-014-0356-8

14. Jaulin, L., Kieffer, M., Didrit, O., Walter, É.: Applied Interval Analysis. Springer, London (2001)

15. Just, R.: The major mutation framework: efficient and scalable mutation analysis for java. In: Proceedings of the International Symposium on Software Testing and Analysis, ISSTA, July 23–25, pp. 433–436, San Jose, CA, USA (2014)

16. Ma, Y.S., Offutt, J., Kwon, Y.R.: MuJava: An Automated Class Mutation System: Research Articles. Softw. Test. Verif. Reliab. **15**(2), 97–133 (2005). http://dx.doi.org/10.1002/stvr.v15:2

17. Object Management Group: OMG Unified Modeling Language (OMG UML), superstructure, version 2.4.1. Tech. rep., OMG (2011)

18. Object Management Group: OMG Systems Modeling Language (OMG SysML^{TM}), Version 1.3. Tech. rep., Object Management Group (2012). http://www.omg.org/spec/SysML/1.3

19. Peleska, J., Siegel, M.: Test automation of safety-critical reactive systems. South African Computer Journal **19**, 53–77 (1997)

20. Peleska, J.: Industrial-strength model-based testing - state of the art and current challenges. In: Petrenko, A.K., Schlingloff, H. (eds.) Proceedings Eighth Workshop on Model-Based Testing. Electronic Proceedings in Theoretical Computer Science, vol. 111, pp. 3–28. Open Publishing Association, Rome (2013)

21. Petrenko, A., Simao, A., Maldonado, J.C.: Model-based testing of software and systems: Recent advances and challenges. Int. J. Softw. Tools Technol. Transf. **14**(4), 383–386 (2012). http://dx.doi.org/10.1007/s10009-012-0240-3

22. Springintveld, J., Vaandrager, F., D'Argenio, P.: Testing timed automata. Theoretical Computer Science **254**(1–2), 225–257 (2001)

23. Tretmans, J.: Model based testing with labelled transition systems. In: Hierons, R.M., Bowen, J.P., Harman, M. (eds.) FORTEST. LNCS, vol. 4949, pp. 1–38. Springer, Heidelberg (2008)

24. UNISIG: ERTMS/ETCS System Requirements Specification, Chapter 3, Principles, vol. Subset-026-3, chap. 3, issue 3.3.0 (February 2012)

25. Vasilevskii, M.P.: Failure diagnosis of automata. Kibernetika (Transl.) **4**, 98–108 (1973)

Testing Functional Requirements in UML Activity Diagrams

Stefan Mijatov, Tanja Mayerhofer[✉], Philip Langer, and Gerti Kappel

Business Informatics Group, Vienna University of Technology, Vienna, Austria
{mijatov,mayerhofer,langer,gerti}@big.tuwien.ac.at

Abstract. In model driven engineering (MDE), models constitute the main artifacts of the software development process. From models defining structural and behavioral aspects of a software system implementation artifacts, such as source code, are automatically generated using model transformation techniques. However, a crucial issue in MDE is the quality of models, as any defect not captured at model level is transferred to the code level, where it requires more time and effort to be detected and corrected. This work is concerned with testing the functional correctness of models created with a subset of UML called fUML comprising class and activity diagrams. We present a testing framework for fUML, which enables modelers to verify the correct behavior of fUML activities.

Keywords: Functional testing · UML activity diagrams · fUML

1 Introduction

In model driven engineering (MDE), models are the main artifacts of the development process. Using model transformations, code and other implementation artifacts are automatically produced from models improving the productivity of the software development process, as well as the quality, portability, and maintainability of the developed system [2]. As the development process shifts from being code-centric to being model-centric, the quality of the models used in an MDE-based software development process becomes essential. Any defect not captured at model level will be propagated to the code level, where it will require more time and effort to be detected and corrected.

This work is concerned with verifying the *functional correctness* of models created with UML [14], which is the most widely adopted modeling language in MDE. More precisely, we focus on fUML [16], which is an executable subset of UML (cf. also xUML [10]) comprising class diagrams for defining the structure of systems and activity diagrams for defining the behavior of systems. For fUML, a standardized virtual machine exists that gives precise operational semantics to the included subset of UML. The standardization of fUML's semantics provides the basis for developing model analysis techniques and tools for UML models.

In general, it can be distinguished between two main analysis techniques for verifying the functional correctness of software artifacts, namely formal analysis and testing techniques. These two techniques are not mutually exclusive,

© Springer International Publishing Switzerland 2015
J.C. Blanchette and N. Kosmatov (Eds.): TAP 2015, LNCS 9154, pp. 173–190, 2015.
DOI: 10.1007/978-3-319-21215-9_11

but instead complement each other. While several approaches applying formal analysis techniques on fUML have been proposed in the past, to the best of our knowledge only first ideas and intents on applying testing techniques on fUML have been published (cf. Sect. 6).

In this paper, we present a fully functional and implemented *testing framework for fUML*, which is based on first ideas and an early prototype presented in [12]. The framework comprises a test specification language, which enables modelers to express assertions on the behavior of a system defined in fUML, as well as a test interpreter, which evaluates these assertions. Besides giving an overall overview of our testing framework, we present *three newly developed testing features*. These new features address three requirements on testing fUML models: *(i)* Specifying assertions on the behavior of a system requires the capability to evaluate complex conditions on the system's runtime state, such as iterations over existing objects and calculations over their feature values. *(ii)* Temporal expressions allowing precise selections of the runtime states to be asserted are required. *(iii)* Because fUML models can be used to specify concurrent behavior, the existence of a potentially large number of possible execution paths has to be considered in the test evaluation. To address these requirements, we extended our initial testing framework with *(i)* support for OCL [15] allowing the specification of complex assertions on the runtime state of a system, *(ii)* a set of temporal operators and temporal quantifiers allowing a more precise selection of the runtime states to be asserted, and *(iii)* an improved test evaluation algorithm taking concurrent behavior into account. We evaluated our testing framework with these newly introduced features in a *user study* concerning the properties *ease of use* and *usefulness*. The evaluation results on the one hand indicate that the testing framework is both easy to adopt and useful for testing fUML models, and on the other hand enabled us to identify potential for improvement.

The remainder of the paper is structured as follows. In Sect. 2, we introduce an example for motivating and illustrating the newly developed features of our testing framework. In Sect. 3 and Sect. 4, we provide an overview of our testing framework and describe its new features in detail. The results of our user study and related work are discussed in Sect. 5 and Sect. 6, respectively. In Sect. 7, we conclude the paper and outline future work.

2   Motivating Example

In this section, we want to motivate our testing approach based on the example of an automatic teller machine (ATM) system. The structure of the ATM system is depicted in Fig. 1. The ATM can be used to perform withdrawals from a bank account. The process of performing a withdrawal (operation *ATM.withdraw*) is realized by the activity *ATM.withdraw* shown in Fig. 2. For starting a withdrawal, the user has to provide an ATM card, the pin assigned to the card, and the amount of money to be withdrawn from the user's account. Once the withdrawal is started, first a new transaction is created and set as current transaction (action *startTransaction*). Next, the provided pin is validated (action *validatePin*). If the pin is valid, the withdrawal is performed (action *makeWithdrawal*).

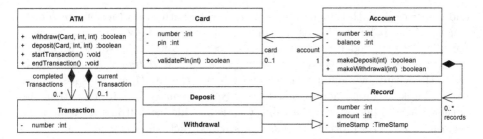

Fig. 1. Class diagram of the ATM system

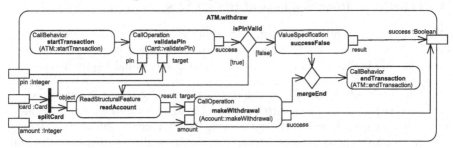

Fig. 2. Activity diagram of the operation *ATM.withdraw*

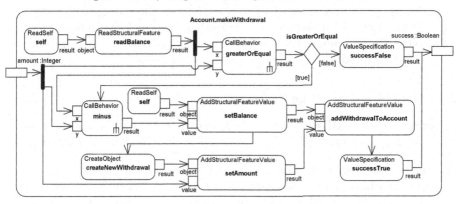

Fig. 3. Activity diagram of the operation *Account.makeWithdrawal*

This in turn causes the balance of the account to be updated and a corresponding withdrawal record to be created. Once the withdrawal has been completed, the transaction is ended and recorded (action *endTransaction*).

Please note that the actions *startTransaction*, *validatePin*, *makeWithdrawal*, and *endTransaction* are call actions calling the declared operations. The explained functionality of these operations are implemented by dedicated activities. In the following, we discuss the implementation of the operation *makeWithdrawal*. The remaining activities are omitted due to space limitations.

Figure 3 shows the activity implementing the operation *Account.makeWithdrawal*. This activity first retrieves the account's balance (action *readBalance*) and compares it with the amount of money to be withdrawn (action *greaterOr-Equal*). If the balance exceeds the amount of money to be withdrawn, the new balance is calculated (actions *minus*) and set (actions *setBalance*). Finally, a new withdrawal record is created (action *createNewWithdrawal*), its amount is set to the withdrawn amount of money (action *setAmount*), and it is associated to the bank account (action *addWithdrawalToAccount*). In the case that the withdrawal was performed, the value *true* is provided as output of the activity (action *successTrue*), otherwise *false* is provided (action *successFalse*).

2.1 Functional Requirements of the ATM System

In the following, we consider the functional correctness of the ATM's withdrawal functionality. For correctly handling withdrawals in case a *correct pin* was provided, the ATM system has to fulfill the following functional requirements.

FR1 The pin has to be validated before the actual withdrawal is performed.
FR2 The account's balance has to be reduced by the provided amount of money.
FR3 After the completion of the withdrawal, the balance of the account should be equal to the difference between the sum of all recorded deposits and the sum of all recorded withdrawals.
FR4 A new withdrawal record has to be created for the account.
FR5 The activity should return *true* indicating a successful withdrawal.
FR6 When the withdrawal is started, a new transaction should be created; once it is completed, the transaction should be ended and recorded.

2.2 Requirements of the Testing Framework

To verify that the fUML model of the ATM system fulfills the specified functional requirements, a testing framework is needed providing the following capabilities.

1. The testing framework shall provide the possibility to test the *chronological order* in which nodes of an activity are executed. Thereby, the framework ensures that the specified order is correct for every possible execution of the activity, taking concurrency into account. (Required for *FR1*)
2. The testing framework shall provide support for testing whether an activity produces the correct *output* for a given input. Also, checking the output of actions within the activity shall be supported. (Required for *FR2* and *FR5*)
3. The testing framework shall provide the possibility to test the *runtime state* of a system during the execution of an activity. Therefore, it has to enable the selection of the relevant runtime states, as well as the evaluation of expressions on these runtime states. (Required for *FR3*, *FR4*, and *FR6*: For *FR6* it has to be tested whether after the execution of the action *startTransaction* of the activity *ATM.withdraw* a new transaction has been created; for the final runtime state it has to checked whether the account's balance and records are consistent (*FR3*), a new withdrawal record has been created (*FR4*), and the started transaction has been recorded (*FR6*))

```
1  scenario atmTestData [
2      object atmTD: ATM {}
3      object cardTD: Card {pin = 1985;}
4      object accountTD: Account {balance = 100;}
5      object depositTD: Deposit {amount = 100;}
6      link card_account {source card = cardTD; target account = accountTD;}
7      link account_record {source account = accountTD; target records = depositTD;}
8  ]
```

Listing 1. Test scenario for testing the ATM system

```
1  test atmTestSuccess activity ATM.withdraw(card=cardTD, pin=1985, amount=100) on
   ↪atmTD {
2      assertOrder *, validatePin, *, makeWithdrawal, *; // FR1
3      finally {
4          readAccount.result::balance = 0; // FR2
5          check 'BalanceRecords' on readAccount.result; // FR3
6          check 'NumOfWithdrawalsSuccess' on readAccount.result; // FR4
7          success = true; // FR5
8      }
9      assertState eventually after constraint 'TransactionCreated' { // FR6
10         check 'TransactionEnded', 'TransactionAdded';
11     }
12 }
```

Listing 2. Test case for testing the ATM system

```
1  context ATM
2      exp TransactionCreated: currentTransaction <> null
3      exp TransactionEnded: currentTransaction = null
4      exp TransactionAdded: completedTransactions -> size() = 1
5  context Account
6      exp NumOfWithdrawalsSuccess: records -> select(oclIsTypeOf(Withdrawal)) -> size()=1
7      exp BalanceRecords:
8      (records -> select(oclIsTypeOf(Deposit)) -> collect(amount) -> sum()) -
9      (records -> select(oclIsTypeOf(Withdrawal)) -> collect(amount) -> sum()) = balance
10 endpackage
```

Listing 3. OCL constraints for testing the ATM system

The early prototype of our testing framework presented in [12] only partially supported these capabilities. In this work, we introduce new testing features that significantly extend the framework's capabilities and enable a more precise and thorough verification of the functional correctness of fUML activities.

3   Overview of the Testing Framework

Our testing framework is composed of a *test specification language* enabling the definition of assertions on the behavior of fUML activities and a *test interpreter* evaluating these assertions. In the following, we briefly introduce these two components and discuss their limitations as presented in [12].

3.1   Test Specification Language

The test specification language enables modelers to define *test suites* composed of test scenarios and test cases.

Test scenarios allow the specification of objects and links, which can be used both as input values and expected output values of activities under test. The definition of a test scenario is composed of the keyword `scenario`, a scenario name, arbitrary many object definitions, and arbitrary many link definitions.

Listing 1 shows the test scenario defined for testing the ATM's functional requirements presented in Sect. 2. The test scenario is called *atmTestData* and defines four objects (keyword `object`), namely one *ATM* object, one *Card* object with the pin *1985*, one *Account* object with the balance *100*, and one *Deposit* object with the deposit amount *100*. Furthermore, it defines two links (keyword `link`), namely between the specified *Card* and *Account* objects, as well as between the *Account* and *Deposit* objects.

A *test case* tests the behavior of an activity. Its definition consists of the keyword `test`, a test name, the keyword `activity`, the name of the activity under test, an optional list of input parameter value assignments for the activity, an optional declaration of a context object for the activity, and a body. In the body an arbitrary number of order assertions and state assertions can be declared.

Listing 2 shows the test case *atmTestSuccess* asserting the functional requirements of the ATM's withdraw functionality defined by the activity *ATM. withdraw*. For the input parameters, the *Card* object *cardTD* defined in the test scenario (cf. Listing 1), the correct pin *1985*, and the amount to be withdrawn of *100* are provided. The activity is executed for the *ATM* object *atmTD* also defined in the test scenario. The test case consists of one order assertion (line 2) and two state assertions (lines 3-8 and 9-11), which are explained in the following.

Order assertion can be used to test the order in which the nodes of the activity under test are executed. To specify an order assertion, the keyword `assertOrder` is used followed by the list of nodes in their expected execution order. It is also possible to specify a relative order of nodes by the use of jokers for skipping exactly one ('_') or zero to many ('*') nodes.

The order assertion of the test case *atmTestSuccess* (cf. Listing 2, line 2) tests whether the action *validatePin* is executed before the action *makeWithdrawal* with arbitrary many nodes being executed before, in between, or after them.

State assertions can be used to check the runtime state of the tested system during the execution of the activity under test. The definition of a state assertion consists of the keyword `assertState`, a temporal expression selecting the runtime state to be checked, and arbitrary many state expressions defining the expected properties of the selected runtime state. The temporal expressions provided by the test specification language have been substantially extended and improved compared to our early prototype presented in [12]. They will be extensively discussed in Sect. 4.2. In line 4 of the test case *atmTestSuccess* (cf. Listing 2) we see an example of a state expression. It checks in the final runtime state of the ATM system whether the account's balance has been updated to 0. Please note that the test input for the activity *ATM.withdraw* defines that a withdrawal of the amount 100 should be performed for the account associated with the card *cardTD*. The card *cardTD* and its associated account *accountTD* have been defined in the test scenario shown in Listing 1. Because the initial balance of the account is specified to be 100 (cf. Listing 1, line 4), it is asserted whether after the withdrawal of 100, the account's balance is equal to 0.

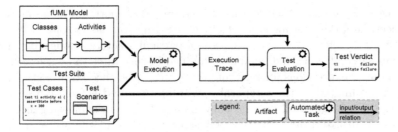

Fig. 4. Test interpreter

The test case shown in Listing 2 tests the fulfillment of all functional requirements defined in Sect. 2. The correspondences are provided in the comments in Listing 2. Please note that the test case uses the objects defined in the test scenario shown in Listing 1 as input values for the tested activity *ATM.withdraw*, and the OCL expressions shown in Listing 3 for several state assertions. We will discuss the test case in more detail in Sect. 4. A thorough discussion of the test specification language is also provided on our project website [13].

3.2 Test Interpreter

The test interpreter is responsible for evaluating test cases specified in the presented test specification language. The process of evaluating test cases is shown in Fig. 4. The input provided to the test interpreter consists of the fUML model to be tested and the test suite to be evaluated on this model. Each test case in the test suite is evaluated by executing the activity under test for the input values defined by the test case using the extended fUML virtual machine elaborated in previous work [9]. This extended fUML virtual machine captures execution traces reflecting the runtime behavior of the executed activity. In particular, an execution trace provides detailed information about the execution order of activities and activity nodes, inputs and outputs of activities and activity nodes, as well as the runtime state of the system at any point in time of the execution. The execution traces are analyzed by the test interpreter for evaluating every assertion defined by a test case. The output of the evaluation is a test report providing the information which assertions succeeded, which assertions failed, and further information on failing assertions, such as invalid execution orders of activity nodes and invalid system states.

3.3 Limitations

While the early prototype of our testing framework as presented in [12] supports assertions of a system's runtime state and the correct execution order of activity nodes, it has the following major limitations:

1. State assertions are restricted to simple equality checks of objects and their feature values. Complex expressions, such as iterations over a set of objects

or calculations over their feature values are not supported. Furthermore, the selection of the runtime states to be checked by state assertions can be only defined by referring to the execution of particular activity nodes, but not by defining conditions that should be fulfilled in the states to be selected.

2. Temporal expressions for selecting the states to be checked in a state assertion are limited to the temporal operators *after* and *before*, as well as the quantifiers *always* and *exactly*. They are insufficient for expressing more complex state assertions, such as that some property of the state eventually becomes *true* or that a certain property is valid in only some states.

3. Furthermore, order assertions are evaluated on a single execution path of the activity under test, which is insufficient in the presence of concurrency.

4   Extensions of the Testing Framework

To overcome the aforementioned limitations of the early prototype of our testing framework, we have extended it with support for OCL, additional temporal operators and quantifiers, as well as a new test evaluation algorithm accounting for concurrent behavior. These extensions are subject of this section.

4.1   OCL Expressions

With state expressions it is tested whether the runtime state of a tested system fulfills certain properties. In the early prototype of our testing framework, state expressions were restricted to simple equality checks. With this restriction, complex properties, such as needed for verifying the consistency of an account's balance with its deposit and withdrawal records (*FR3*), are not possible.

Supporting the definition of complex properties in state expressions requires the extension of our testing framework with a suitable expression language. Thereby, concepts allowing iterations over objects existing in a system's runtime states, calculations over these objects' feature values, and comparisons of values are of particular interest. This includes especially operations for the predefined types of fUML, such as *Collection* operations (e.g., *select()*, *forAll()*).

The integration of these concepts requires an extension of our test specification language with complex grammar concepts, as well as an extension of our test interpreter for evaluating expressions defined with these concepts. Both extensions are expensive to achieve without using an already existing expression language with supporting infrastructure. Thus, we decided against building our own expression language and interpreter, but instead integrated OCL with our testing framework. OCL [15] is a formal language providing concepts for defining expressions on UML models. Like UML, it is standardized by OMG and most of the experts in the modeling domain are familiar with OCL.

We integrated OCL with our testing framework, such that OCL expressions can be used for defining *complex conditions* on a system's runtime state as state expressions in state assertions, as well as for specifying *temporal expressions* selecting the runtime states to be asserted. This integration was achieved using the DresdenOCL framework [7], which provides extension mechanisms that allow the integration of OCL into the abstract and concrete syntax of an existing modeling language, such as our test specification language, as well as the evaluation of OCL expressions on any model instances, such as the runtime state of a model represented with fUML as required by our test interpreter. Details about how such an integration of OCL may be achieved can be found in [7].

The OCL expressions used in the test cases for the ATM system are given in Listing 3. For instance, the OCL expression *BalanceRecords* (lines 7-9) specifies that the balance of an account should be equal to the difference between the sum of all recorded deposits and the sum of all recorded withdrawals. This OCL expression is used in the test case (cf. Listing 2, line 5) to test that the account's balance and its withdrawal and deposit records are consistent.

4.2   Temporal Expressions

Temporal expressions are used in state assertions for selecting the runtime states of a tested system that have to be checked for expected properties. Thereby, runtime states are generated during the execution of activities and capture the system's state after a certain action has been executed. For instance, as illustrated in Fig. 5, the states *S1*, *S2*, *S3*, and *S4* resulted from the execution of the actions *actionA*, *actionB*, *actionC*, and *actionD*, respectively. The values *a*, *b*, and *c* in each state represent the results of evaluating conditions on these states.

Temporal expressions are composed of temporal operators, temporal quantifiers, and actions or alternatively OCL constraints. In the early prototype of our testing framework, OCL constraints were not supported for selecting runtime states, and important temporal quantifiers, such as *eventually*, were missing. As part of our extensions, we also refined the supported temporal operators. In the following, we discuss the temporal operators and quantifiers based on Fig. 5.

Temporal operators in combination with the specification of actions are used for selecting the runtime states to be considered in a state assertion. We support the temporal operators *after* and *until* defining that all runtime states after or until an action has been executed shall be considered. If OCL constraints are used instead of actions, they are evaluated in each runtime state starting with the first one. Those states in which the constraints are evaluated to *true* for the first time are select, as well as all runtime states between them.

Temporal quantifiers are used for specifying in which of the selected runtime states the state expressions of a state assertion should evaluate to *true*. Our test specification language provides the temporal quantifiers *always*, *eventually*, *immediately*, and *sometimes* described in the following.

The temporal quantifier *always* defines that the state expressions should evaluate to *true* in all selected runtime state. For instance, the temporal expression *(1a)* specifies that in each state starting from the first one until the state produced by *actionB*, the value of the state expression *c* should evaluate to *false*.

The temporal quantifier *eventually* defines that each state expression should evaluate to *true* in one of the selected runtime states and should remain *true* in all of the following selected runtime states. For instance, the temporal expression

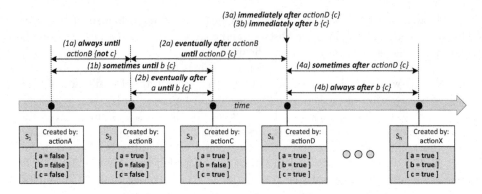

Fig. 5. Combinations of temporal operators and temporal quantifiers in state assertions

(2b) specifies that from the first state in which *a* becomes *true*, until the first state in which *b* becomes *true*, the value of the state expression *c* should become *true* in one state and remain *true* in each of the following selected states.

The temporal quantifier *immediately* specifies that each state expression should be *true* in either a runtime state created by the specified action or the one right before this state, depending on whether the temporal operator *after* or *until* is used. If an OCL constraint is used instead, the state expression should be fulfilled in the first state where the specified constraint evaluates to *true* or the state right before it. For instance, the temporal expression *(3a)* specifies that the value of the state expression *c* should be *true* in the state caused by *actionD*.

The temporal quantifier *sometimes* defines that each state expression should evaluate to *true* in at least one of the selected runtime states. The temporal expression *(1b)* specifies that the state expression *c* should evaluate to *true* in at least one of the states from the first state until the state where *b* becomes *true*.

We also introduced the keyword *finally* as a shorthand for `always after actionX` where *actionX* is the last executed action of the activity under test.

Looking back at the test case for the ATM system in Listing 2, the state assertion in lines 9-11 specifies that after the constraint *TransactionCreated* (cf. Listing 3) is evaluated to *true*, the constraints *TransactionEnded* and *TransactionAdded* should eventually evaluate to *true*. Thus, it is tested whether during the execution of the activity *ATM.withdraw*, a transaction is created, which is afterwards ended and recorded.

With the newly introduced and improved temporal operators and temporal quantifiers, and the capability to use OCL conditions in temporal expressions, a system's runtime states can be much more precisely selected for testing purposes than has been possible with the early prototype of our testing framework.

4.3   Concurrency

Concurrency in an activity leads to the existence of a potentially large or even infinite number of possible execution paths of that activity, which have to be

	st	sc	vp	ipv	ra	mw	me	et
startTransaction (st)			T					
splitCard (sc)			T		T			
validatePin (vp)				I				
isPinValid (ipv)					I			
readAccount (ra)						I		
makeWithdrawal (mw)							T	
mergeEnd (me)								T
endTransaction (et)								

Fig. 6. Adjacency matrix for evaluating order assertions on the activity *ATM.withdraw*

considered in the test evaluation. In particular, order assertions checking the correct execution order of activity nodes have to be evaluated for every possible execution path of the activity under test.

The early prototype of our testing framework did not account for concurrent execution paths of activities and thus reported false positive evaluation results for order assertions. This is because the fUML virtual machine executes concurrent paths sequentially, and thus the trace used for evaluating order assertions reflects only one possible execution order of activity nodes lying on concurrent paths. The early prototype checked order assertions only on this single sequential execution order. To overcome this limitation, we implemented a new evaluation algorithm for order assertions, which correctly deals with concurrent paths.

As a first step, the algorithm transforms the execution trace of the activity under test into an adjacency matrix. The execution trace from which we construct the matrix is like in the former version of the evaluation algorithm obtained from a single execution of the activity under test for the given input defined by the test case. However, the new algorithm also takes the input/output dependencies between executed activity nodes into account, which are also captured by the execution trace. Thereby, an activity node B depends on an activity node A, if B received an object token or control token from A as input. In this case, B is added as being adjacent to A in the adjacency matrix.

Figure 6 shows the adjacency matrix constructed for the execution of the activity *ATM.withdraw* (cf. Fig. 2) with the input values defined in our test case *atmTestSuccess* (cf. Listing 2). For instance, the activity node *validatePin* is adjacent to the activity node *startTransaction*, because it received a control token from *validatePin* via the defined control flow edge. Thus, the matrix contains a *true* value (abbreviated with T) in the first row and third column.

Based on the constructed adjacency matrix, order assertions can be evaluated efficiently by analyzing the dependencies between activity nodes specified in the order assertions. For instance, to evaluate an order assertion `assertOrder *,` `A, B, *`, we have to check whether B depends on A, i.e., whether a *true* value in the adjacency matrix indicates B as being adjacent to A. If this is not the case, there exists no input/output dependency between A and B and, hence, they may be executed in reverse order. Furthermore, we have to check that there are no other nodes independent of both A and B, i.e., nodes that lie on parallel paths.

For the evaluation of the jokers '_' and '*', also indirect input/output dependencies between activity nodes have to be considered, which can also be efficiently calculated from the adjacency matrix. For instance, to evaluate an order assertion `assertOrder A, _, B`, we have to check whether an arbitrary activity node X exists on which B depends and which itself depends on A, i.e., X provided input to B and received input from A.

Looking back at our test case defined for the ATM system (cf. Listing 2), the order assertion defined in line 2 is evaluated by checking in the adjacency matrix (cf. Fig. 6) whether *makeWithdrawal* is directly or indirectly adjacent to *validatePin*. Because this is the case, indicated by the underlined *true* values in the matrix, the order assertion evaluates to *true*.

4.4   Implementation

We provide an open source implementation of our testing framework integrated with EMF. The testing framework is part of the larger project *moliz* [13], which is concerned with executing, testing, and debugging models based on the fUML standard. For implementing the grammar and editor of our test specification language, we have used the Xtext framework. The test interpreter is implemented in Java and based on an extended version of the reference implementation of the fUML virtual machine elaborated in previous work [9]. For the integration of OCL with our testing framework, we have used the DresdenOCL framework [7].

5   Evaluation

We evaluated our testing framework with the presented new functionality concerning *ease of use* and *usefulness* by carrying out a user study. In the following, we present the user study setup, as well as the results and lessons learned.

5.1   User Study Setup

The user study consisted of the following four steps, which were carried out with each participant individually.

(i) Introduction. At the beginning of the user study, the participant was given an introduction to fUML and our testing framework. This included the most important concepts of fUML comprising fUML's class concepts, activity concepts, and action language. Furthermore, a simple exemplary fUML model was introduced and used to explain the main concepts of our test specification language.

(ii) Skills questionnaire. The target group of users of our testing framework are practitioners in the MDE domain using UML activity diagrams to define the behavior of systems. Thus, in order to obtain relevant results, our selection of participants was based on their background in UML, OCL, and unit testing.

The participants' skills in these languages were collected using a questionnaire. Most of the participants had a good background in UML being slightly more experienced with class diagrams than with activity diagrams. The knowledge of the UML action language was balanced from having no experience to being an expert. Most of the participants declared their experience with OCL at the beginner level, while unit testing knowledge was declared as average by most participants. The participants of the user study consisted of post-doctoral researchers, PhD students, and master students of the Vienna University of Technology.

(iii) Testing tasks. The participants were asked to complete two tasks with our testing framework. Therefore they used our implementation of the testing framework, including an editor for writing test cases and the test interpreter running test cases and providing the results as console output.

The aim of the *first task* was to evaluate the *ease of use* of our testing framework. Therefore, the participants had to define a test suite implementing predefined functional requirements for two given and correct activities. For the first activity, the participants had to specify a test scenario with one object, and two test cases with two different order assertions and two different state assertions. The activity comprised nine nodes and included simple fUML action types, such as *value specification action.* For the second activity, the participants had to specify a test scenario with several objects and links, two state assertions, and one OCL expression. The activity was composed of fourteen activity nodes and included slightly more complex fUML concepts, such as *expansion regions.*

With the *second task,* we aimed at evaluating the *usefulness* of our testing framework, in particular, the usefulness of test results for detecting and correcting defects in UML activity diagrams. In this task, the participant was given a defective activity diagram, two test cases testing the activity diagram, and the test results. Based on the test cases and test results, the participant had to locate the defects and suggest corrections. The activity consisted of nine activity nodes and included simple fUML action types. Two defects were introduced into the UML activity diagram. One defect consisted of wrong guards for a decision node, which led to the execution of a wrong path. This defect was detectable from the test result of a failing order assertion. The second defect consisted of a missing merge node, which led to an activity node not being executed. This defect was detectable from the test result of a failing state assertion.

(iv) Opinion questionnaire. Finally, the participants rated the ease of use and usefulness of the testing framework in a questionnaire.

More details about the case study setup including the used fUML models, test suits, and task descriptions may be found at our project website [13].

5.2   Results and Lessons Learned

We observed the participants during performing the given tasks to find out *(i)* how easy our testing framework is to use for testing UML activity diagrams (first task), and *(ii)* whether test results are useful for detecting and correcting defects in UML activity diagrams (second task).

(i) Ease of use. For the first task, where the participants had to define test cases, we made the following observations.

Test scenarios. Most of the participants had at the beginning problems to understand the purpose of test scenarios, because they tried to define the test scenarios before thinking about and writing the actual test cases. However, after having defined the first test case, the participants understood how to use test scenarios for providing input to the activities under test.

Order assertions. Another frequently observed problem encountered by the participants was to correctly specify order assertions. Several participants specified the expected order of activity nodes incorrectly, as they forgot to use jokers for allowing arbitrary nodes to be executed between two nodes of interest. However, after running the order assertion and reading the failing test result, all participants were able to correct the order assertion.

State assertions. A third recurring issue was related to understanding the relation between temporal expressions and state expressions. More precisely, several participants specified each state expression separately in a distinct state assertion, even though the temporal expressions of these state assertions were identical (i.e., only one state assertion would have been required).

OCL expressions. Several participants had issues with specifying the OCL expression required for one of the test cases. However, this was due to the fact that these participants had little experience with OCL. Connecting the OCL expression with a test case was not an issue for any of the participants.

Overall, we observed that after each written test case, the participants were making fewer mistakes in specifying the next one. By the time they got to the second task, all participants had a clear understanding about all the concepts provided by the test specification language. From this observation, we conclude that our test specification language has a gentle learning curve. One of the possible improvements that we discovered during the user study is that some concepts of the test specification language, such as the specification of links in test scenarios, could be improved. Furthermore, additional validations by the editor would significantly improve the specification of test cases, as it prevents defects in the test cases themselves.

(ii) Usefulness. In the second task, the participants had to detect and correct defects in a UML activity diagram based on test cases and test results. We made the following observations for this task.

Understanding test cases. The participants had no problems in understanding the given test cases and their purpose. They were able to correctly explain the functional requirements tested by the test cases.

Understanding test results. Out of the eleven participants, five were able to locate both introduced defects, three were able to locate the first defect only, and three were not able to locate any of the defects.

For identifying the first defect, we provided the participants with a test case testing the expected execution order of activity nodes with an order assertion, as well as the test result of running the test case on the defective activity. The test result listed the actually executed path, which allowed all of the participants to detect that a wrong path was executed. Eight of the participants were also able to identify the related defect, namely wrongly defined guard conditions. Three participants were not able to locate this defect, because they were not familiar with how guard conditions are evaluated in UML based on object flows.

The second defect was a missing merge node, which impeded the execution of an activity node and consequently resulted in a wrong final runtime state of the tested system. For identifying this defect, we provided a test case checking the final runtime state with a state assertion, as well as the test result. The test result showed both the actually last executed activity node and the actual final runtime state. Neither of them was as expected by the state assertion. For identifying the causing defect, the participants had to detect that the activity node leading to the expected final runtime state was not executed and that the reason for this was the missing merge node. This was not as obvious as in the former example, where the result of an order assertion clearly showed which nodes of the tested activity were executed and which were not. Furthermore, identifying that a merge node has to be introduced to correct the defect requires the knowledge that alternative branches in UML activities always have to be explicitly merged by a merge node. Thus, the participants who did not have this knowledge were not able to identify the missing merge node as defect.

With this task, we aimed at evaluating how useful test results are for detecting and resolving defects in UML activity diagrams. We define the property *usefulness* as the average percentage of defects resolved by participants based on test results. Let D be the number of defects introduced into an activity, and RD_i the number of defects resolved by participant i. Then, the percentage of resolved defects by user i is $X_i = RD_i/D * 100$. The metric for measuring usefulness is $U = \sum X_i/n$, where n is the number of participants. According to this metric, the usefulness measured through the user study is $U = (5 * 100\% + 3 * 50\% + 3 * 0\%)/11 = 59.09\%$. This measure indicates a positive result for the usefulness of test results for detecting defects in activities. However, it also indicates that further improvements are needed.

Our conclusion drawn from these observations is that the visualization of test results is crucial for making them useful for locating defects. Therefore, providing more effective means for visualizing test results have to be investigated in future work. For instance, we intend to investigate the integration of the visualization of test results with UML modeling editors, such that test results can be presented on the tested activity diagrams themselves. Furthermore, presenting the states of a system occurred during the execution of an activity under test in the form of UML object diagrams could be useful, as it may provide more insight into the cause of failing test cases. Furthermore, for localizing a defect and deriving valid corrections, debugging is essential. Providing users with the possibility to step through the execution of an activity and observe the state of the system after each step may facilitate the localization of defects causing failing test cases.

Table 1 shows the results of the opinion questionnaire filled in by the participants to rate how difficult it was to accomplish the given tasks. As can be seen from the results, our observations and conclusions correspond to the participants' opinion.

Table 1. Results of the opinion questionnaire

Task	very easy	easy	medium	hard	very hard
Read class diagrams	7	4			
Read activity diagrams	3	7		1	
Write test cases		8		3	
Read test cases	3	4	2	2	
Read test results	3	4	2	2	
Correct activity diagrams	1	3	2	2	3

Threats to Validity. There are several threats to the validity of the evaluation results. First, in order to make the evaluation feasible in the described setup, the examples given to participants were of low complexity. Having more complex examples might give better insights into the ease of use of the test specification language and the usefulness of test results for detecting defects. Another threat to validity is the selection of participants. The participants consisted of researchers and students, but participants from industry were missing. Furthermore, also the fairly low number of participants influences the validity of the results. As future work, we intend to perform a larger user study with more participants having different background and knowledge, as well as with more complex examples.

6   Related Work

Until now, testing UML activity diagrams conforming to the fUML standard has not been investigated intensively. We are only aware of the work by Craciun *et al.* [4], who propose to develop a virtual machine for fUML models using the K-framework for efficiently testing fUML models. However, this work is still in its early stage and there is yet no information about an existing implementation.

For UML 2 activities and actions, Crane and Dingel [5] present an interpreter, which offers several dynamic analysis capabilities, such as reachability and dead lock analysis, as well as assertions on objects during the execution of activities. The latter capability is similar to the state assertions provided by our testing framework. However, only some simple expressions on objects are supported. In contrast, our testing framework supports the full power of OCL.

Another interesting line of work related to state assertions is temporal OCL. It is an extension of OCL with temporal operators and quantifiers (e.g., [3]) enabling not only the evaluation of OCL expressions on a single state of a system but also on its evolution. Thus, temporal OCL could be used in a similar way as our state assertions for testing purposes. However, our testing framework does not extend OCL with temporal expressions, but rather uses it as is and instead provides temporal expressions as part of the test specification language.

Contrary to testing techniques, several approaches applying formal analysis techniques on fUML activities have been proposed. Romero *et al.* [18] show how the standardized formal semantics of fUML can be utilized to perform formal verification through theorem proving. Abdelhalim *et al.* [1] developed a framework that automatically formalizes fUML models as CSP processes and analyzes them for deadlocks. Laurent *et al.* [8] define a first-order logic formalization for a subset of fUML and apply model checking techniques for verifying the correctness of process models defined with fUML. Their formalization covers control and data flows, as well as resource and timing constraints. Properties that are verified include termination and dead lock freeness. Planas *et al.* [17] propose a verification method for fUML models, which focuses on the property *strong executability*. This property guarantees that every time an activity is executed, the system's state is changed in a way consistent with all defined integrity constraints. Micskei *et al.* [11] propose a transformation chain from UML models to formal verification tools using fUML and Alf as intermediary languages. In particular, they propose to translate UML state machines into the formal language of the UPPAAL tool environment, which provides a model checker allowing the formal verification of the modeled behavior.

Further approaches dealing with the formal analysis of UML activity diagrams exist, which, however, do not consider the full power of fUML. For instance, Eshuis and Wieringa [6] present a formalization of workflow models specified as UML activity diagrams for verifying functional requirements. In their approach, activity diagrams are translated into transition systems, functional requirements are defined as LTL formulas, and these LTL formulas are evaluated on the obtained transition systems using the NuSMV model checker.

7   Conclusion and Future Work

In this paper, we have presented a testing framework for fUML models, which allows modelers to verify the correct behavior of fUML activities. Besides giving an overview of the testing framework, we have explained three newly introduced features in detail, which significantly extend the framework's testing capabilities. In particular, we introduced support for OCL allowing the evaluation of more complex conditions on the expected runtime state of a system under test. Furthermore, our testing framework now provides additional temporal operators and quantifiers for more precisely selecting the runtime states to be asserted by test cases. Finally, we developed a new algorithm for verifying the correct execution order of activity nodes in the presence of concurrent behavior.

Based on the lessons learned from evaluating our testing framework in a user study, we intend to improve the ease of use of our test specification language by adapting its textual syntax, as well as the usefulness of test results by investigating more effective visualization techniques. Furthermore, we plan to further improve the evaluation of assertions taking into account concurrency. In particular, concurrent paths also have to be considered when evaluating state assertions, as actions modifying and accessing the same values concurrently might lead to nondeterminism. Another interesting feature that we have identified for future work is the support of comparisons between distinct runtime states of the tested system, i.e., the comparison of runtime states at different points in time.

References

1. Abdelhalim, I., Schneider, S., Treharne, H.: An Integrated Framework for Checking the Behaviour of fUML Models using CSP. International Journal on Software Tools for Technology Transfer **15**(4), 375–396 (2013)
2. Bézivin, J.: On the unification power of models. Software and Systems Modeling **4**(2), 171–188 (2005)
3. Bill, R., Gabmeyer, S., Kaufmann, P., Seidl, M.: OCL meets CTL: Towards CTL-Extended OCL model checking. In: Proc. of 14th Int. Workshop on OCL, OCL 2013. CEUR WS, vol. 1092, pp. 13–22. CEUR-WS.org. (2013)
4. Craciun, F., Motogna, S., Lazar, I.: Towards better testing of fUML models. In: Proc. of 6th Int. Conf. on Software Testing, Verification and Validation, ICST 2013, pp. 485–486. IEEE Computer Society (2013)
5. Crane, M.L., Dingel, J.: Towards a UML virtual machine: implementing an interpreter for UML 2 actions and activities. In: Proc. of 2008 Conf. of the Center for Advanced Studies on Collaborative Research, CASCON 2008, pp. 8:96–8:110. ACM (2008)
6. Eshuis, R., Wieringa, R.: Tool Support for Verifying UML Activity Diagrams. IEEE Transactions on Software Engineering **30**(7), 437–447 (2004)
7. Heidenreich, F., Johannes, J., Karol, S., Seifert, M., Thiele, M., Wende, C., Wilke, C.: Integrating OCL and textual modelling languages. In: Dingel, J., Solberg, A. (eds.) MODELS 2010. LNCS, vol. 6627, pp. 349–363. Springer, Heidelberg (2011)
8. Laurent, Y., Bendraou, R., Baarir, S., Gervais, M.-P.: Formalization of fUML: an application to process verification. In: Jarke, M., Mylopoulos, J., Quix, C., Rolland, C., Manolopoulos, Y., Mouratidis, H., Horkoff, J. (eds.) CAiSE 2014. LNCS, vol. 8484, pp. 347–363. Springer, Heidelberg (2014)
9. Mayerhofer, T., Langer, P., Kappel, G.: A runtime model for fUML. In: Proc. of 7th Workshop on Models@run.time, MRT 2012, pp. 53–58. ACM (2012)
10. Mellor, S.J., Balcer, M.: Executable UML: A Foundation for Model-Driven Architectures. Addison-Wesley Longman Publishing Co., Inc. (2002)
11. Micskei, Z., Konnerth, R., Horváth, B., Semeráth, O., Vörös, A., Varró, D.: On open source tools for behavioral modeling and analysis with fUML and Alf. In: Proc. of 1st Workshop on Open Source Software for Model Driven Engineering, OSS4MDE 2014. CEUR WS, vol. 1290, pp. 31–41. CEUR-WS.org. (2014)
12. Mijatov, S., Langer, P., Mayerhofer, T., Kappel, G.: A framework for testing UML activities based on fUML. In: Proc. of 10th Int. Workshop on Model Driven Engineering, Verification and Validation, MoDeVVa 2013. CEUR WS, vol. 1069, pp. 1–10. CEUR-WS.org. (2013)
13. Moliz Project. http://www.modelexecution.org
14. OMG: OMG Unified Modeling Language (OMG UML), Superstructure, Version 2.4.1 (August 2011). http://www.omg.org/spec/UML/2.4.1
15. OMG: OMG Object Constraint Language (OCL), Version 2.3.1 (January 2012). http://www.omg.org/spec/OCL/2.3.1
16. OMG: Semantics of a Foundational Subset for Executable UML Models (fUML), Version 1.1 (August 2013). http://www.omg.org/spec/FUML/1.1
17. Planas, E., Cabot, J., Gómez, C.: Lightweight verification of executable models. In: Jeusfeld, M., Delcambre, L., Ling, T.-W. (eds.) ER 2011. LNCS, vol. 6998, pp. 467–475. Springer, Heidelberg (2011)
18. Romero, A., Schneider, K., Gonçalves Vieira Ferreira, M.: Using the base semantics given by fUML for verification. In: Proc. of 2nd Int. Conf. on Model-Driven Engineering and Software Development, MODELSWARD 2014, pp. 5–16. SCITEPRESS Digital Library (2014)

Coverage of OCL Operation Specifications and Invariants

Mathias Soeken[1,2(✉)], Julia Seiter[1], and Rolf Drechsler[1,2]

[1] Faculty of Mathematics and Computer Science,
University of Bremen, Bremen, Germany
{msoeken,jseiter,drechsle}@cs.uni-bremen.de
[2] Cyber-Physical Systems, DFKI GmbH, Bremen, Germany

Abstract. We consider operation coverage of OCL operation specifications and invariants in class diagrams with respect to sequence diagrams. The coverage criteria are based on the operations that are executed from the sequence diagrams and their asserted OCL subexpressions. We propose an algorithm that automatically generates a set of sequence diagrams in order to maximise these coverage criteria. A model finder is leveraged for this purpose. As a result, also operations and constraints can be determined that can never be executed and asserted, respectively. Our algorithm has been implemented in the UML specification tool USE.

1 Introduction

Given a class diagram with OCL operation specifications, invariants and a set of sequence diagrams, we define two coverage metrics that measure (1) how many operations of the class diagram have been called and (2) how many OCL subexpressions evaluated to true for this purpose. We define the coverage semantics on top of the precise modelling approach that has been presented by Mark Richters in [11]. As a result, the coverage metrics can readily be integrated in the context of formal analysis tools.

We demonstrate this by utilising model finders for behavioural modelling tasks to automatically generate sequence diagrams to increase coverage with respect to the defined metrics. Since model finders traverse the complete search space (and often efficiently), also "dead" operations or "dead" subexpressions can be found with our algorithm. Analogously to "dead code" in software development, these refer to operations that can never be called or subexpressions that never evaluate to true.

We have integrated the coverage metrics in the UML specification tool USE [6]. When starting the program with a class diagram and some initial sequence diagrams, the initial coverage is reported. The user of the tool can then start the

This work was supported by the German Federal Ministry of Education and Research (BMBF) (01IW13001) within the project SPECifIC, by the German Research Foundation (DFG) (DR 287/23-1), and by the University of Bremen's graduate school SyDe, funded by the German Excellence Initiative.

© Springer International Publishing Switzerland 2015
J.C. Blanchette and N. Kosmatov (Eds.): TAP 2015, LNCS 9154, pp. 191–207, 2015.
DOI: 10.1007/978-3-319-21215-9_12

model finder to generate new sequence diagrams which successively increase the coverage or pinpoint the user to "dead" operations or subexpressions.

Coverage metrics for modelling languages have been considered in the past, but rarely have methods been provided to automatically increase the proposed coverage criteria. In [12] coverage criteria based on the execution traces of sequence diagrams have been defined, but no algorithm has been provided that generates input data to increase the coverage. An approach very similar to ours has been proposed in [17] where model finders are exercised in order to find sequence diagrams that adhere to a given specification. However, coverage has not been considered in this context.

The remainder of the paper is structured as follows. The next section reviews class diagrams, system states, and model finding and introduces the formal notation that is used as a basis in the paper. Section 3 proposes two coverage criteria and in Sect. 4 it is described how model finding can be utilised in order to automatically find sequence diagrams to increase the coverage of a class diagram. The implementation in USE is illustrated in Sect. 5 before related work is discussed in Sect. 6. Section 7 concludes the paper.

2   Preliminaries

This section introduces a notation that is used to describe class diagrams and system states in the remainder of the paper. Also, model finding is reviewed.

2.1   Class Diagrams and System States

We are making use of the notation that has been introduced in [11]. Associations have no immediate influence on our proposed coverage metric and therefore we use simpler definitions that omit details on associations.

Definition 1 (Class diagram). *A* class diagram *is denoted as*

$$\mathcal{M} = (\text{CLASS}, \text{ATT}_c, \text{OP}_c, \prec) \ , \tag{1}$$

where

- CLASS *is a finite set of class names,*
- ATT_c *are sets of attributes for each class* $c \in$ CLASS *defined as signatures* $a : t_c \to t$, *where* a *is the attribute name,* t_c *is the type of class* c, *and* t *is the attribute type,*
- OP_c *are sets of operations for each class* $c \in$ CLASS *defined as signatures* $\omega : t_c \times t_1 \times \cdots \times t_n \to t$, *where* ω *is the operation name,* t_c *is the type of class* c, $t_1, \ldots, t_n$ *are the types of the operation's* n *parameters, and* t *is the operation's return type,*
- *and* $\prec$ *is a partial order on* CLASS *to reflect the generalisation hierarchy.*

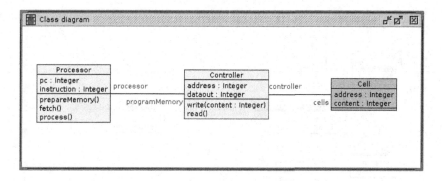

Fig. 1. Class diagram

We define

$$\text{ops}(\mathcal{M}) \overset{\text{def}}{=} \bigcup_{c \in \text{CLASS}} \text{OP}_c \ . \tag{2}$$

For ATT_c and OP_c their reflexive closures

$$\text{ATT}_c^* \overset{\text{def}}{=} \text{ATT}_c \cup \bigcup_{c' \in \text{parents}(c)} \text{ATT}_{c'} \quad \text{and}$$

$$\text{OP}_c^* \overset{\text{def}}{=} \text{OP}_c \cup \bigcup_{c' \in \text{parents}(c)} \text{OP}_{c'} \tag{3}$$

are defined with $\text{parents}(c) \overset{\text{def}}{=} \{c' \mid c' \in \text{CLASS} \wedge c \prec c'\}$.

Example 1. Figure 1 shows a class diagram that will serve as running example throughout the paper. It models the memory access part of a processor architecture. The processor which has a program counter and a current instruction is connected to a memory controller which offers operations to read and write to memory which is represented in terms of cells.[1] The precise formal notation of the class diagram is

$$\text{CLASS} = \{Processor, \ Controller, \ Cell \ \}$$

$$\text{ATT}_{Processor} = \{ \qquad \text{pc} : Processor \rightarrow Integer,$$
$$\text{instruction} : Processor \rightarrow Integer \ \}$$

$$\text{ATT}_{Controller} = \{ \ \text{address} : Controller \rightarrow Integer,$$
$$\text{dataout} : Controller \rightarrow Integer \ \}$$

$$\text{ATT}_{Cell} = \{ \ \text{address} : Cell \rightarrow Integer,$$
$$\text{content} : Cell \rightarrow Integer \ \}$$

---

[1] The class diagram can be downloaded as a model for USE at www.informatik. uni-bremen.de/agra/files/memory.use

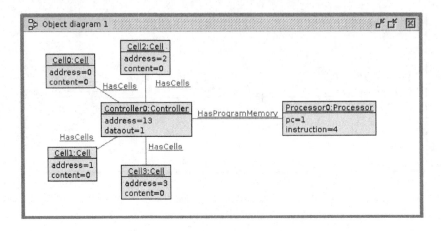

Fig. 2. System state

$$\mathrm{OP}_{Processor} = \{\ \mathrm{prepareMemory} : Processor \rightarrow VoidType,$$
$$\mathrm{fetch} : Processor \rightarrow VoidType,$$
$$\mathrm{process} : Processor \rightarrow VoidType\ \}$$

$$\mathrm{OP}_{Controller} = \{\ \mathrm{write} : Controller \times Integer \rightarrow VoidType,$$
$$\mathrm{read} : Controller \rightarrow VoidType\ \}\ .$$

Definition 2 (Class domain). *The set of object identifiers of a class $c \in \mathrm{CLASS}$ is given by an infinite set $\mathrm{oid}(c) = \{\underline{c}_1, \underline{c}_2, \dots\}$. Then, the domain of c is defined as*

$$I_{\mathrm{CLASS}}(c) \stackrel{\mathrm{def}}{=} \bigcup_{\substack{c' \in \mathrm{CLASS} \\ c' \preceq c}} \{\mathrm{oid}(c')\}\ . \tag{4}$$

In general, we will use the letter I to denote an interpretation mapping [11] that defines the semantics of OCL expressions.

Definition 3 (System state). *A system state for a class diagram $\mathcal{M}$ is a structure*

$$\sigma(\mathcal{M}) = (\sigma_{\mathrm{CLASS}}, \sigma_{\mathrm{ATT}})\ , \tag{5}$$

with

- *finite sets $\sigma_{\mathrm{CLASS}}(c) \subset \mathrm{oid}(c)$ containing all objects of class $c \in \mathrm{CLASS}$ in the system state and*
- *functions $\sigma_{\mathrm{ATT}}(a) : \sigma_{\mathrm{CLASS}}(c) \rightarrow I(t)$ for each $a : t_c \rightarrow t \in \mathrm{ATT}_c^*$.*

$I(t)$ is an interpretation function for variables of types t.

If the context is clear, $\mathcal{M}$ can be omitted and a system state is simply written as σ.

Example 2. A valid system state for the class diagram in Fig. 1 is shown in Fig. 2.

Class diagrams can be accompanied by expressions in the object constraint language (OCL, [15]) that is part of the UML standard. OCL allows the specification of formal constraints in the context of a model. Since constraints are conditions on all system states and transitions between states, a set of constraints therefore restricts the set of valid system states. In the extreme case, the set of possible system states is empty; in this case the model is called *inconsistent*. Constraints are primarily used to express invariants which are global constraints that hold in every system state and operation specifications in terms of pre- and postconditions that are evaluated locally in the context of an operation call. An operation can only be called if the preconditions hold and must ensure that after execution its postconditions evaluate to true. In general an OCL expression that evaluates to a value of type t is an element of the set Expr_t. The following definitions provide notation for invariants and operation specifications.

Definition 4 (Invariants). *All* invariants *of a class* c *are contained in the set* $\mathcal{I}(c) \subset \mathrm{Expr}_{\mathrm{Boolean}}$. *All these Boolean OCL expressions contain a variable* self *that is of type* c. *All invariants of a model are denoted*

$$\mathcal{I}(\mathcal{M}) \stackrel{\mathrm{def}}{=} \bigcup_{c \in \mathrm{CLASS}} \mathcal{I}(c) \ , \tag{6}$$

and as in the notation for system states the $\mathcal{M}$ *can be omitted, i.e., we write* $\mathcal{I}$, *if the use is clear from the context.*

Example 3. One invariant for the memory controller model from Fig. 1 is:

```
context Controller
inv uniqueCells: cells->forAll(c1, c2 |
    c1 <> c2 implies c1.address <> c2.address)
```

This invariant states that the cells that are associated to a memory controller must have a unique address.

Definition 5 (Pre- and postconditions). *Given an operation* $\omega \in \mathrm{ops}(\mathcal{M})$, *the sets* $\lhd(\omega) \subseteq \mathrm{Expr}_{\mathrm{Boolean}}$ *and* $\rhd(\omega) \subseteq \mathrm{Expr}_{\mathrm{Boolean}}$ *are the* pre- *and* postconditions *of* ω. *The notation is borrowed from* [13].

Example 4. The operation specification for the operation *write* of class *Controller* is:

```
context Controller::write(content: Integer)
    pre: address < 10
    pre: content < 4
    post: cells->one(c | c.address = address and c.content =
content)
    post: cells->forAll(c | c.address = c.address@pre)
    post: cells->forAll(c | c.address <> address implies
                        c.content = c.content@pre)
```

The two preconditions ensure that a valid address and content have been assigned to the attributes of the *Controller* object. The first postcondition ensures that the cell at the given address has the new content after the operation has been called. The second postcondition ensures that the cell's addresses were not changed by the operation call and the last postcondition ensures that the content of the non-addressed cells is not changed. The model finder cannot *guess* the developer's intention. To ensure that non-related attributes are not changed frame constraints need to be added. Either automatic tools are used that assist the developer in finding them [10] or they are provided manually:

```
post: processor.pc = processor.pc@pre
post: dataout = dataout@pre
post: address = address@pre
```

When evaluating OCL expressions in the context of a system state σ one needs to consider assignments to variables that appear in the OCL expressions. For this purpose, let Var_t be the set of variables of type t, then $\beta : \mathrm{Var}_t \to I(t)$ is a variable assignment. A context for the evaluation of an OCL expression is given by an environment $\tau = (\sigma, \beta)$. Let 'Env' be the set of environments $\tau = (\sigma, \beta)$, then the semantics of an expression $e \in \mathrm{Expr}_t$ is provided by a mapping $I[\![e]\!] : \mathrm{Env} \to I(t)$.

In this paper we make heavy use of the notation that has been introduced in [11] to formalise UML class diagrams and OCL expressions. The meaning of the notation should be comprehensible from the context, however, for more precise definitions the reader is referred to [11].

2.2 Model Finding

Model finding describes the problem of finding a system state σ to a given model $\mathcal{M}$ with invariants $\mathcal{I}$ such that

$$I[\![\mathcal{I}]\!](\sigma) \stackrel{\mathrm{def}}{=} \bigwedge_{c \in \mathrm{CLASS}} \bigwedge_{e \in \mathcal{I}(c)} \bigwedge_{\underline{c} \in \sigma_{\mathrm{CLASS}}(c)} I[\![e]\!]((\sigma, \mathtt{self} \mapsto \underline{c})) = \mathrm{true} \ , \tag{7}$$

i.e., all invariants hold for all objects in the system state. Such a system state σ is called *valid* and witnesses the consistency of $\mathcal{M}$. Usually the size of σ_{CLASS} is predefined such that the model finding problem becomes decidable [2]. This assumption is reasonable, since often the size bounds of the model are known in advance. Similar restrictions are assumed for associations, but not discussed in this paper. We refer to this problem also as *structural* model finding since only one system state is considered. Different implementations for the model finding problem have been proposed in the past [3,7,9,14]. The problem can be extended to consider the class diagram's operations which is described in the following. For this purpose, some additional notation to formalise operation calls is required.

An operation call $\underline{\omega} = (\underline{c}, \omega)$ is a tuple consisting of an operation $\omega \in \mathrm{OP}_c$ and an object $\underline{c} \in \sigma_{\mathrm{CLASS}}(c)$. How parameters are bound to operation calls is described later in Sect. 3. For interpreting an operation call, both a pre-state σ_{pre} and a post-state and σ_{post} need to be considered. Consequently, also two environments $\tau_{\text{pre}} = (\sigma_{\text{pre}}, \beta_{\text{pre}})$ and $\tau_{\text{post}} = (\sigma_{\text{post}}, \beta_{\text{post}})$ are required to formalise the semantics of a postcondition. Then, the interpretation of an operation call $\underline{\omega} = (\underline{c}, \omega)$ is

$$I[\![\underline{\omega}]\!](\sigma, \sigma') \stackrel{\text{def}}{=} \bigwedge_{e \in \triangleleft(\omega)} I[\![e]\!](\tau_{\text{pre}}) \bigwedge_{e \in \triangleright(\omega)} I[\![e]\!](\tau_{\text{pre}}, \tau_{\text{post}}) , \qquad (8)$$

with $\{\texttt{self} \mapsto \underline{c}\} \in \beta_{\text{pre}}$ and $\{\texttt{self} \mapsto \underline{c}'\} \in \beta_{\text{post}}$ where $\underline{c}'$ refers to $\underline{c}$ in the post-state.

Given a Boolean expression e_{task}, the *behavioural* model finding problem [13] asks to find a set of system states $\sigma_1, \ldots, \sigma_T$ and a set of operation calls $\underline{\omega}_1, \ldots \underline{\omega}_{T-1}$ such that

$$\bigwedge_{t=1}^{T} I[\![\mathcal{I}]\!](\sigma_t) \wedge \bigwedge_{t=1}^{T-1} I[\![\underline{\omega}_t]\!](\sigma_t, \sigma_{t+1}) \wedge e_{\text{task}} = \text{true} . \qquad (9)$$

Also for this problem, T is usually predefined, since otherwise the problem is undecidable. This assumption is reasonable, since one is interested in a short sequence diagram. The common practice is to increase T in an iterative manner until a solution is found. This is similar to reachability analysis with bounded model checking [4]. Furthermore, the initial state σ_1 is typically preassigned by the developer to exclude false positives, i.e., system states that cannot be reached. Verification tasks in behavioural model checking can, e.g., be the check for a deadlock, i.e., a final system state in which no operation can be called since no preconditions can be asserted, or it can be checked whether an operation is executable by preassigning one of the operation call variables. Besides these, a variety of other reachability tasks can be formulated. Implementations for behavioural model finders have been realised, e.g., in [5,13].

3   Operation Coverage

In this section, two coverage criteria are defined. Since coverage is witnessed and increased in terms of sequence diagrams, we first need to formalise them analogously to the definitions of the previous section. In this paper, we only consider very simple sequence diagrams with no nested operation calls and no control structures. Consequently, these can also be represented by a sequence of operations.

Definition 6 (Operation sequence). *Given a class diagram $\mathcal{M}$ and a sequence of system states $\sigma_i(\mathcal{M}) = (\sigma_{\text{CLASS},1}, \sigma_{\text{ATT},1})$ for $1 \leq i \leq n$, an operation sequence is an ordered set*

$$S = \langle r_1 \leftarrow \underline{\omega}_1(\boldsymbol{p}_1), r_2 \leftarrow \underline{\omega}_2(\boldsymbol{p}_2), \ldots, r_n \leftarrow \underline{\omega}_n(\boldsymbol{p}_n) \rangle . \qquad (10)$$

The ith operation call in the sequence S is of the form $r \leftarrow \underline{\omega}(\boldsymbol{p})$ with $\underline{\omega} = (\underline{c}, \omega)$ stating that an operation $\omega : t_c \times t_1 \times \cdots \times t_k \to t \in \text{OP}_c$ is called on an *object $\underline{c} \in \sigma_{\text{CLASS},i}(c)$ of class c with parameters $\boldsymbol{p} = (p_1, \ldots, p_k)$ with $p_i \in t_i$ and returns a value $r \in t$. We define*

$$\text{ops}(S) \stackrel{\text{def}}{=} \{\omega_1, \ldots, \omega_n\} \ . \tag{11}$$

An operation sequence may not necessarily be executable since invariants and operation specifications could prevent the OCL expressions from being asserted.

Definition 7 (Validity of operation sequences). *Operation sequences are executed with respect to some given valid initial system state σ_1. An operation sequence is called* valid *if, and only if there exist valid system states $\sigma_2, \ldots, \sigma_{n+1}$ such that*

$$\bigwedge_{i=1}^{n} I[\![\underline{\omega}_i]\!](\sigma_i, \sigma_{i+1}) = \text{true} \ . \tag{12}$$

Example 5. Figure 3 shows a valid system state for the running example written in the USE syntax. First, the initial state is prepared which includes object creation and linking. The command `!openter` initiates the operation call and also the preconditions are evaluated. Afterwards, the post-state is prepared before the operation call is finished using `!opexit`, which also evaluates the operation's postcondition.

3.1   Operation Call Coverage

Now that operation sequences are formally defined, we can formalise the coverage metrics. The first coverage metric, called *operation call coverage*, checks how many of the model's operations have been called in a given set of operation sequences.

Definition 8 (Operation call coverage). *Given a class diagram $\mathcal{M}$ and valid operation sequences $S_1, \ldots, S_n$, the* operation call coverage *is defined as*

$$\sum_{i=1}^{n} \frac{|\text{ops}(S_i)|}{|\text{ops}(\mathcal{M})|} \ . \tag{13}$$

3.2   Subexpression Coverage

The second coverage metric is based on an expression's subexpressions and should first be illustrated by means of an example.

Example 6. The operation *process* from the class *Processor* has among other the following two postconditions:

```
post: pc@pre < 9 implies pc = pc@pre + 1
post: pc@pre = 9 implies pc = 0
```

They ensure that the program counter *pc* overflows to 0 if its value is 9 before the operation is called.

```
!create Controller0: Controller
!create Cell0: Cell
!create Cell1: Cell
!create Cell2: Cell
!create Cell3: Cell
!create Processor0: Processor
!set Controller0.address := 13
!set Controller0.dataout := 1
!set Cell0.address := 0
!set Cell0.content := 0
!set Cell1.address := 1
!set Cell1.content := 0
!set Cell2.address := 2
!set Cell2.content := 0
!set Cell3.address := 3
!set Cell3.content := 0
!set Processor0.pc := 0
!set Processor0.instruction := 4
!insert (Controller0, Cell0) into HasCells
!insert (Controller0, Cell1) into HasCells
!insert (Controller0, Cell2) into HasCells
!insert (Controller0, Cell3) into HasCells
!insert (Processor0, Controller0) into HasProgramMemory
```

σ_1 (Initial state)

```
!openter Processor0 process()
!set Processor0.pc := 1
!set Processor0.instruction := Undefined
!opexit
```

σ_2 e_1

```
!openter Processor0 fetch()
!set Processor0.instruction := 1
!set Controller0.dataout := Undefined
!opexit
```

σ_3 e_2

Fig. 3. Valid operation sequence

An implication expression always evaluates to true if the antecedent is false. Hence, one is interested in finding operation sequences that assert many subexpressions. The same argument holds for expressions of the form e_1 or e_2. Even expressions of the form e_1 and e_2 need to be considered although in this case, both e_1 and e_2 must have been true in order to assert the overall conjunction. However, the expression can be more complicated if nested expressions are used as, e.g., in $(e_1$ or $e_2)$ and $(e_3$ or $e_4)$. Also here, it is desired that all subexpressions have been asserted once in some sequence diagram.

For this purpose, we define a function 'sub' that returns all Boolean subexpressions of a given expression $e \in \text{Expr}$:

$$\text{sub}(e) \stackrel{\text{def}}{=} \begin{cases} \{e\} \cup \bigcup\{\text{sub}(e') \mid e' \text{ is subexpression of } e\} & \text{if } e \in \text{Expr}_{\text{Boolean}}, \\ \bigcup\{\text{sub}(e') \mid e' \text{ is subexpression of } e\} & \text{otherwise .} \end{cases}$$

$$(14)$$

Before we define the second coverage metric, we define the evaluation of a Boolean expression $e \in \text{Expr}_{\text{Boolean}}$ in the context of a valid operation sequence $S = \langle \underline{\omega}_1 = (\underline{c}_1, \omega_1), \ldots, \underline{\omega}_n = (\underline{c}_n, \omega_n) \rangle$ as defined in (10) (For brevity we omitted parameters and return values from the operation sequence). The operation sequence implies $n + 1$ valid system states $\sigma_1, \ldots, \sigma_{n+1}$ as defined in (12). The evaluation of e depends on whether it is part of an invariant, a precondition, or a postcondition. If e is part of an invariant, it is checked whether e evaluates to true in some of these system states for some object, i.e.,

$$I_{\text{inv}}[\![e]\!](S) \stackrel{\text{def}}{=} \bigvee_{i=1}^{n} \bigvee_{\underline{c} \in \sigma_{\text{CLASS}}(c)} I[\![e]\!]((\sigma_i, \texttt{self} \mapsto \underline{c})) \ . \tag{15}$$

If e is part of a precondition of some operation ω, it is checked whether it evaluates to true if the operation has been called, i.e.,

$$I_{\text{pre}}[\![e]\!](S) \stackrel{\text{def}}{=} \bigvee_{i=1}^{n} (\omega_i \equiv \omega) \wedge I[\![e]\!]((\sigma_i, \texttt{self} \mapsto \underline{c}_i)) \ . \tag{16}$$

Finally, if e is part of a postcondition of some operation ω, it is checked whether it evaluates to true in the state after the operation has been called, i.e.,

$$I_{\text{post}}[\![e]\!](S) \stackrel{\text{def}}{=} \bigvee_{i=1}^{n} (\omega_i \equiv \omega) \wedge I[\![e]\!]((\sigma_i, \texttt{self} \mapsto \underline{c}_i), (\sigma_{i+1}, \texttt{self} \mapsto \underline{c}_i')) \ , \tag{17}$$

where $\underline{c}_i'$ refers to $\underline{c}_i$ in state σ_{i+1}.

We also define a partition over all subexpressions in a model based on their context, i.e., whether the expression is part of an invariant or of an operation specification:

$$\text{sub}_{\text{inv}} \stackrel{\text{def}}{=} \bigcup_{e \in \mathcal{I}} \text{sub}(e),$$

$$\text{sub}_{\text{pre}} \stackrel{\text{def}}{=} \bigcup_{\omega \in \text{ops}(\mathcal{M})} \bigcup_{e \in \triangleleft(\omega)} \text{sub}(e), \text{ and}$$

$$\text{sub}_{\text{post}} \stackrel{\text{def}}{=} \bigcup_{\omega \in \text{ops}(\mathcal{M})} \bigcup_{e \in \triangleright(\omega)} \text{sub}(e)$$

Definition 9 (Subexpression coverage). *Given a class diagram $\mathcal{M}$ and valid operation sequences $S_1, \ldots, S_n$, the subexpression coverage is defined as*

$$\frac{\left| \bigcup_{x \in \{\text{inv}, \text{pre}, \text{post}\}} \{e \in \text{sub}_x \mid \exists S_i : I_x[\![e]\!](S_i)\} \right|}{|\text{sub}_{\text{inv}} \cup \text{sub}_{\text{pre}} \cup \text{sub}_{\text{post}}|} \ . \tag{18}$$

The formal definition for subexpression coverage is a bit tedious, however, the intuitive idea can readily be stated in an informal manner. We take all subexpressions from the model's invariants and operation specifications. Then for each of them we check whether they evaluate to true in some intermediate state of the given operation sequences. The number of such subexpressions is divided by the total amount of subexpressions. It is important to ensure that a subexpression of a pre- or postcondition is only checked for a positive evaluation if the respective operation has been called.

Example 7. The operation sequence in Fig. 3 leads to an operation call coverage of 0.4 since 2 out of 5 operations have been called. Furthermore, the subexpression coverage is approximately 0.3 as 14 out of 46 subexpressions are asserted. For instance, the second postcondition of Example 6 is not covered by the operation sequence in Fig. 3 since the program counter pc is initially set to 0. Consequently, the subexpression pc@pre = 9 evaluates to false.

4   Algorithm to Automatically Enhance Coverage

Now that the coverage criteria have been defined, in this section we are proposing methods that aim at automatically increasing the coverage by generating new sequence diagrams. Since model finders are used for this purpose, always the whole solution space is considered. Consequently, the algorithm either yields a sequence diagram that indeed increases the coverage or finds that some operation is not executable or some subexpression cannot be asserted by any sequence diagram. Hence, the algorithm is able to determine "dead" model code (analogously to dead code in programs that can never be executed).

The model finder is utilised by choosing an appropriate expression for e_{task} as described in (9). To increase operation call coverage the model finder is used to find an operation sequence that contains an operation ω that has not been executed thus far. In order to constrain the model finder to call an operation in an operation sequence one needs to assign

$$e_{\text{task}} = \bigvee_{t=1}^{T-1} (\omega_t \equiv \omega) \ . \tag{19}$$

When increasing subexpression coverage a task needs to be formalised for each subexpression e that is not covered yet. Again, the description of the task expression depends on the origin of the subexpression. If e is part of an invariant of class c, we assign

$$e_{\text{task}} = \bigvee_{t=1}^{T} \bigvee_{\underline{c} \in \sigma_{\text{CLASS}}(c)} I[\![e]\!]((\sigma_t, \texttt{self} \mapsto \underline{c})) \ . \tag{20}$$

For the case if e is part of an operation specification, we could also find a suitable task expression, however, instead we are making use of a small trick. We are using the same task expression as in (19) but additionally add e as pre- or postcondition to the considered model. Since the task forces the operation to be called also e must evaluate to true.

It can easily be seen that many sequence diagrams may need to be generated in order to obtain full coverage if initially many operations and subexpressions are uncovered. The first measure to avoid this is to recompute the coverage metrics after each generated sequence diagram, since other uncovered elements may be covered by the newly generated sequence diagram. Furthermore, one can also try to cover multiple uncovered elements at once by combing the task expressions that have been introduced above. As an example one can try to find a sequence diagram in which three uncovered operations ω_1, ω_2, and ω_3 are called by assigning

$$e_{\text{task}} = \bigvee_{t=1}^{T-1} (\omega_t \equiv \omega_1) \wedge \bigvee_{t=1}^{T-1} (\omega_t \equiv \omega_2) \wedge \bigvee_{t=1}^{T-1} (\omega_t \equiv \omega_3) \ .$$

However, this approach needs to be applied with care since it may lead to false negatives, since operations may be executable independently but not in combination. A strategy can be to first try to generate sequence diagrams that cover a lot of operations and then decrease the number if no more sequence diagrams can be found.

Alternatively, one can make use of Boolean *select variables* $s_1, \ldots, s_\ell$ for each uncovered operation $\omega_1, \ldots, \omega_\ell$. Then these can be considered at once in a single task expression and let the model finder decide which ones to use in the sequence diagram and which ones not:

$$e_{\text{task}} = \bigwedge_{i=1}^{\ell} \left(s_i \Rightarrow \bigvee_{t=1}^{T-1} (\omega_t \equiv \omega_i) \right) \wedge \sum_{i=1}^{\ell} s_i \geq k \ . \tag{21}$$

If a select variable s_i is assigned 1, then the operation ω_i must be called in the sequence diagram. Since e_{task} can easily be satisfied by assigning all select variables to 0, a cardinality constraint ensures that at least k select variables must be assigned 1 and hence at least k operations must be called in the operation sequence. The value for k can be initially set high and then decreased successively if e_{task} cannot be satisfied.

5 Tool Support

We implemented the proposed algorithm as a plugin of the UML specification tool USE [6]. Consequently, models in the form of class diagrams as well as sequence diagrams are to be provided in the USE format (.use and .cmd to specify class diagrams and operation sequences, respectively). We have used the SMT-based behavioural model finder that has been proposed in [13].

The features realised in the plugin are the following:[2]

1. computation of the initial coverage of operations and constraints based on the provided sequence diagram(s) (Fig. 4)

---

[2] A USE plugin for computing and displaying coverage information can be downloaded from www.informatik.uni-bremen.de/agra/files/coverage-plugin.zip

Coverage	⌐ᵏ ⌐ᵏ ⊠
Initial Coverage	Maximum Coverage

read	Not Covered
pre3: self.address.isDefined	Not Covered
post8: self.cells->forAll(c : Cell	((c.address = c.address@pre) and (c.content = c.content@pre)))	Not Covered
post9: self.cells->one(c : Cell	((c.address = self.address@pre) and (c.content = self.dataout)))	Not Covered
post10: self.address.isUndefined	Not Covered
post11: (self.processor.instruction = self.processor.instruction@pre)	Not Covered
post12: (self.processor.pc = self.processor.pc@pre)	Not Covered
write	Not Covered
pre1: (self.address < 10)	Not Covered
pre2: (content < 4)	Not Covered
post1: self.cells->one(c : Cell	((c.address = self.address) and (c.content = content)))	Not Covered
post2: self.cells->forAll(c : Cell	(c.address = c.address@pre))	Not Covered
post3: self.cells->forAll(c : Cell	((c.address <> self.address) implies (c.content = c.content@pre)))	Not Covered
post4: (self.processor.instruction = self.processor.instruction@pre)	Not Covered
post5: (self.processor.pc = self.processor.pc@pre)	Not Covered
post6: (self.dataout = self.dataout@pre)	Not Covered
post7: (self.address = self.address@pre)	Not Covered
fetch	Not Covered
pre5: self.programMemory.dataout.isDefined	Not Covered
post18: (self.instruction = self.programMemory.dataout@pre)	Not Covered
post19: (self.pc = self.pc@pre)	Not Covered
post20: self.programMemory.cells->forAll(c : Cell	((c.address = c.address@pre) and (c.content = c.content@pre)))	Not Covered
post21: self.programMemory.address = self.programMemory.address@pre)	Not Covered
post22: self.programMemory.dataout.isUndefined	Not Covered
prepareMemory	Not Covered
pre4: self.programMemory.address.isUndefined	Not Covered
post13: (self.programMemory.address = self.pc)	Not Covered
post14: (self.instruction = self.instruction@pre)	Not Covered
post15: (self.pc = self.pc@pre)	Not Covered
post16: (self.programMemory.dataout = self.programMemory.dataout@pre)	Not Covered
post17: self.programMemory.cells->forAll(c : Cell	((c.address = c.address@pre) and (c.content = c.content@pre)))	Not Covered
process	Covered
pre6: self.instruction.isDefined	Covered
post23: ((self.pc@pre < 9) implies (self.pc = (self.pc@pre + 1)))	Maybe Covered
post24: ((self.pc@pre = 9) implies (self.pc = 0))	Maybe Covered
post25: self.programMemory.cells->forAll(c : Cell	((c.address = c.address@pre) and (c.content = c.content@pre)))	Covered
post26: self.instruction.isUndefined	Covered
post27: (self.programMemory.address = self.programMemory.address@pre)	Covered
post28: (self.programMemory.dataout = self.programMemory.dataout@pre)	Covered

Initial: Covered 6/39 Elements	15%
Maximum: Covered 14/39 Elements	36%

Fig. 4. Initial coverage

2. computation of the maximal possible coverage of operations and constraints using a model finder in the background (Fig. 5)
3. display of the results

Both types of coverage are computed upon start of the plugin in the background if a model is provided. Without given sequence diagrams, the initial status of each operation and each constraint is displayed as *not covered*. If coverage of the respective operation or constraint has been reached, the mark is changed to *covered*. The remaining constraints are marked as *maybe covered* in the initial computation and as *partially covered* in the final state.

A constraint is *maybe covered* if the respective operation has been executed but the constraint contains subexpressions which might not hold, e.g., a part of a disjunction where the whole constraint can evaluate to true while a single subexpression evaluates to false. A constraint is eventually *partially covered* when it was not possible to find an operation sequence such that all subexpressions

Coverage	
Initial Coverage Maximum Coverage	
read	Not Covered
pre3: self.address.isDefined	Not Covered
post8: self.cells->forAll(c : Cell	((c.address = c.address@pre) and (c.content = c.content@pre)))	Not Covered
post9: self.cells->one(c : Cell	((c.address = self.address@pre) and (c.content = self.dataout)))	Not Covered
post10: self.address.isUndefined	Not Covered
post11: (self.processor.instruction = self.processor.instruction@pre)	Not Covered
post12: (self.processor.pc = self.processor.pc@pre)	Not Covered
write	Not Covered
pre1: (self.address < 10)	Not Covered
pre2: (content < 4)	Not Covered
post1: self.cells->one(c : Cell	((c.address = self.address) and (c.content = content)))	Not Covered
post2: self.cells->forAll(c : Cell	(c.address = c.address@pre))	Not Covered
post3: self.cells->forAll(c : Cell	((c.address <> self.address) implies (c.content = c.content@pre)))	Not Covered
post4: (self.processor.instruction = self.processor.instruction@pre)	Not Covered
post5: (self.processor.pc = self.processor.pc@pre)	Not Covered
post6: (self.dataout = self.dataout@pre)	Not Covered
post7: (self.address = self.address@pre)	Not Covered
fetch	Covered
pre5: self.programMemory.dataout.isDefined	Covered
post18: (self.instruction = self.programMemory.dataout@pre)	Covered
post19: (self.pc = self.pc@pre)	Covered
post20: self.programMemory.cells->forAll(c : Cell	((c.address = c.address@pre) and (c.content = c.content@pre)))	Covered
post21: (self.programMemory.address = self.programMemory.address@pre)	Covered
post22: self.programMemory.dataout.isUndefined	Covered
prepareMemory	Not Covered
pre4: self.programMemory.address.isUndefined	Not Covered
post13: (self.programMemory.address = self.pc)	Not Covered
post14: (self.instruction = self.instruction@pre)	Not Covered
post15: (self.pc = self.pc@pre)	Not Covered
post16: (self.programMemory.dataout = self.programMemory.dataout@pre)	Not Covered
post17: self.programMemory.cells->forAll(c : Cell	((c.address = c.address@pre) and (c.content = c.content@pre)))	Not Covered
process	Covered
pre6: self.instruction.isDefined	Covered
post23: ((self.pc@pre < 9) implies (self.pc = (self.pc@pre + 1)))	Covered
post24: ((self.pc@pre = 9) implies (self.pc = 0))	Partially Covered
post25: self.programMemory.cells->forAll(c : Cell	((c.address = c.address@pre) and (c.content = c.content@pre)))	Covered
post26: self.instruction.isUndefined	Covered
post27: (self.programMemory.address = self.programMemory.address@pre)	Covered
post28: (self.programMemory.dataout = self.programMemory.dataout@pre)	Covered
Initial: Covered 6/39 Elements	15%
Maximum: Covered 14/39 Elements	36%

Fig. 5. Maximised coverage

eventually hold, i.e., one part of the constraint is covered and one part of it is not covered.

During computation of the maximum coverage, sequence diagrams for the not yet covered operations and constraints are produced and printed to the USE shell. The overall results of the coverage enhancement are always displayed at the bottom of the window. Here, the amount of initially and finally covered elements are provided as well as a progress bar depicting the coverage percentage.

5.1   Experimental Evaluation

For an experimental evaluation, the approach has been applied to several models which have been provided with the tool USE or have been written by the authors. Table 1 shows the results of said evaluation. The first column gives the names of the models. In the second and third column, their initial and maximal coverage is stated. Then, the amount of generated sequences is provided and the last column contains the required run-times.

In all cases except for one, an increase in coverage up to 94–100% could be achieved. Only for the test case *CPU*, the initial coverage of 0% remained unchanged. This means that no operation sequences could be generated and, consequently, none of the constraints were triggered. This scenario may occur due to two reasons: (1) The initial state may be chosen poorly so that no operation's pre-condition evaluates to true. (2) The post-conditions of the operations may be contradictory, preventing the operation's execution even if a pre-condition is satisfied. In both cases, the model as well as the initial state have to be revised.

With regard to the run-time, it can be stated that only the test case *Memory* required a slightly longer execution time than the remaining examples. Since this example is by far the largest one in terms of OCL constraints and has a relatively low initial coverage of 15%, a slight increase in run-time was to be expected.

Overall, it was possible to reach high coverage percentages in negligible run-time by generating a maximum of 6 operation call sequences. In two cases, constraints and/or operations could be detected thanks to our approach which could not be covered by sequences starting in the initial state. These constraints/operations would result in dead code, so by uncovering them, the quality of the resulting implementation can be improved.

6   Related Work

In [12] coverage criteria are defined based on sequence diagrams which are extracted by reverse engineering of existing Java source code. Branches in the source code are mapped to guarded messages in the sequence diagram and therefore each sequence diagram defines a set of possible execution paths. Coverage criteria are based on these paths. The authors have not provided methods to automatically increase the coverage criteria.

The authors of [1] propose three test coverage criteria for class diagrams. These criteria specify a certain structure of an object diagram which has to be created by a test case in order to reach full coverage. In two cases, this structure is determined by constructing representative values for association-end multiplicities and attributes. The third criterion considers generalisation relationships. All three criteria do not consider behavioural aspects and only one criterion takes OCL constraints into consideration.

Table 1. Experimental results

Model	Initial	Maximal	#Sequences	Run-time
CPU	0%	0%	0	<0.01s
Traffic	35%	94%	4	<0.01s
Memory	15%	97%	6	0.22s
Car	0%	100%	4	<0.01s
Life	0%	100%	3	<0.01s

Scenario-based design analysis (SUDA) is defined in [16]. The authors introduce snapshot models to transform a class model with operations into a static model of behaviour which can be verified against a sequence of operation calls. Based on this technique an automatic approach is presented in [17]. Given a UML class diagram with OCL operation specifications and invariants and a specification for a desired scenario, a scenario is automatically generated using model finding techniques.

In [8] a technique is presented that allows animation of UML class diagrams with OCL operation specifications and invariants. Given a current state, a post-state is computed that satisfies the class diagram's invariants and underspecified postconditions.

7   Conclusions

We concerned ourselves with the question of how to formalise coverage criteria of class diagrams with respect to a set of sequence diagrams in terms of operation sequences. We have defined two coverage criteria, one which checks how many operations are called and another one which considers whether all subexpressions in the involved OCL constraints evaluate to true. Based on the formalisation of UML class diagrams and OCL expressions introduced in [11] we formalised the coverage criteria to enable their application in formal analysis.

We demonstrated how model finders can be utilised in order to automatically generate new sequence diagrams that increase overall coverage of the class diagram. By using the model finder the developer is also pinpointed to operations and OCL subexpressions that can never be executed or asserted, respectively. Our algorithm has been implemented in the UML specification tool USE.

It is a well-known fact that model finders cannot be applied to arbitrarily large models and face scalability problems as the number of classes and constraints increases. Consequently, the efficiency of our approach for automatically generating sequence diagrams heavily depends on the efficiency of the model finder. For now, we have evaluated the generation approach to class diagrams similar to the running example of the paper. For these, sequence diagrams can be generated within a few seconds. In future work we want to evaluate the scalability of the approach in more detail by comparing different model finders. Alternatively, model finders can be tuned to perform well for these kind of problem. Furthermore, more advanced sequence diagrams, e.g., with nested operations, will enhance the usability of the approach.

References

1. Andrews, A., France, R.B., Ghosh, S., Craig, G.: Test adequacy criteria for UML design models. Software Testing, Verification and Reliability **13**, 95–127 (2003)
2. Berardi, D., Calvanese, D., De Giacomo, G.: Reasoning on UML class diagrams. Artificial Intelligence **168**(1–2), 70–118 (2005)

3. Cabot, J., Clarisó, R., Riera, D.: Verification of UML/OCL class diagrams using constraint programming. In: Int'l. Conference on Software Testing Verification and Validation Workshop, pp. 73–80. IEEE (2008)
4. Clarke, Jr., E.M., Grumberg, O., Peled, D.A.: Model Checking. MIT Press (1999)
5. Frias, M.F., Galeotti, J.P., Pombo, C.L., Aguirre, N.: DynAlloy: upgrading alloy with actions. In: Int'l Conf. on Software Engineering, pp. 442–451. ACM (2005)
6. Gogolla, M., Büttner, F., Richters, M.: USE: a UML-based specification environment for validating UML and OCL. Science of Computer Programming **69**, 27–34 (2007)
7. Jackson, D.: Software Abstractions: Logic, Language, and Analysis. MIT Press (2006)
8. Krieger, M.P., Knapp, A.: Executing underspecified OCL operation contracts with a SAT solver. Electronic Communication of the European Association of Software Science and Technology 15 (2008)
9. Kuhlmann, M., Hamann, L., Gogolla, M.: Extensive validation of OCL models by integrating SAT solving into USE. In: Bishop, J., Vallecillo, A. (eds.) TOOLS 2011. LNCS, vol. 6705, pp. 290–306. Springer, Heidelberg (2011)
10. Niemann, P., Hilken, F., Gogolla, M., Wille, R.: Assisted generation of frame conditions for formal models. IEEE (2015)
11. Richters, M.: A Precise Approach to Validating UML Models and OCL Constraints. Ph.D. thesis, University of Bremen, Logos Verlag, Berlin, BISS Monographs, No. 1 (2002)
12. Rountev, A., Kagan, S., Sawin, J.: Coverage criteria for testing of object interactions in sequence diagrams. In: Cerioli, M. (ed.) FASE 2005. LNCS, vol. 3442, pp. 289–304. Springer, Heidelberg (2005)
13. Soeken, M., Wille, R., Drechsler, R.: Verifying dynamic aspects of UML models. In: Design, Automation and Test in Europe. pp. 1077–1082. IEEE (2011)
14. Soeken, M., Wille, R., Kuhlmann, M., Gogolla, M., Drechsler, R.: Verifying UML/OCL models using Boolean satisfiability. In: Design, Automation and Test in Europe, pp. 1341–1344. IEEE (2010)
15. Warmer, J., Kleppe, A.: The Object Constraint Language: Precise Modeling with UML. Addison-Wesley Longman (1999)
16. Yu, L., France, R.B., Ray, I.: Scenario-Based static analysis of UML class models. In: Czarnecki, K., Ober, I., Bruel, J.-M., Uhl, A., Völter, M. (eds.) MODELS 2008. LNCS, vol. 5301, pp. 234–248. Springer, Heidelberg (2008)
17. Yu, L., France, R.B., Ray, I., Sun, W.: Systematic scenario-based analysis of UML design class models. In: Int'l Conf. on Engineering of Complex Computer Systems, pp. 86–95. IEEE Computer Society (2012)

Author Index